D0404277

Splatoon
reads from
right to
left!

This is
the end
of this
graphic
novel.

Splatoon

Volume 14
VIZ Media Edition

Story and Art by
Sankichi Hinodeya

Translation **Tetsuichiro Miyaki**
English Adaptation **Bryant Turnage**
Lettering **John Hunt**
Design **Kam Li**
Editor **Joel Enos**

TM & © 2022 Nintendo. All rights reserved.

SPLATOON Vol. 14 by Sankichi HINODEYA
© 2016 Sankichi HINODEYA
All rights reserved.
Original Japanese edition published by SHOGAKUKAN.
English translation rights in the United States of America,
Canada, the United Kingdom, Ireland, Australia and
New Zealand arranged with SHOGAKUKAN.

The stories, characters and incidents mentioned
in this publication are entirely fictional.

Original Design **100percent**

Printed in the U.S.A.

Published by VIZ Media, LLC
P.O. Box 77010
San Francisco, CA 94107

10 9 8 7 6 5 4 3 2 1
First Printing, April 2022

VIZ MEDIA
viz.com

Splatoon™

VOL. 14

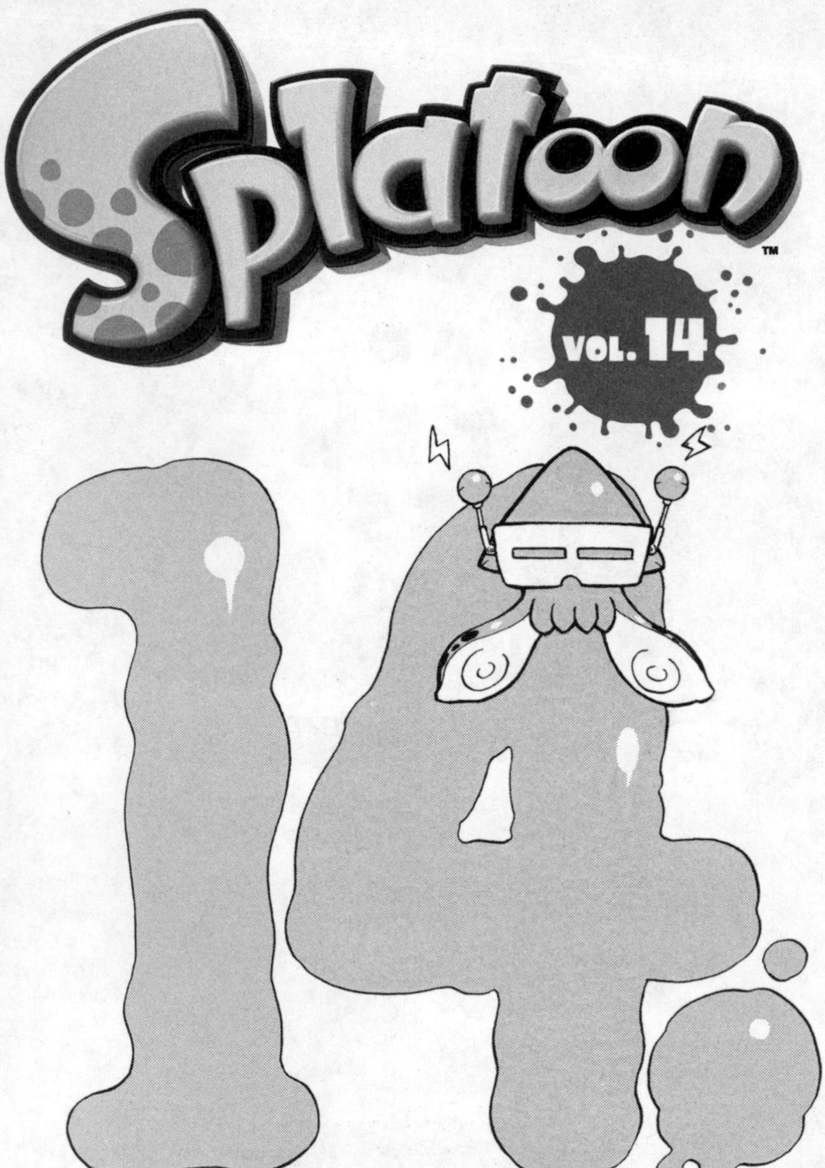

STORY AND ART BY

Sankichi Hinodeya

CONTENTS

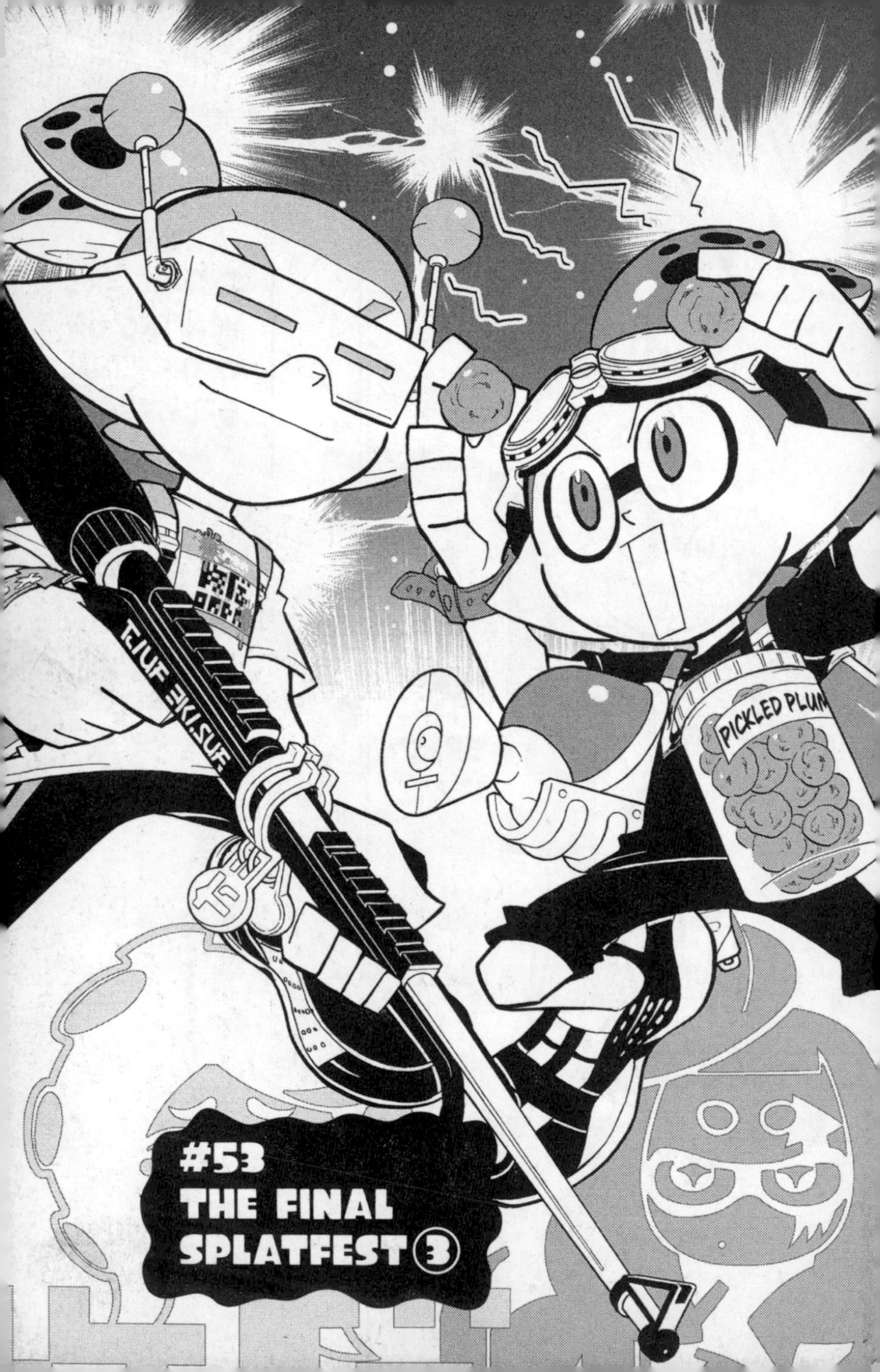
#53
THE FINAL
SPLATFEST 3
PICKLED PLUM

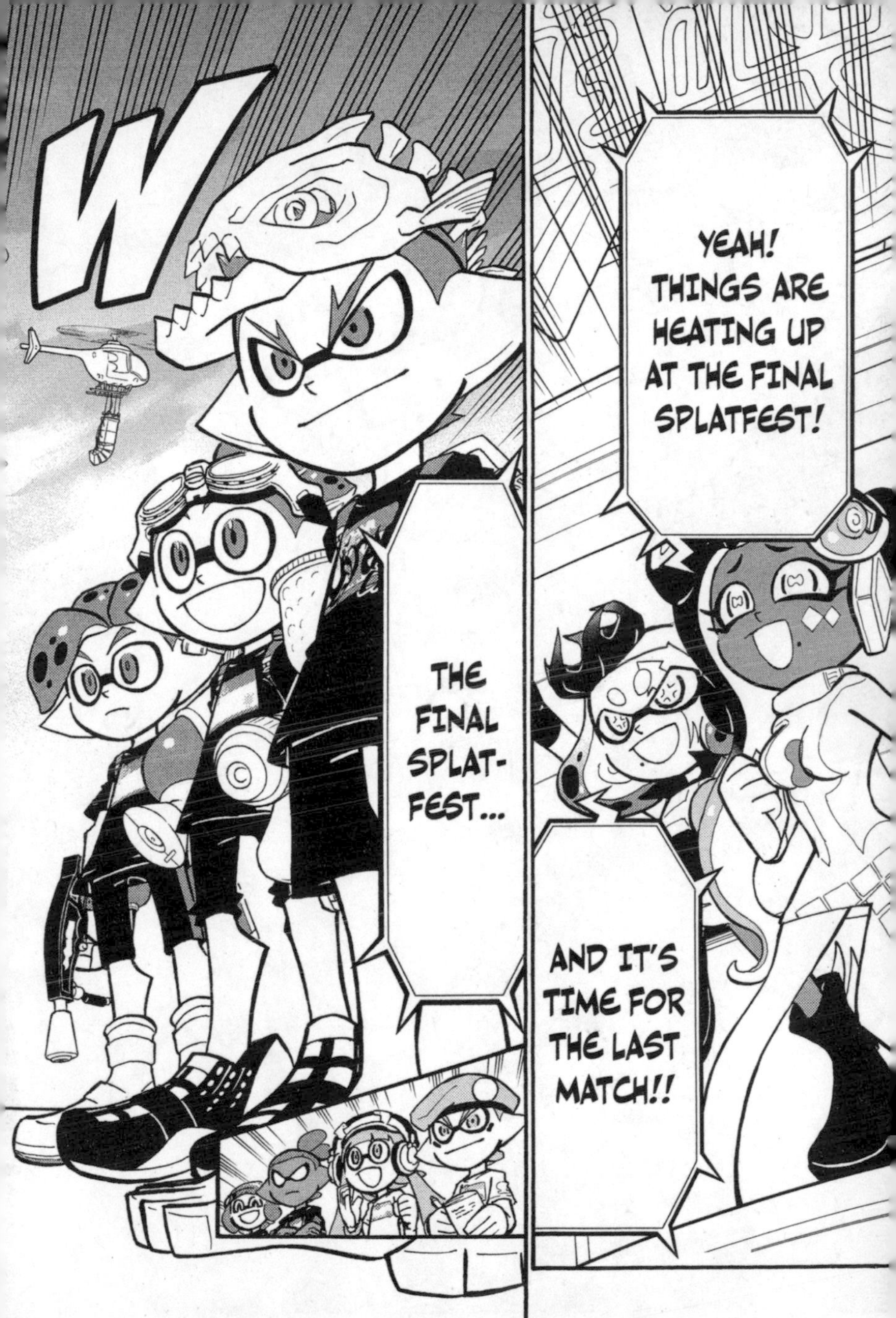
YEAH! THINGS ARE HEATING UP AT THE FINAL SPLATFEST!
AND IT'S TIME FOR THE LAST MATCH!!
W
THE FINAL SPLAT-FEST...

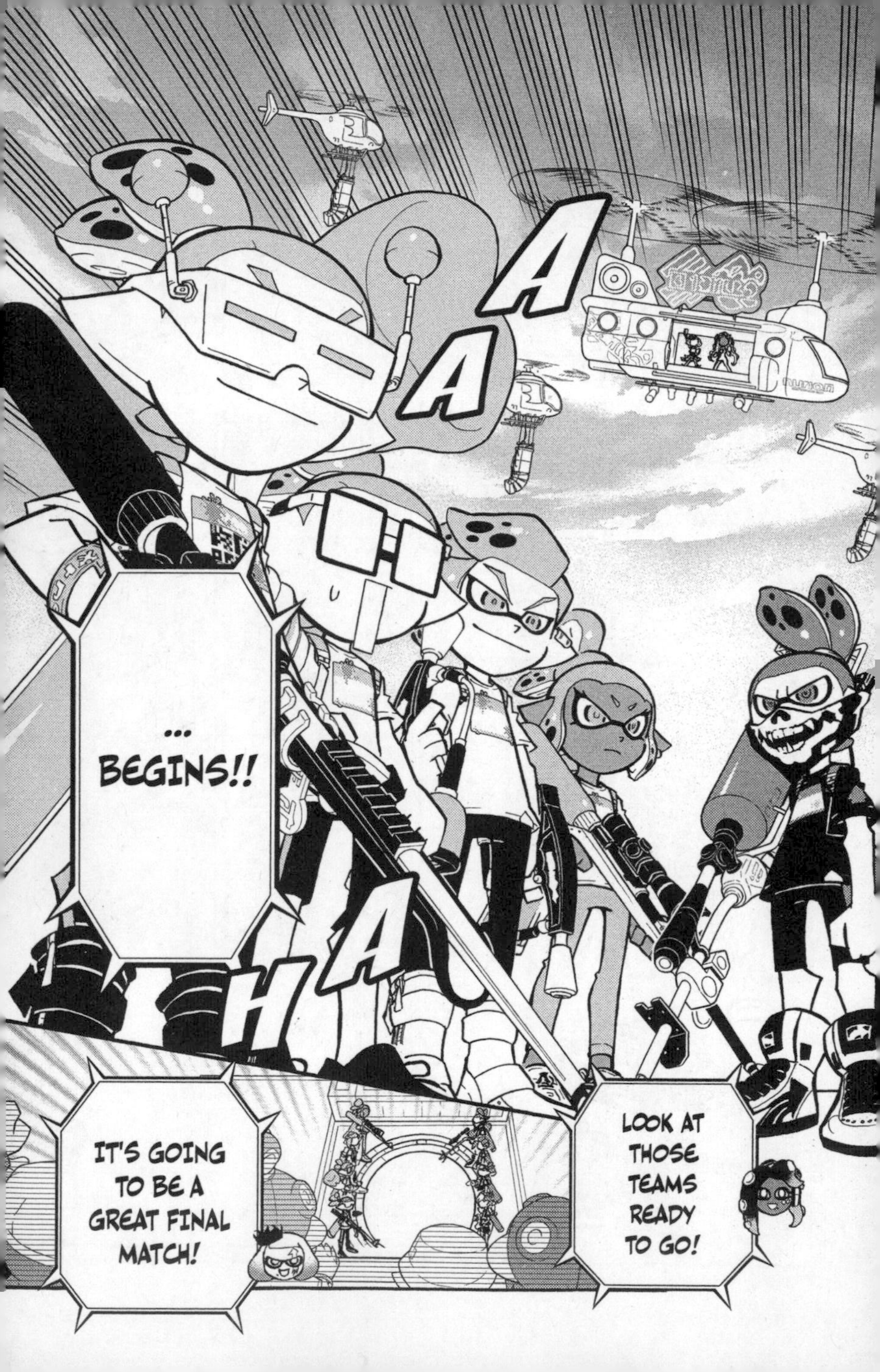
HAAA
... BEGINS!!
LOOK AT THOSE TEAMS READY TO GO!
IT'S GOING TO BE A GREAT FINAL MATCH!

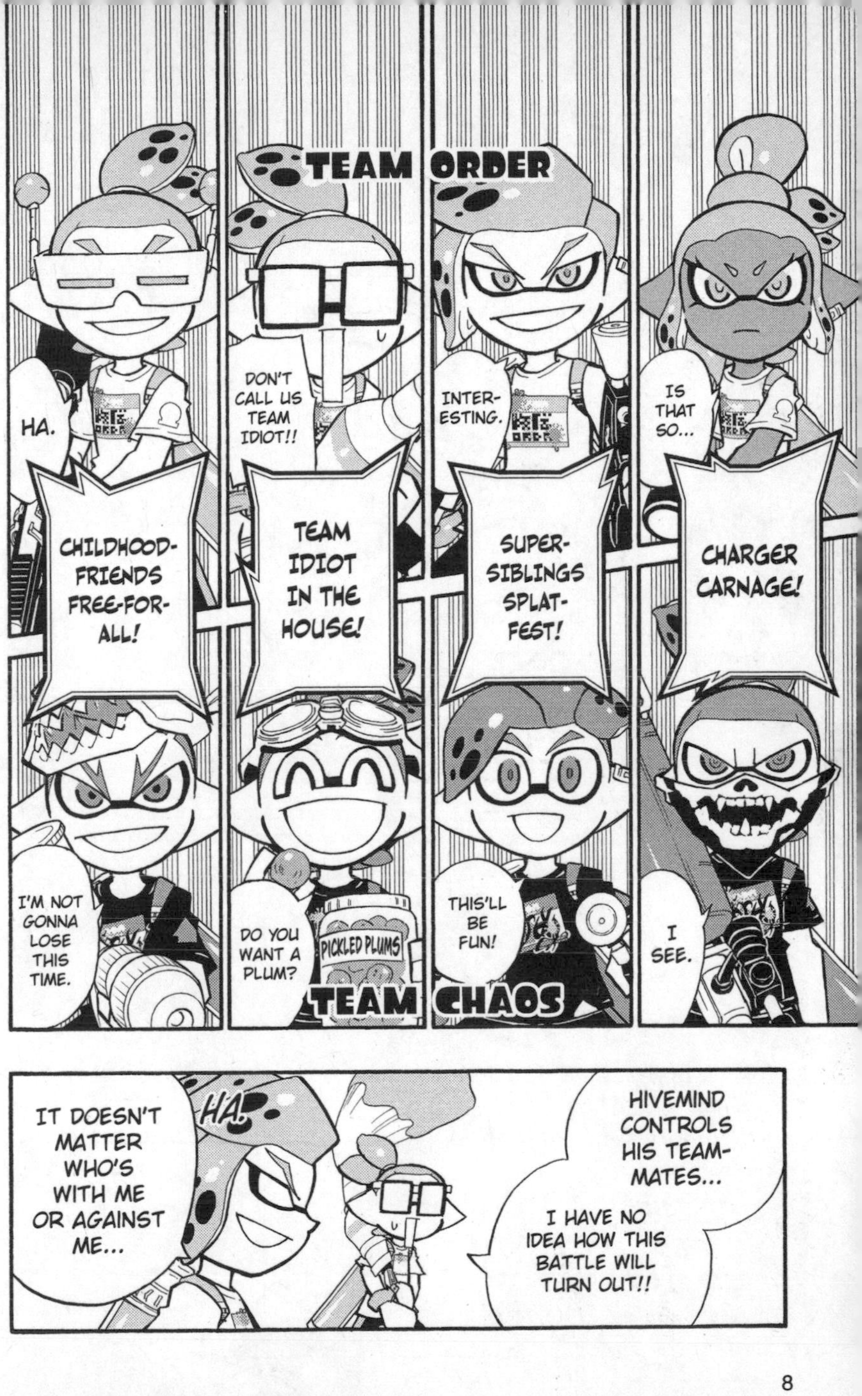
TEAM ORDER
IS THAT SO...
CHARGER CARNAGE!
I SEE.
INTERESTING.
SUPER-SIBLINGS SPLATFEST!
THIS'LL BE FUN!
DON'T CALL US TEAM IDIOT!!
TEAM IDIOT IN THE HOUSE!
DO YOU WANT A PLUM?
PICKLED PLUMS
HA.
CHILDHOOD-FRIENDS FREE-FOR-ALL!
I'M NOT GONNA LOSE THIS TIME.
TEAM CHAOS
HIVEMIND CONTROLS HIS TEAMMATES...
I HAVE NO IDEA HOW THIS BATTLE WILL TURN OUT!!
HA!
IT DOESN'T MATTER WHO'S WITH ME OR AGAINST ME...

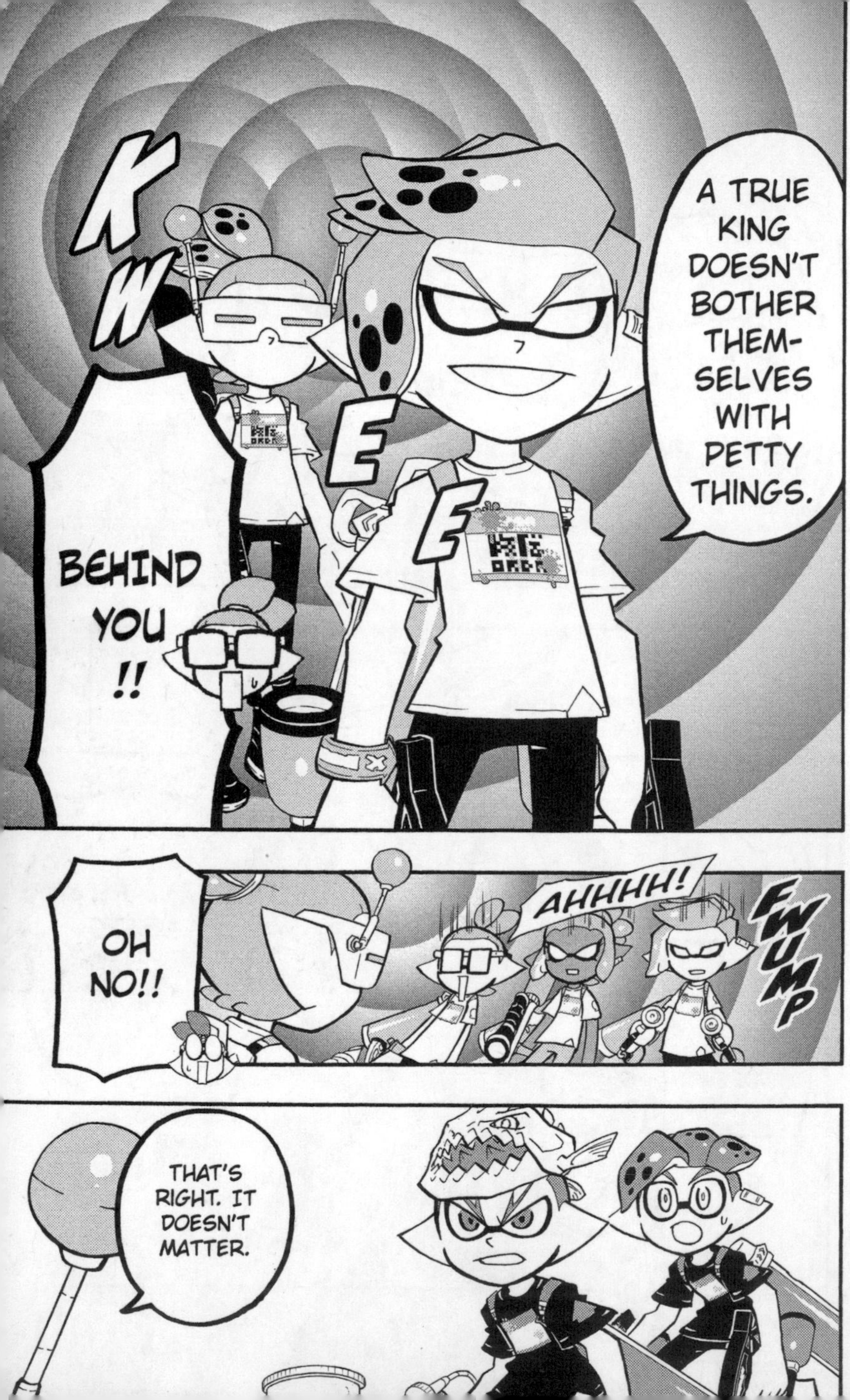
A TRUE KING DOESN'T BOTHER THEMSELVES WITH PETTY THINGS.
KWEE
BEHIND YOU !!
FWUMP
AHHHH!
OH NO!!
THAT'S RIGHT. IT DOESN'T MATTER.

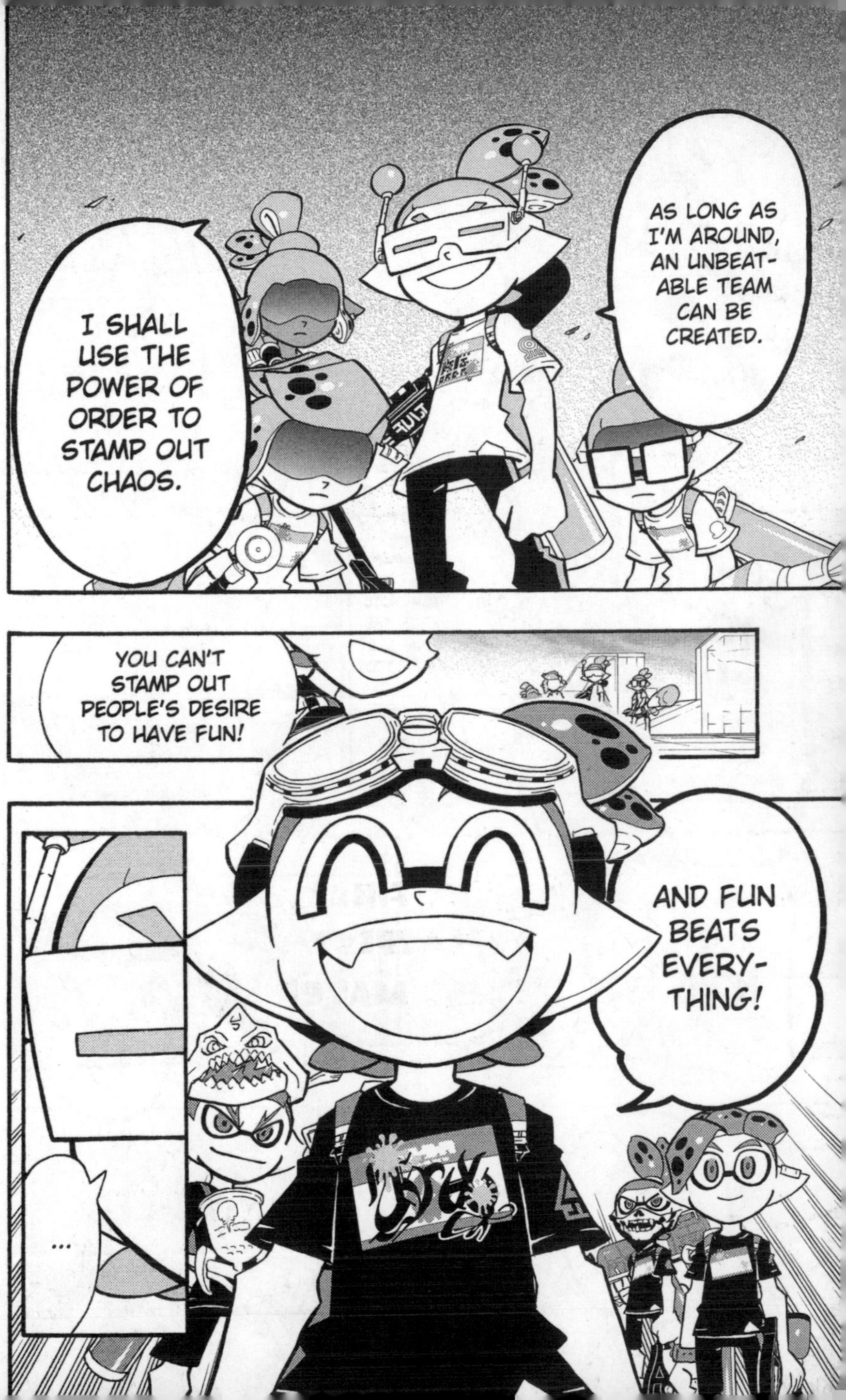
AS LONG AS I'M AROUND, AN UNBEAT-ABLE TEAM CAN BE CREATED.
I SHALL USE THE POWER OF ORDER TO STAMP OUT CHAOS.
YOU CAN'T STAMP OUT PEOPLE'S DESIRE TO HAVE FUN!
AND FUN BEATS EVERY-THING!
...

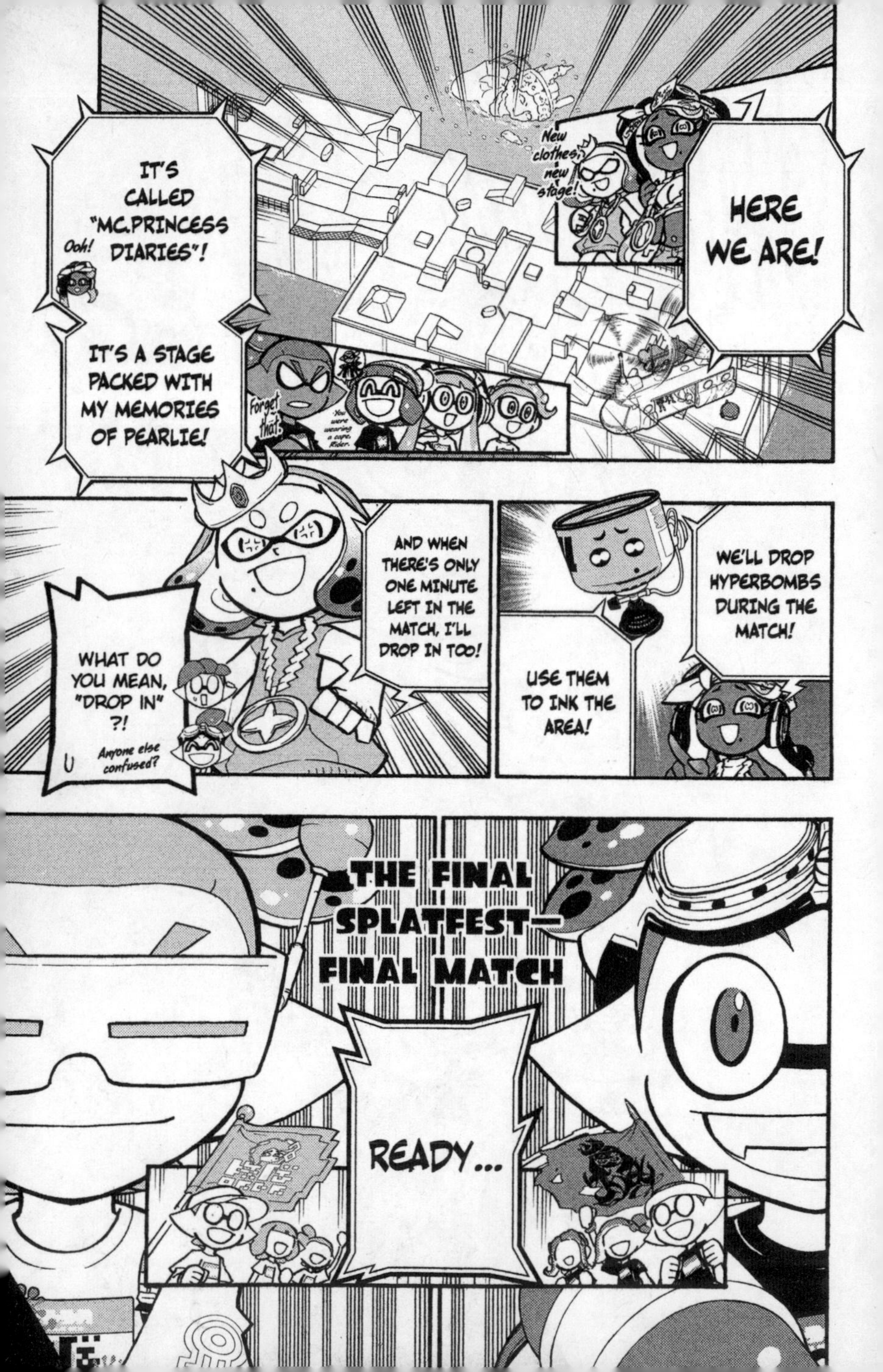
HERE WE ARE!
New clothes, new stage!
IT'S CALLED "MC.PRINCESS DIARIES"!
Ooh!
IT'S A STAGE PACKED WITH MY MEMORIES OF PEARLIE!
Forget that!
You were wearing a cape, Rider.
WE'LL DROP HYPERBOMBS DURING THE MATCH!
USE THEM TO INK THE AREA!
AND WHEN THERE'S ONLY ONE MINUTE LEFT IN THE MATCH, I'LL DROP IN TOO!
WHAT DO YOU MEAN, "DROP IN" ?!
Anyone else confused?
THE FINAL SPLATFEST— FINAL MATCH
READY...

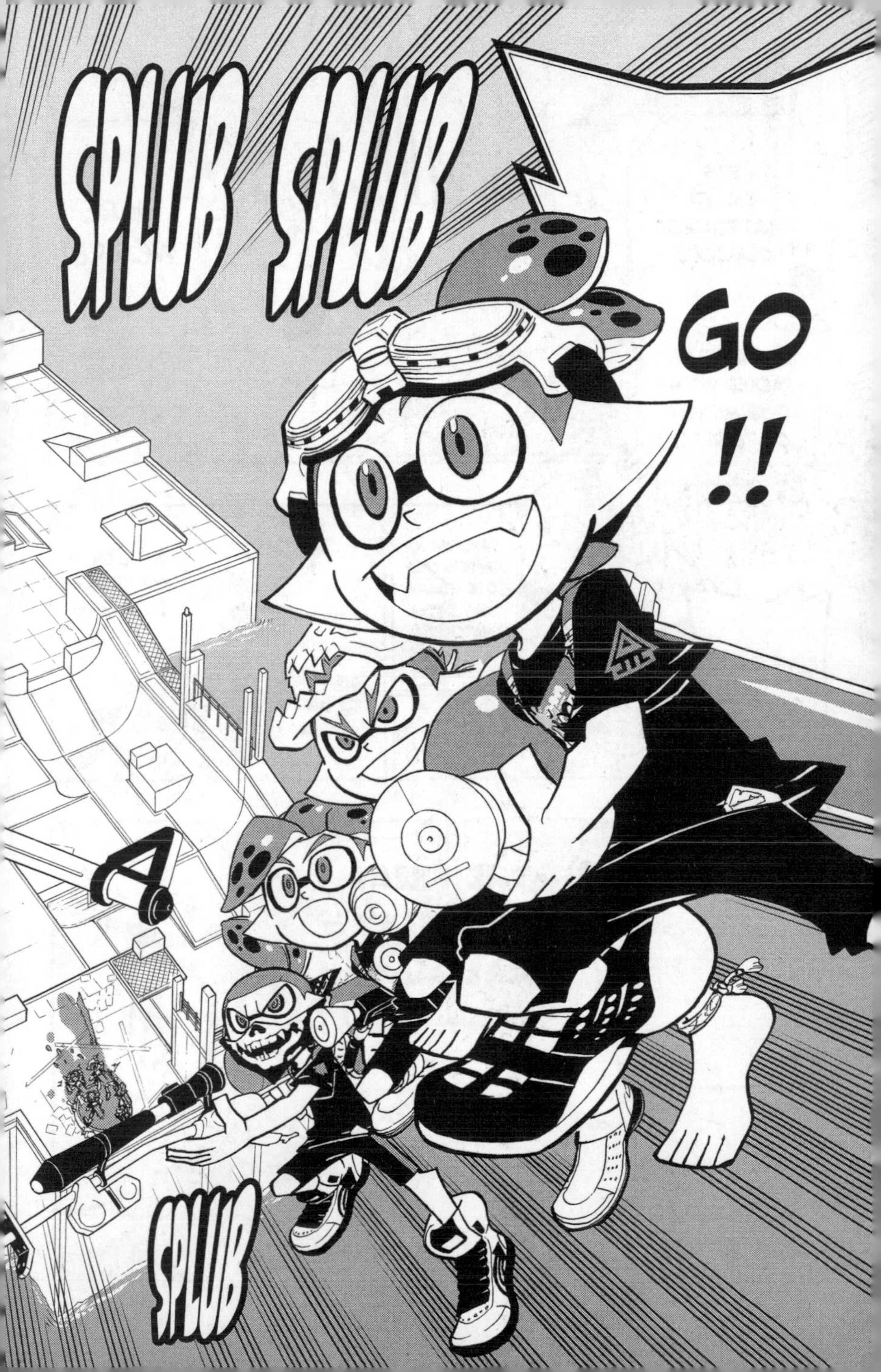
SPLUB SPLUB
GO!!
SPLUB

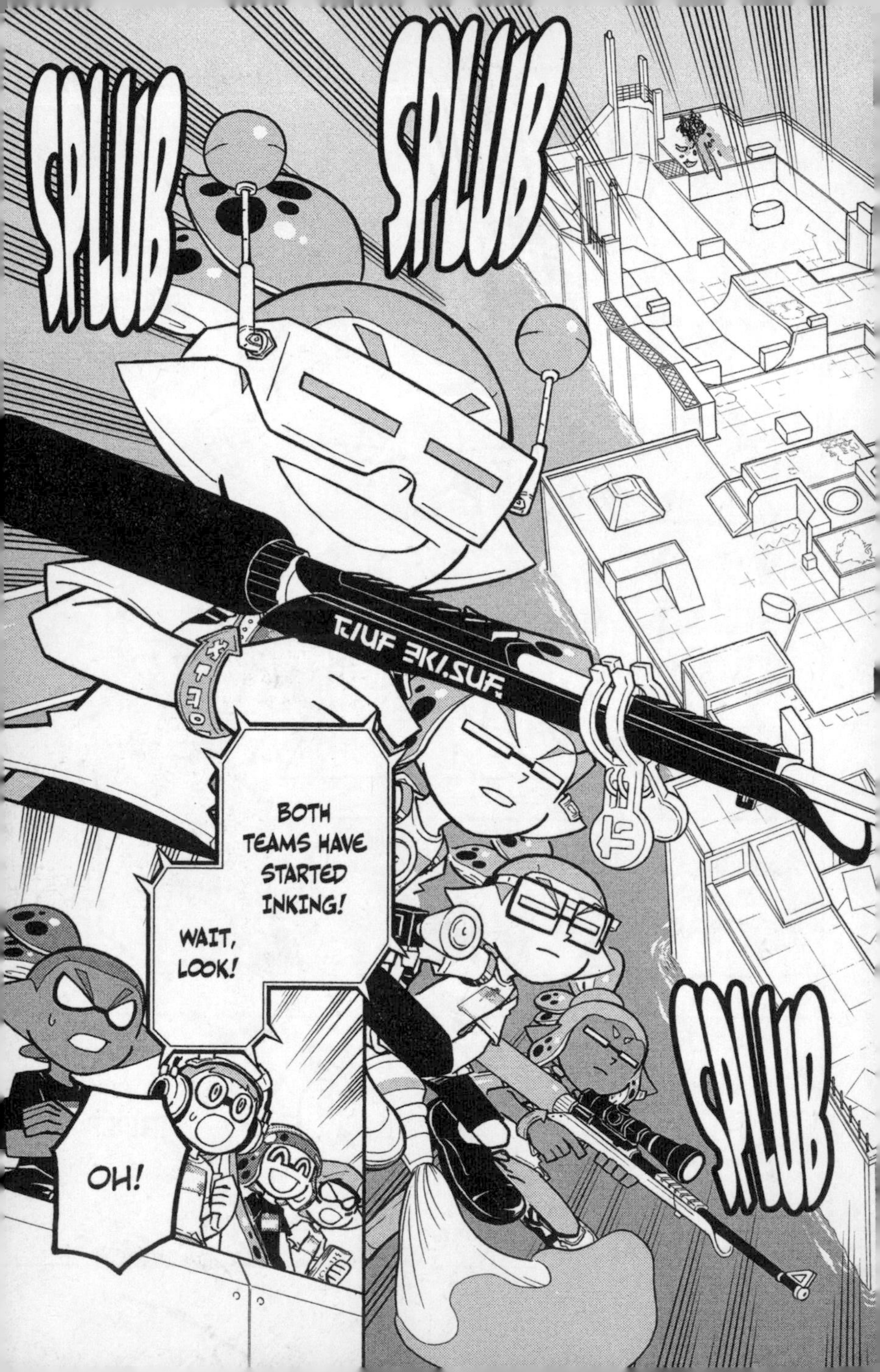
SPLUB
SPLUB
BOTH TEAMS HAVE STARTED INKING!
WAIT, LOOK!
OH!
SPLUB

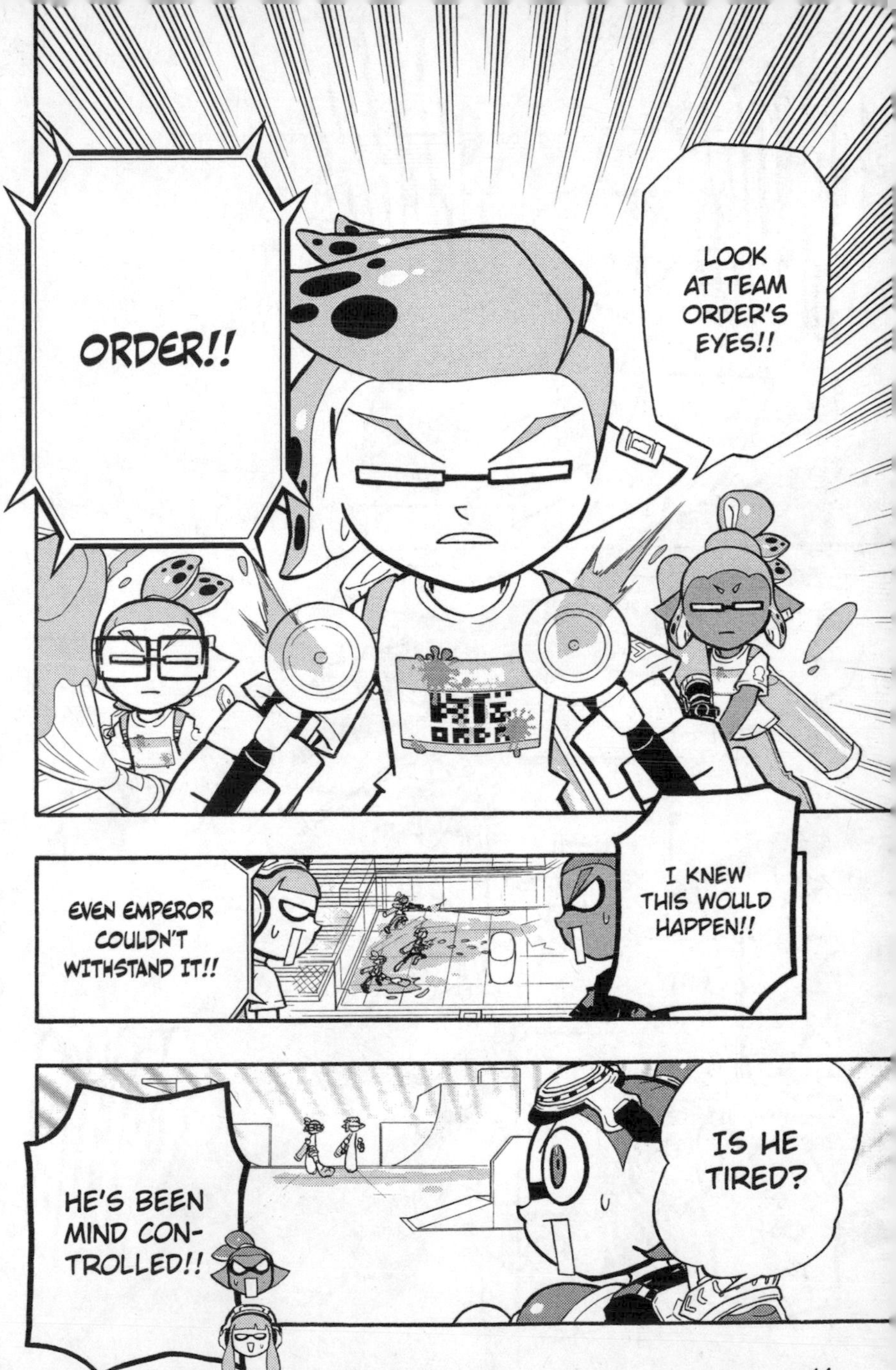
LOOK AT TEAM ORDER'S EYES!!
ORDER!!
I KNEW THIS WOULD HAPPEN!!
EVEN EMPEROR COULDN'T WITHSTAND IT!!
IS HE TIRED?
HE'S BEEN MIND CON-TROLLED!!

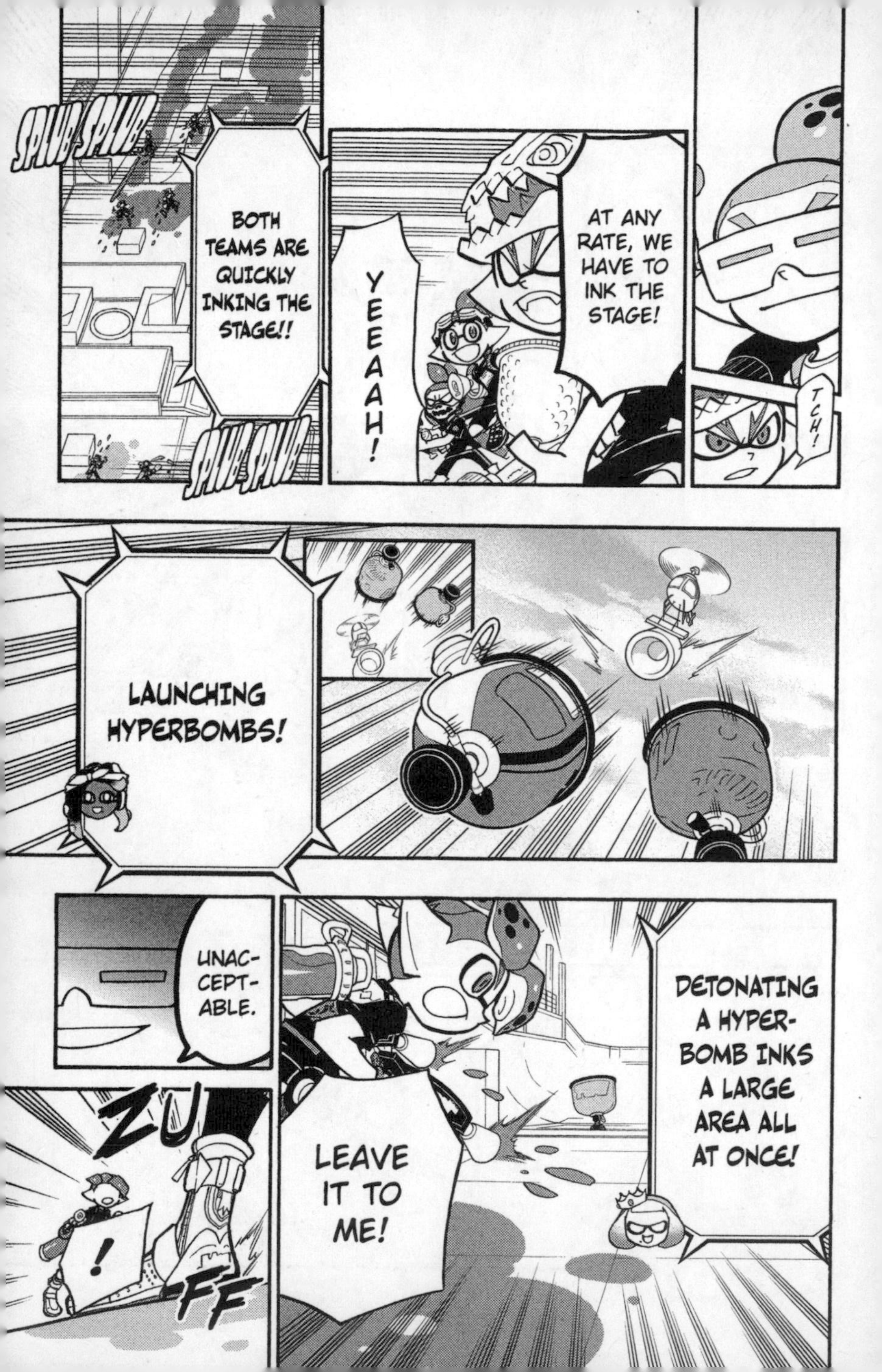
TCH!
AT ANY RATE, WE HAVE TO INK THE STAGE!
YEEEAAAH!
BOTH TEAMS ARE QUICKLY INKING THE STAGE!!
LAUNCHING HYPERBOMBS!
DETONATING A HYPER-BOMB INKS A LARGE AREA ALL AT ONCE!
LEAVE IT TO ME!
UNAC-CEPT-ABLE.
ZU
FF
!

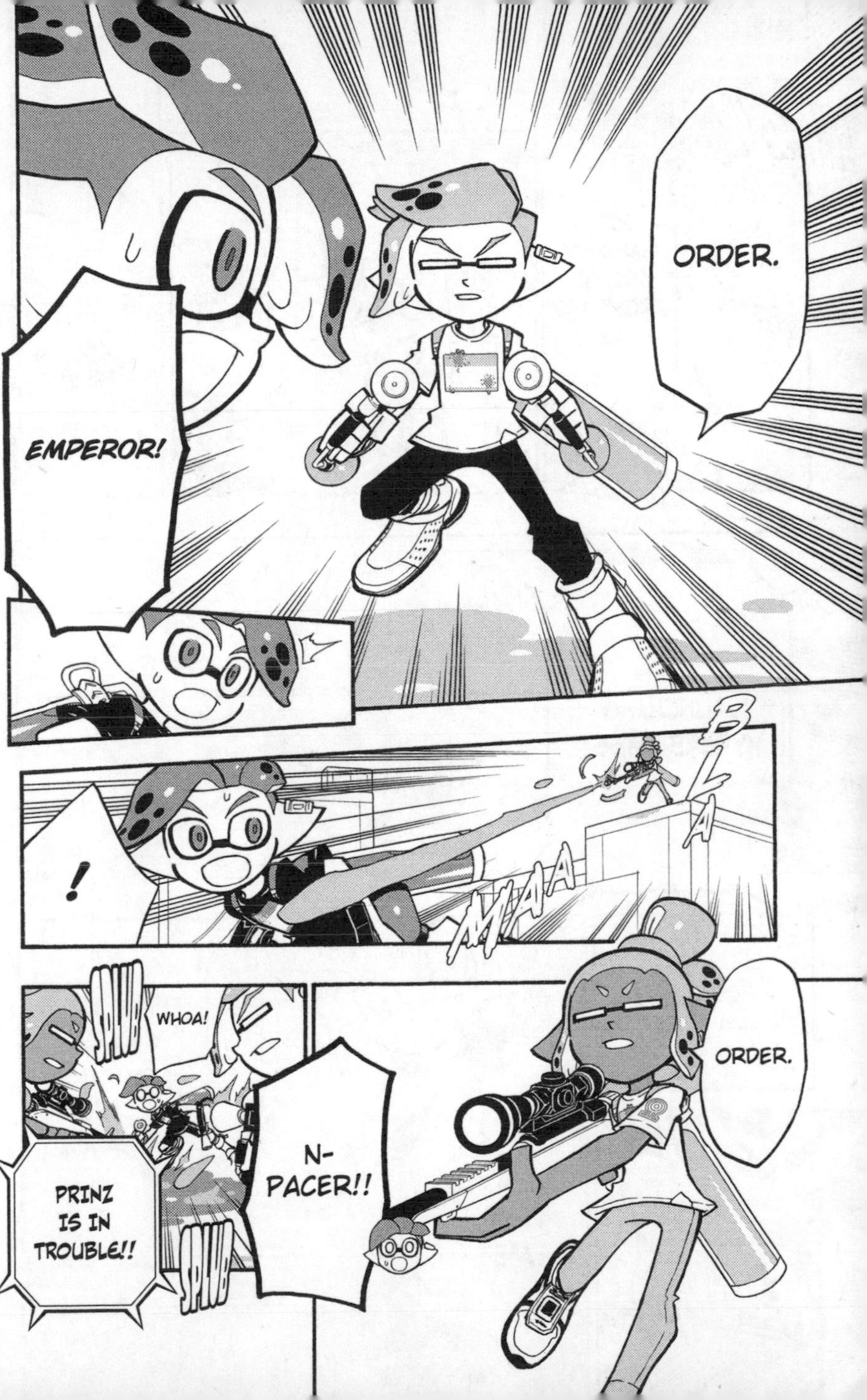
ORDER.
EMPEROR!
!
BLAAAM
ORDER.
N-PACER!!
SPLUB
WHOA!
PRINZ IS IN TROUBLE!!
SPLUB

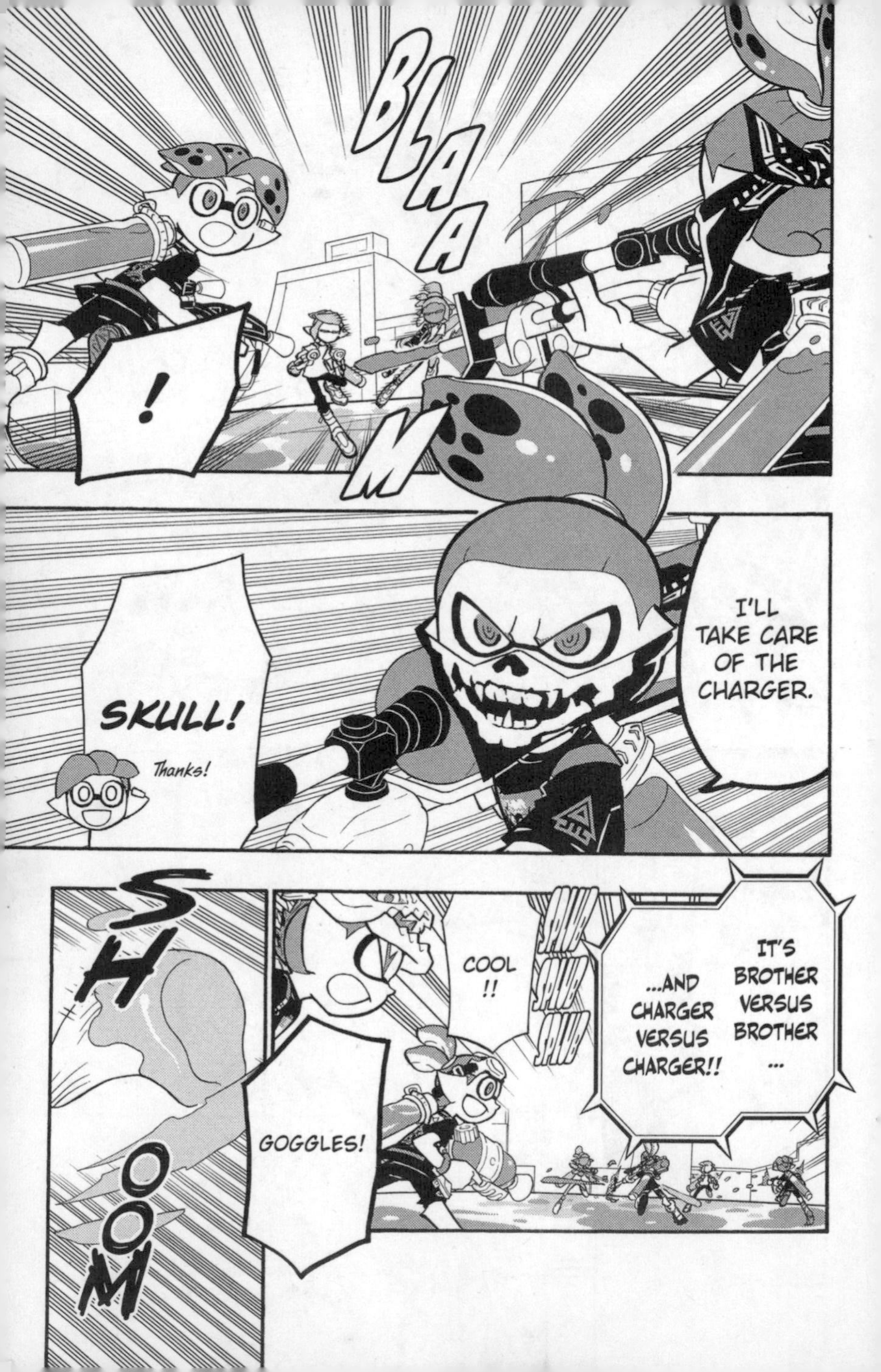
BLAAM
!
I'LL TAKE CARE OF THE CHARGER.
SKULL!
Thanks!
IT'S BROTHER VERSUS BROTHER ...
...AND CHARGER VERSUS CHARGER!!
COOL !!
GOGGLES!
SHOOM

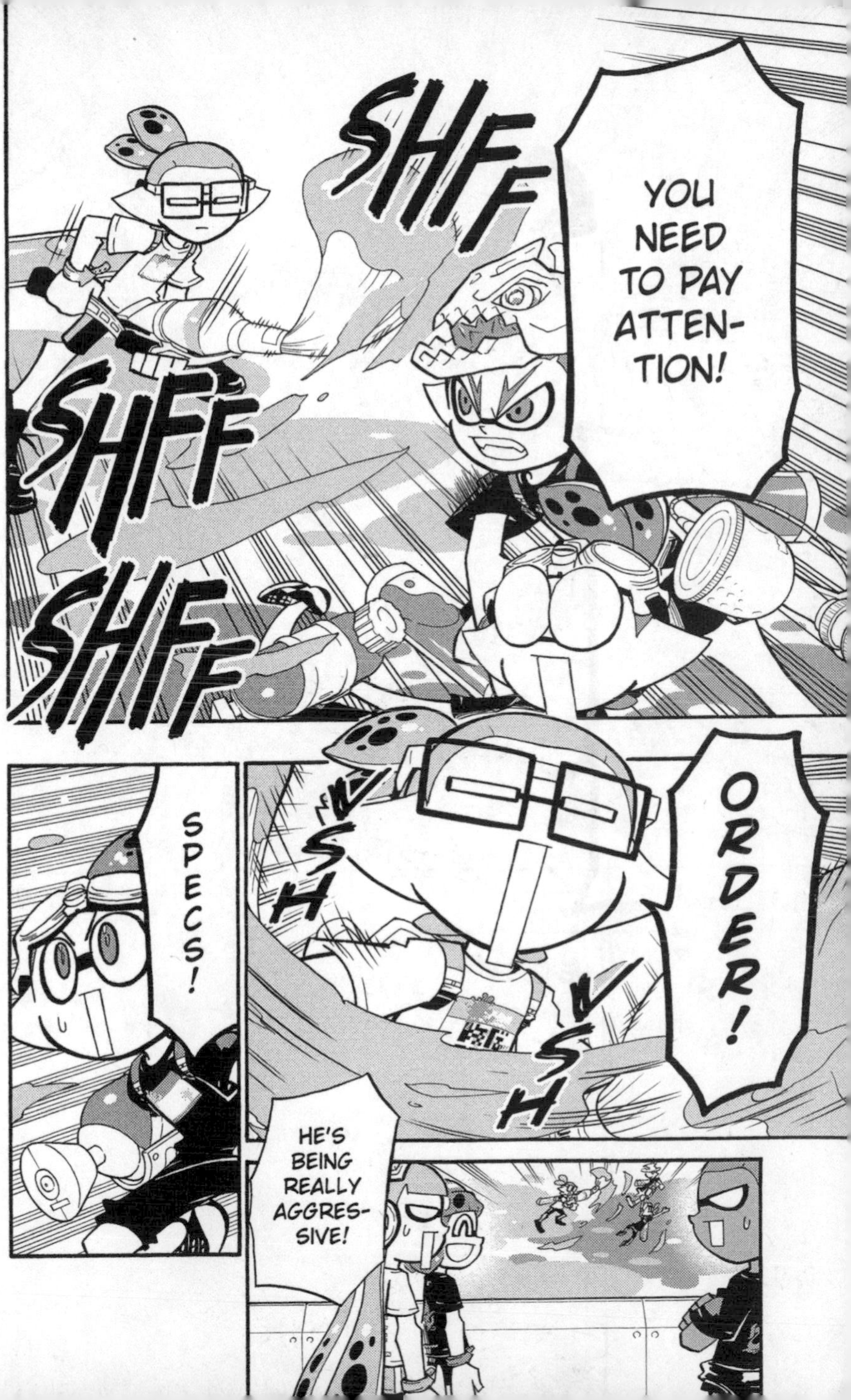
YOU NEED TO PAY ATTEN-TION!
SHFF
SHFF
SHFF
ORDER!
SPECS!
HE'S BEING REALLY AGGRES-SIVE!

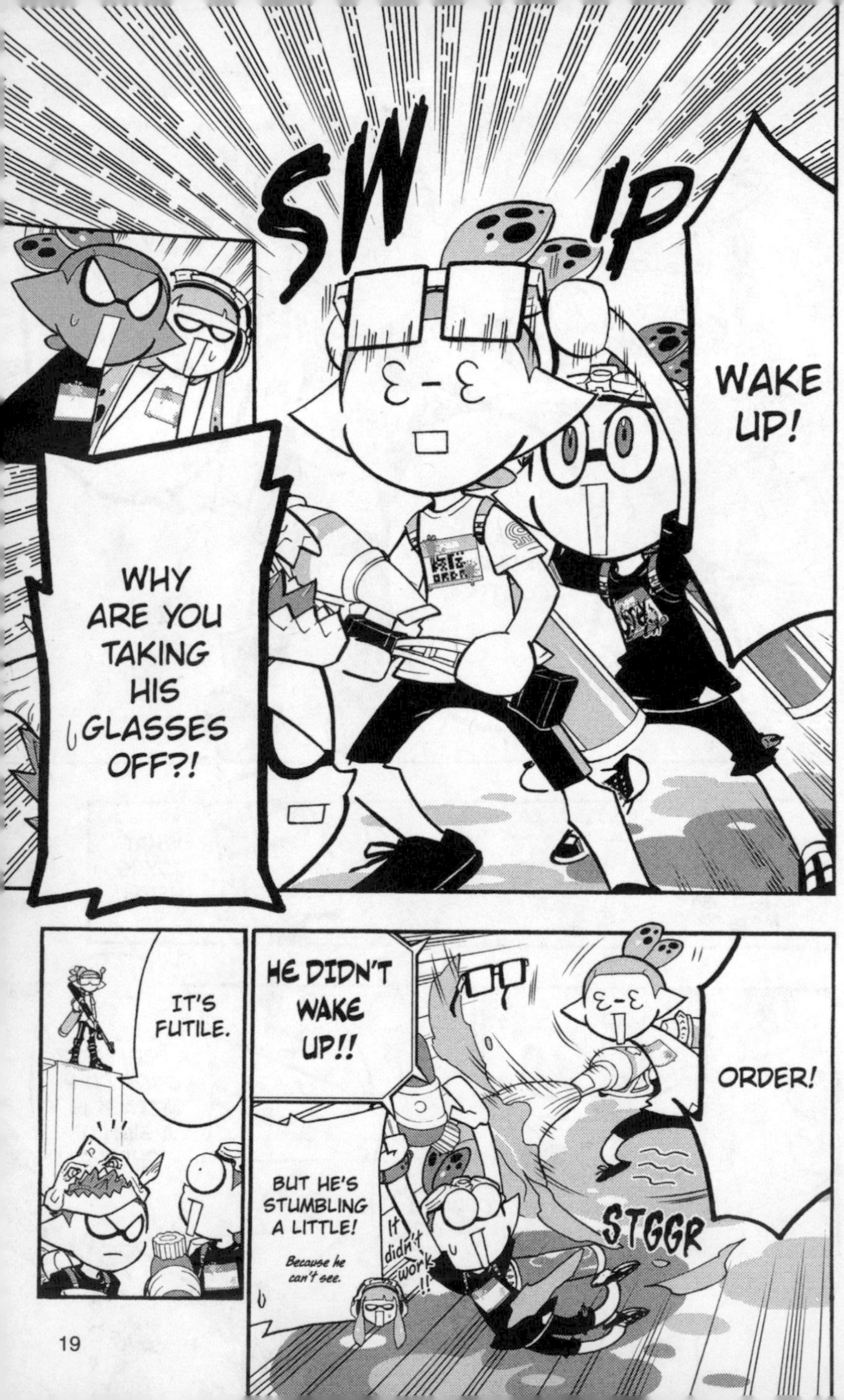
SW IP
WAKE UP!
WHY ARE YOU TAKING HIS GLASSES OFF?!
ORDER!
HE DIDN'T WAKE UP!!
STGGR
BUT HE'S STUMBLING A LITTLE!
It didn't work!!
Because he can't see.
IT'S FUTILE.

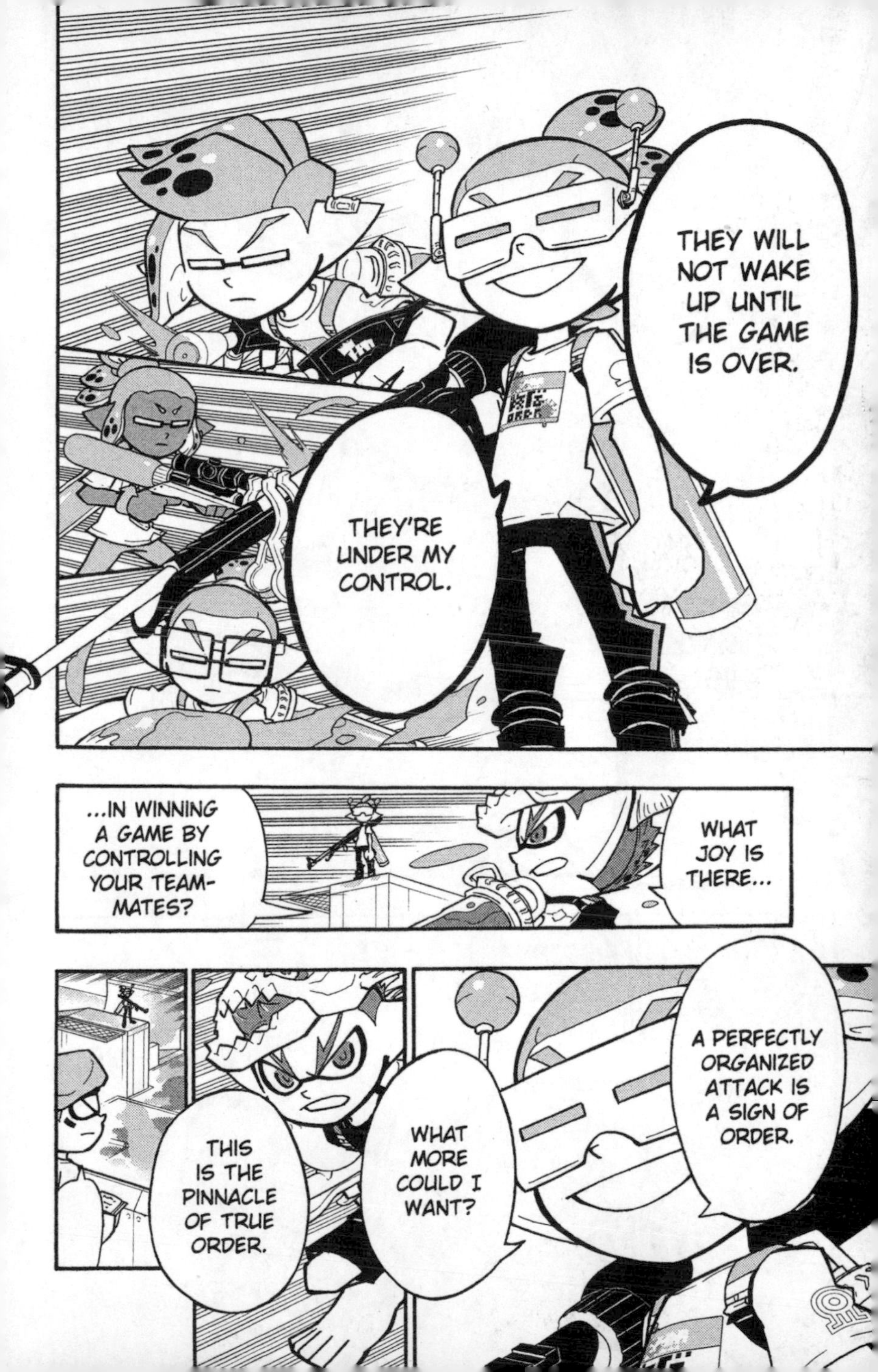
THEY WILL NOT WAKE UP UNTIL THE GAME IS OVER.
THEY'RE UNDER MY CONTROL.
WHAT JOY IS THERE...
...IN WINNING A GAME BY CONTROLLING YOUR TEAM-MATES?
A PERFECTLY ORGANIZED ATTACK IS A SIGN OF ORDER.
WHAT MORE COULD I WANT?
THIS IS THE PINNACLE OF TRUE ORDER.

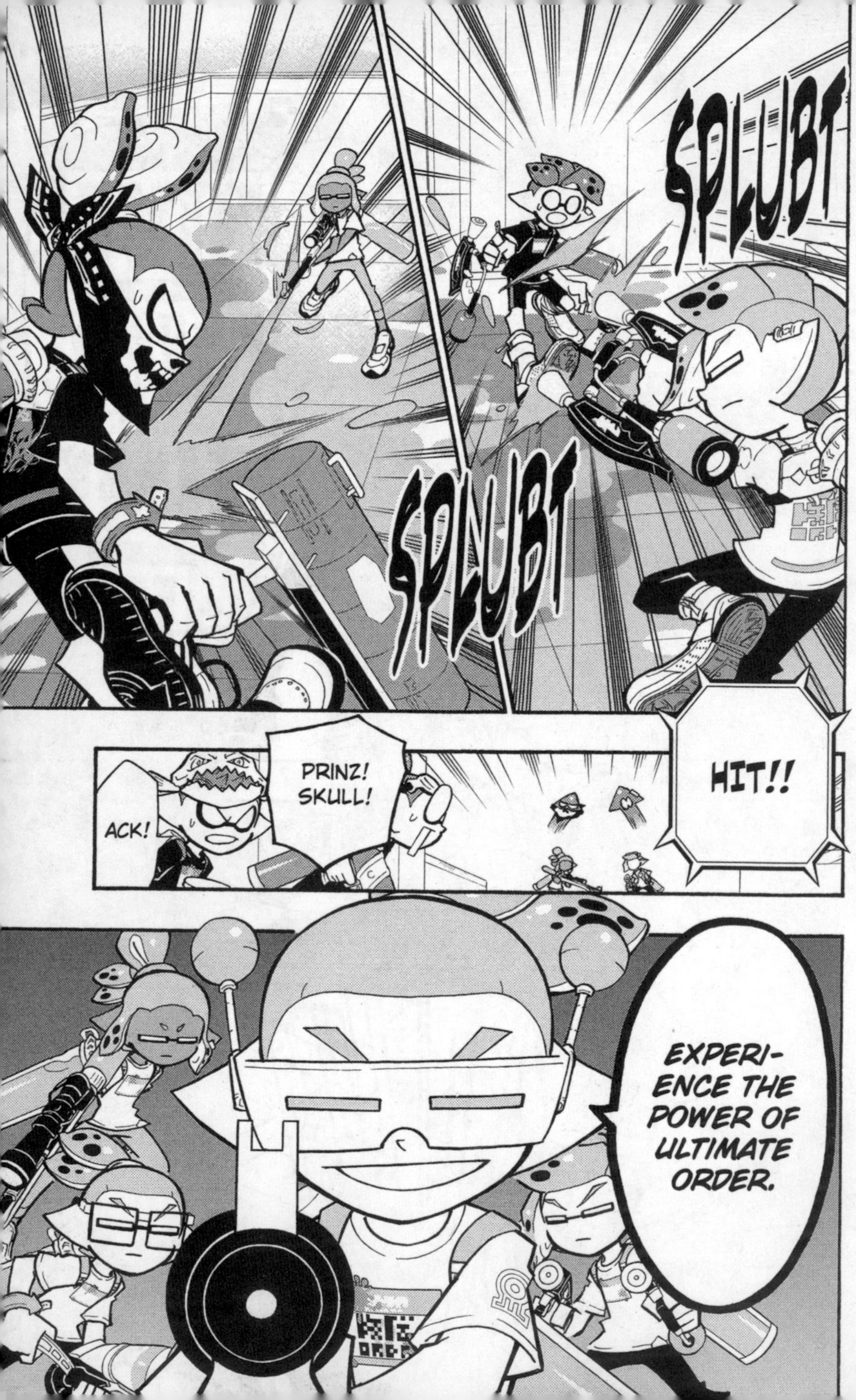
SPLUBT
SPLUBT
HIT!!
PRINZ! SKULL!
ACK!
EXPERIENCE THE POWER OF ULTIMATE ORDER.

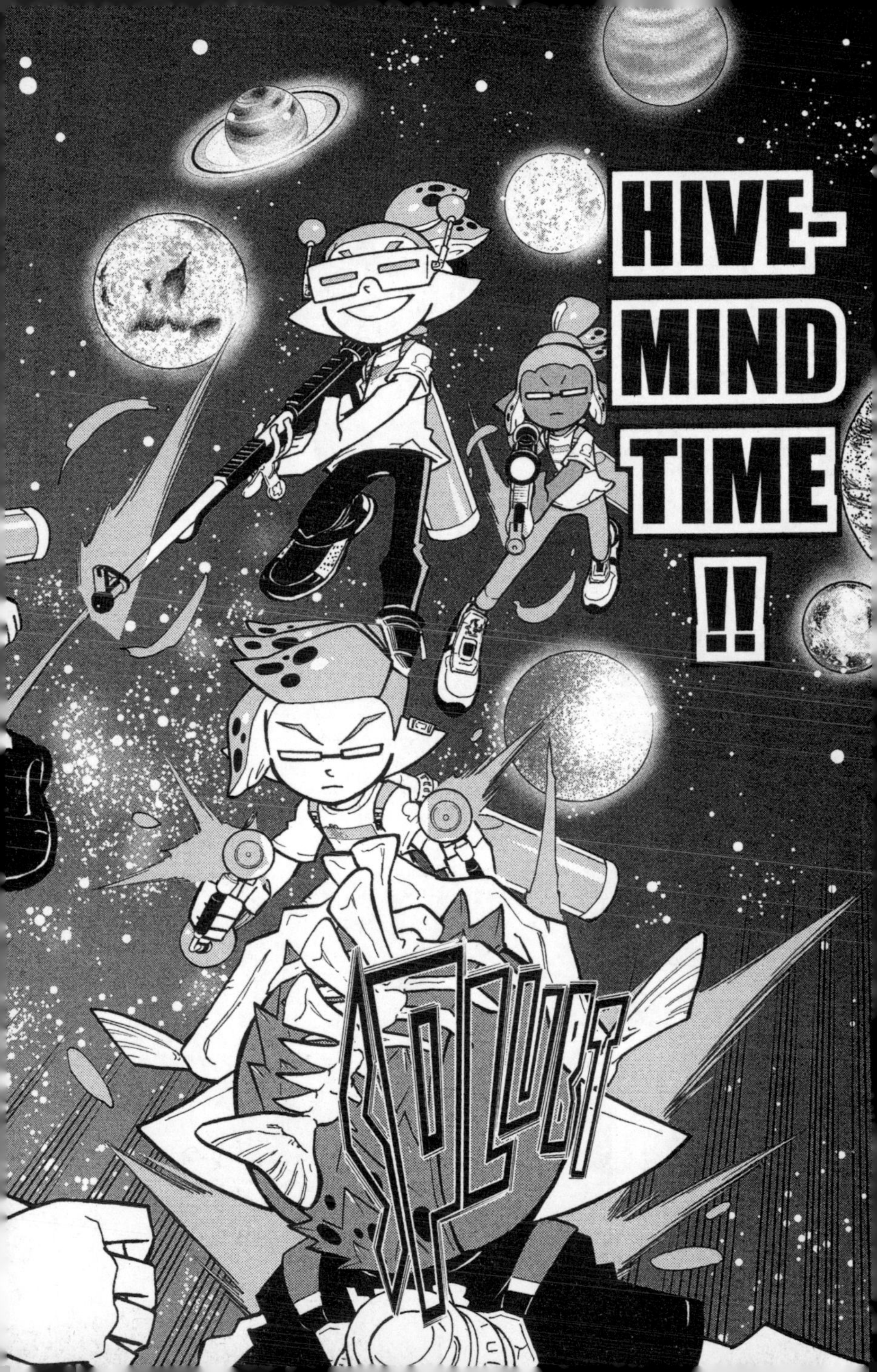
HIVE-MIND TIME !!
SPLURST

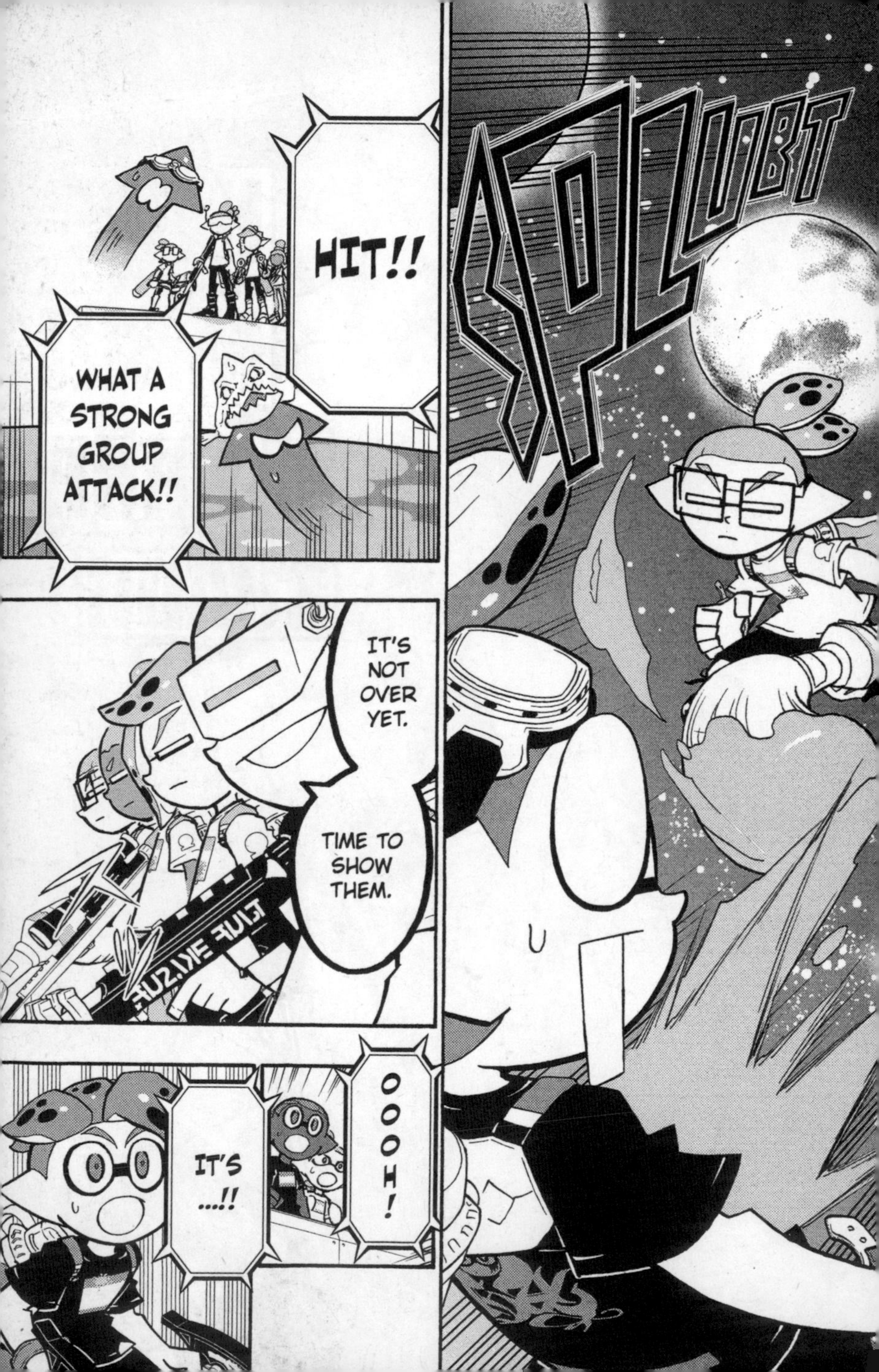
HIT!!
WHAT A STRONG GROUP ATTACK!!
IT'S NOT OVER YET.
TIME TO SHOW THEM.
OOOOH!
IT'S ...!!

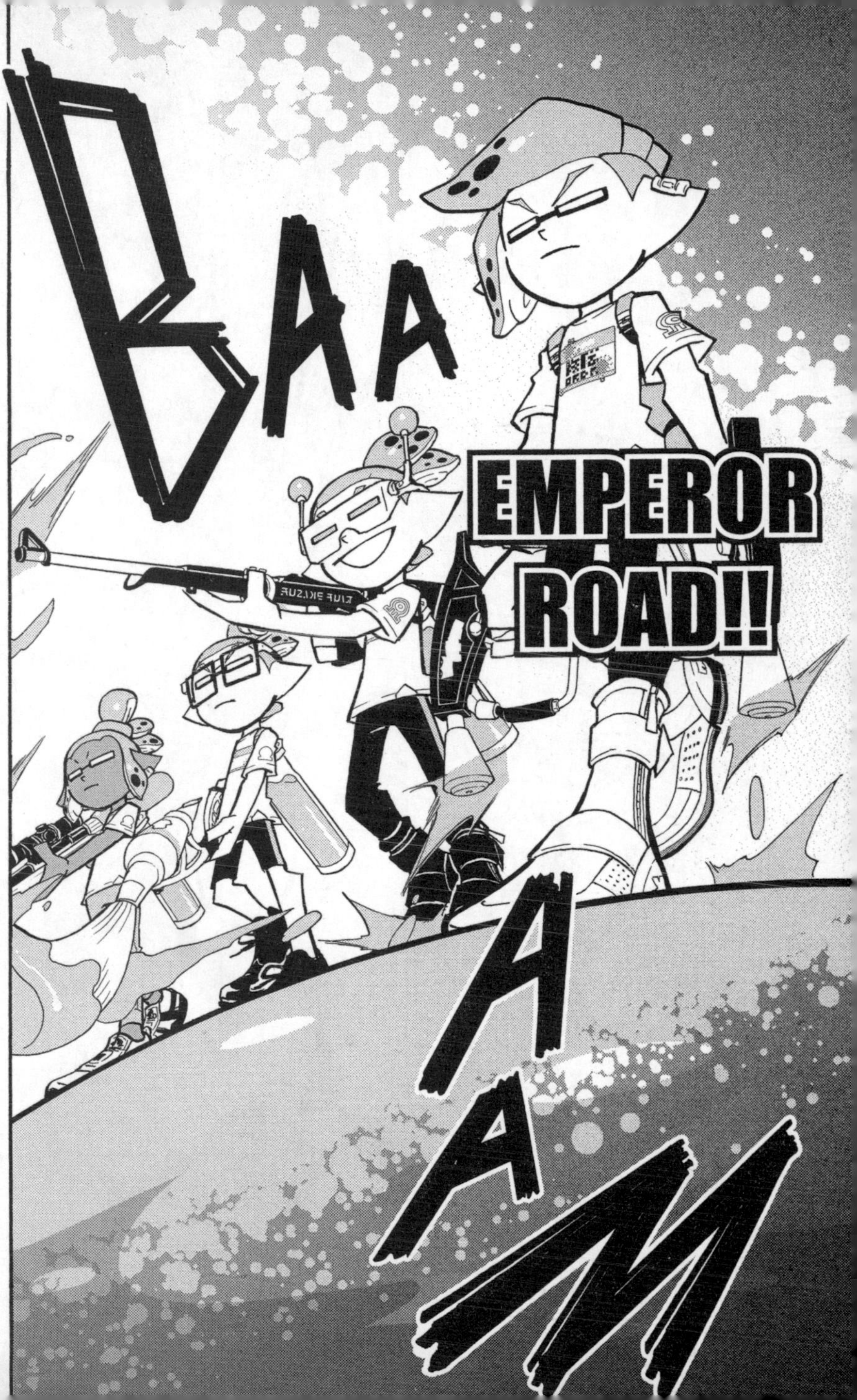
EMPEROR ROAD!!
BAAAAAM

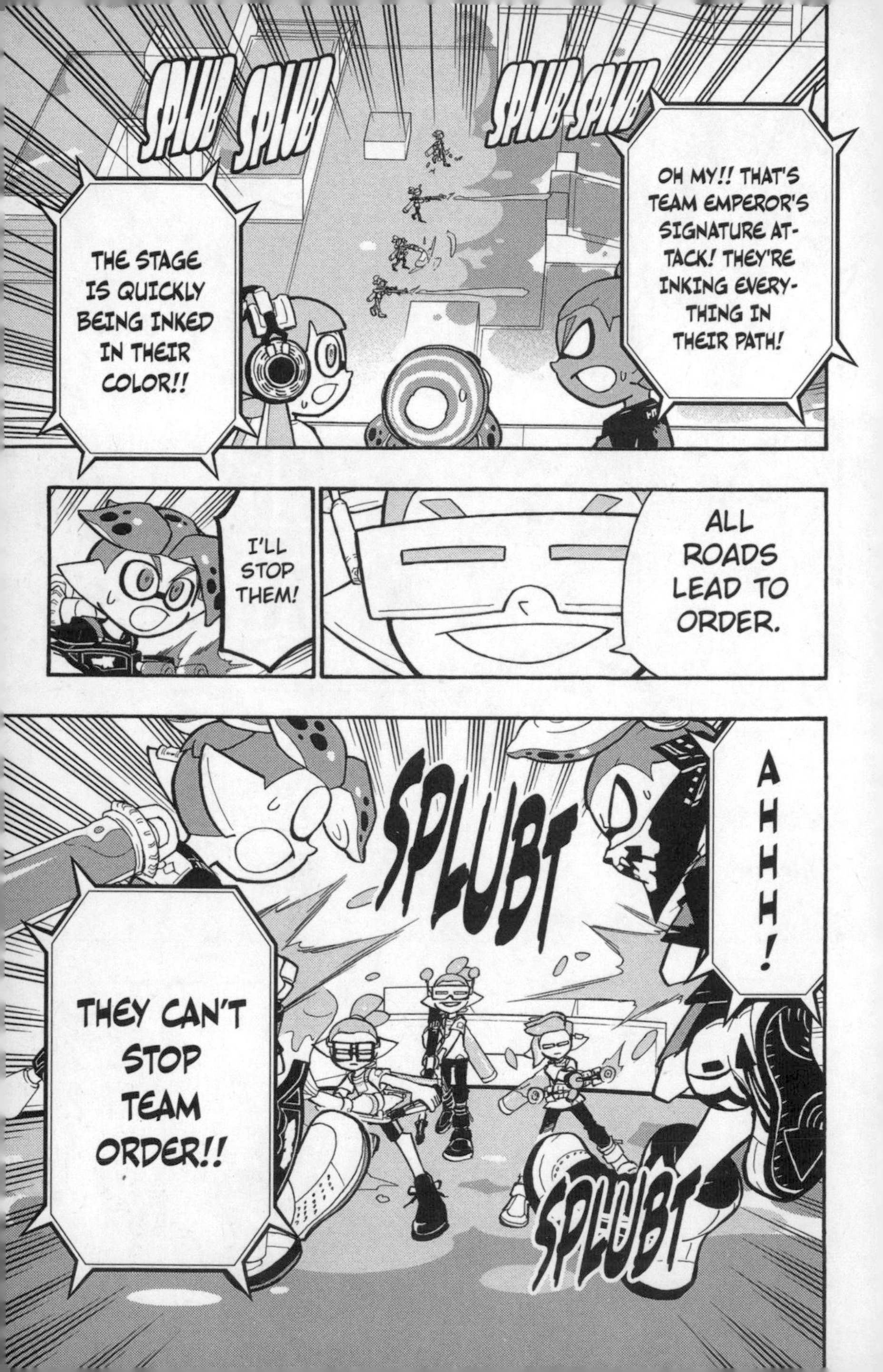
SPLUB SPLUB
OH MY!! THAT'S TEAM EMPEROR'S SIGNATURE AT-TACK! THEY'RE INKING EVERY-THING IN THEIR PATH!
SPLUB SPLUB
THE STAGE IS QUICKLY BEING INKED IN THEIR COLOR!!
ALL ROADS LEAD TO ORDER.
I'LL STOP THEM!
AHHH!
SPLUBT
THEY CAN'T STOP TEAM ORDER!!
SPLUBT

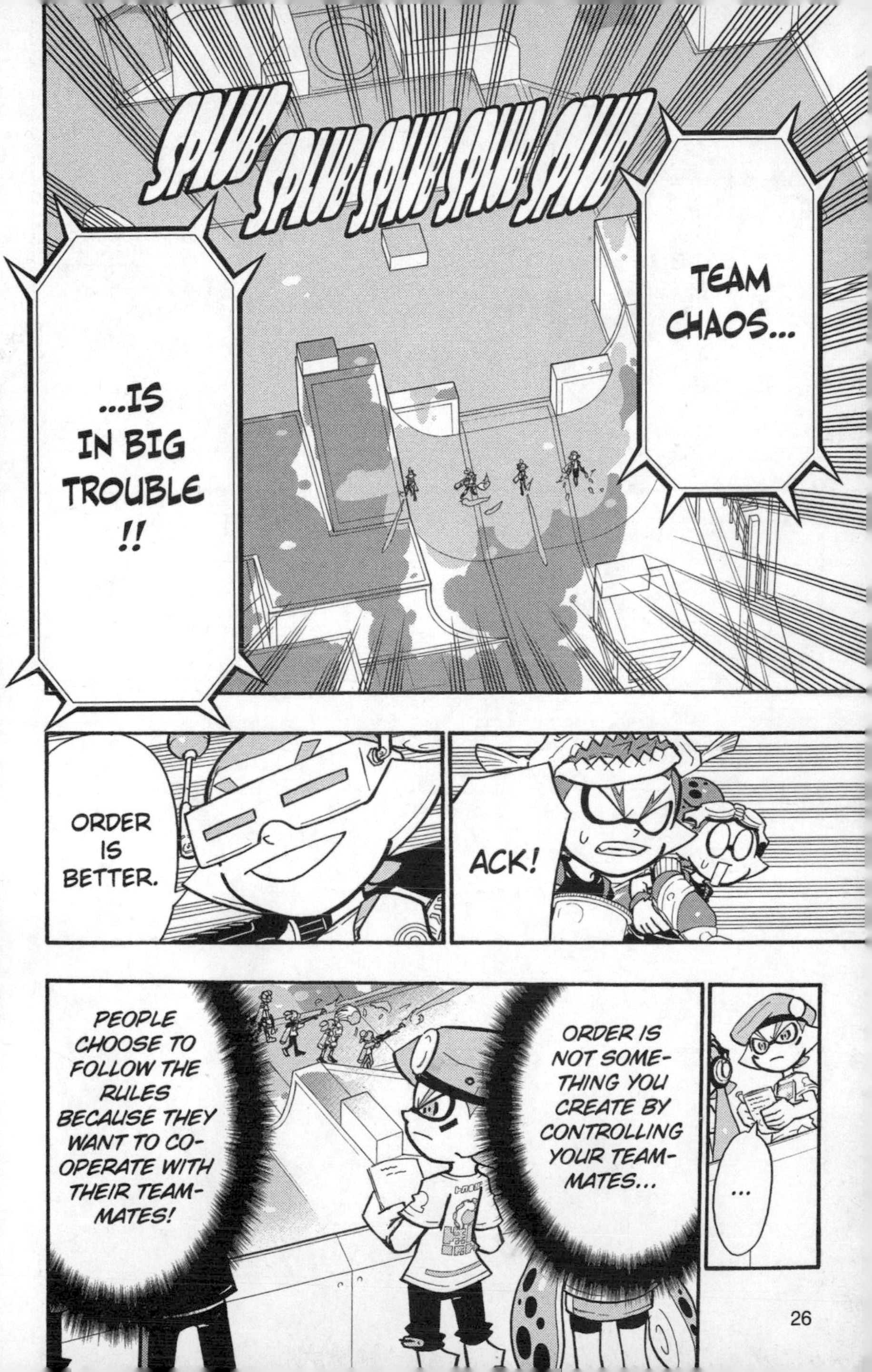
TEAM CHAOS...
...IS IN BIG TROUBLE!!
ACK!
ORDER IS BETTER.
...
ORDER IS NOT SOME-THING YOU CREATE BY CONTROLLING YOUR TEAM-MATES...
PEOPLE CHOOSE TO FOLLOW THE RULES BECAUSE THEY WANT TO CO-OPERATE WITH THEIR TEAM-MATES!

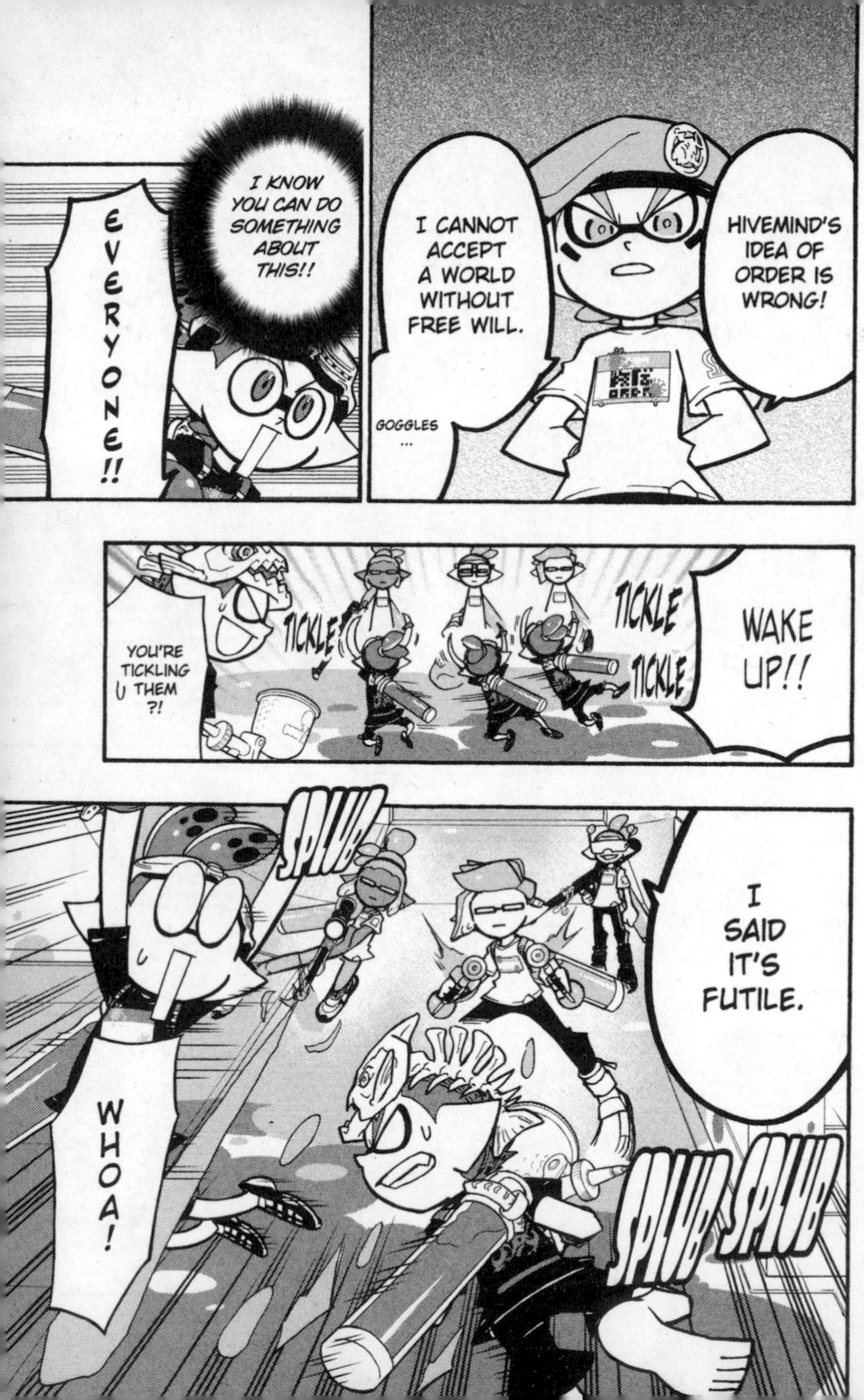
HIVEMIND'S IDEA OF ORDER IS WRONG!
I CANNOT ACCEPT A WORLD WITHOUT FREE WILL.
GOGGLES ...
I KNOW YOU CAN DO SOMETHING ABOUT THIS!!
EVERYONE!!
WAKE UP!!
TICKLE
TICKLE
TICKLE
YOU'RE TICKLING THEM ?!
I SAID IT'S FUTILE.
SPLUB
SPLUB SPLUB
WHOA!

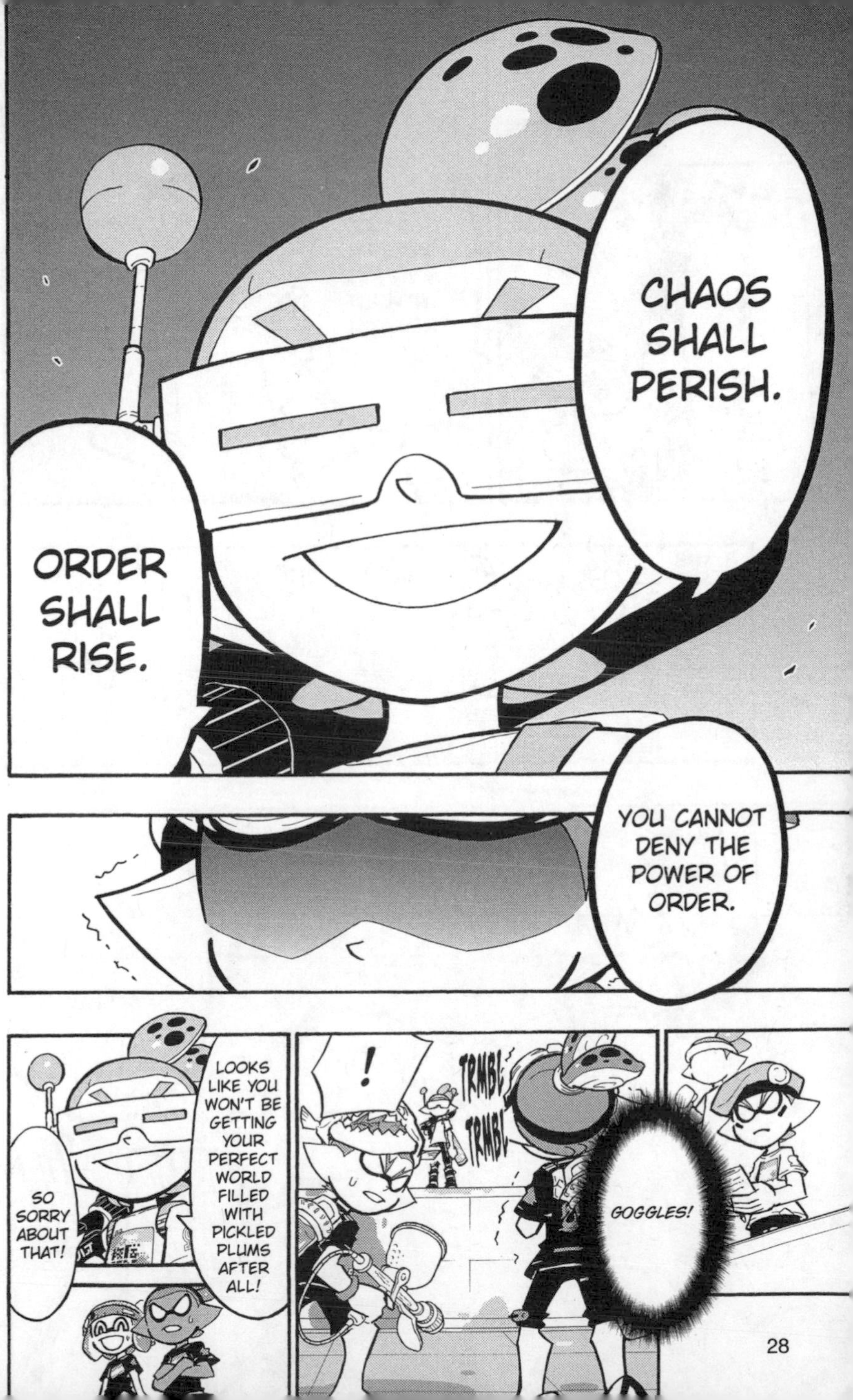
CHAOS SHALL PERISH.
ORDER SHALL RISE.
YOU CANNOT DENY THE POWER OF ORDER.
TRMBL TRMBL
!
GOGGLES!
LOOKS LIKE YOU WON'T BE GETTING YOUR PERFECT WORLD FILLED WITH PICKLED PLUMS AFTER ALL!
SO SORRY ABOUT THAT!

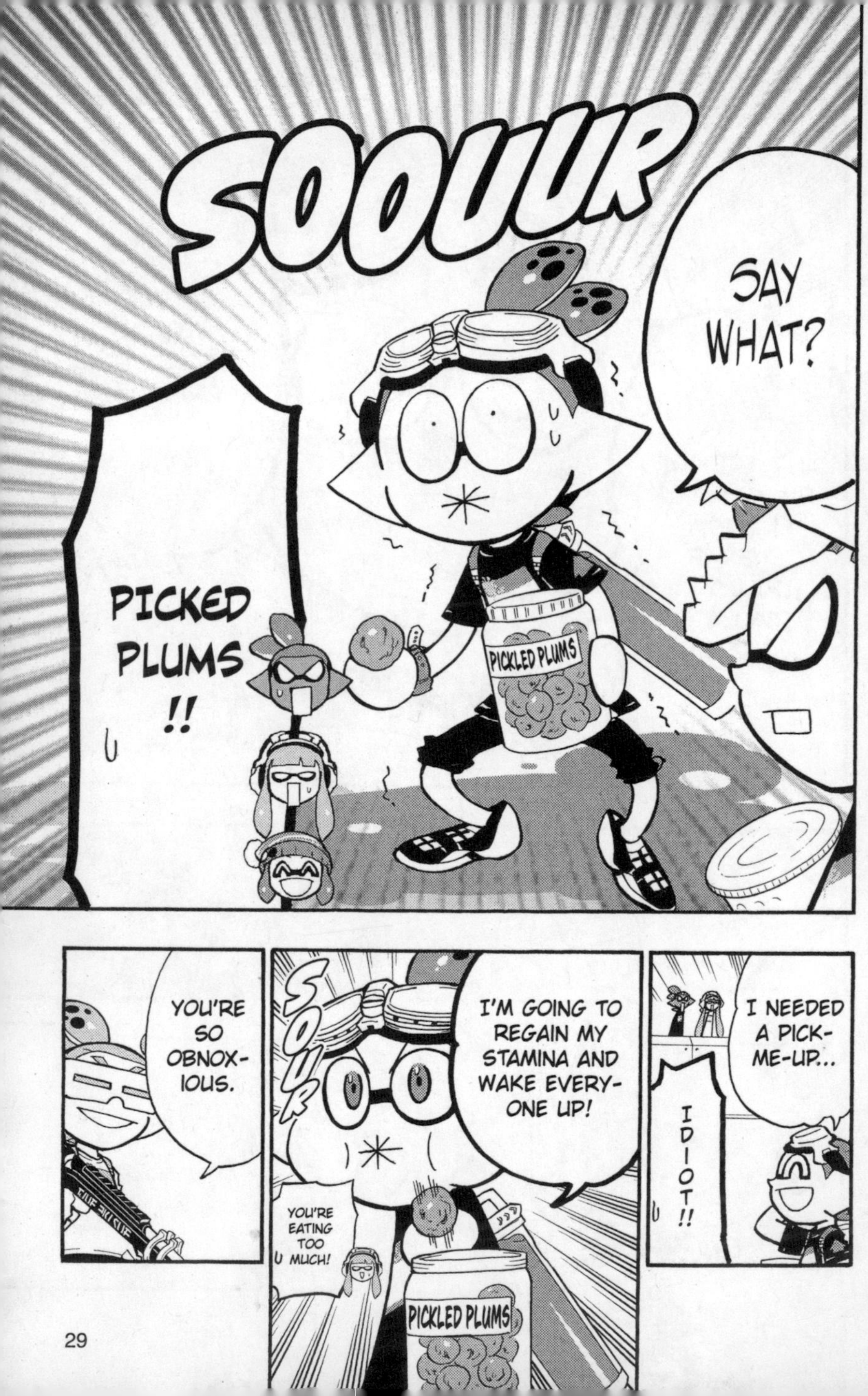
SOOUUR
SAY WHAT?
PICKLED PLUMS
PICKED PLUMS !!
I NEEDED A PICK-ME-UP...
IDIOT!!
SOUR
I'M GOING TO REGAIN MY STAMINA AND WAKE EVERY-ONE UP!
YOU'RE EATING TOO MUCH!
PICKLED PLUMS
YOU'RE SO OBNOX-IOUS.

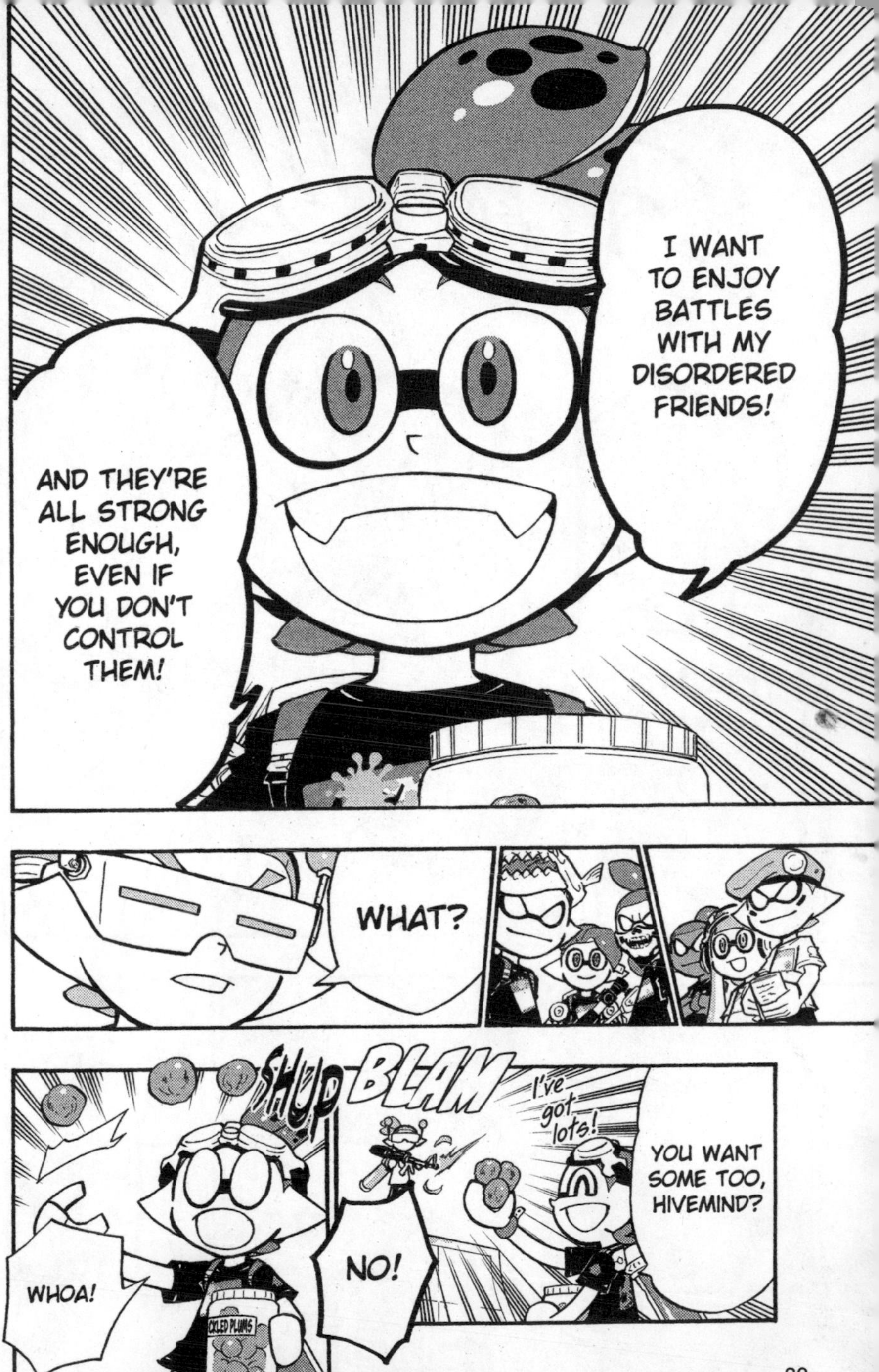
I WANT TO ENJOY BATTLES WITH MY DISORDERED FRIENDS!
AND THEY'RE ALL STRONG ENOUGH, EVEN IF YOU DON'T CONTROL THEM!
WHAT?
YOU WANT SOME TOO, HIVEMIND?
I've got lots!
BLAM
SHUP
NO!
WHOA!

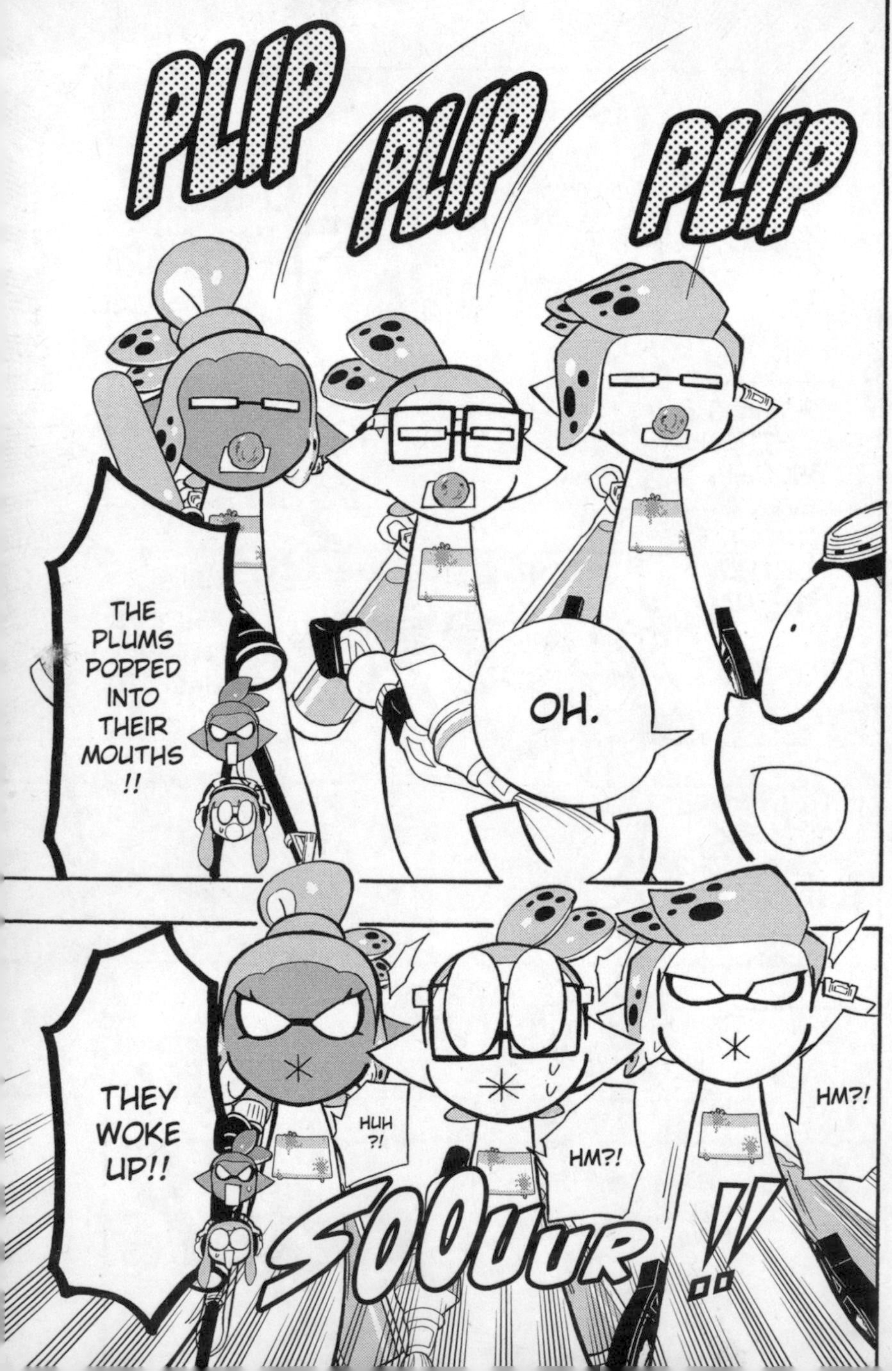
PLIP
PLIP
PLIP
OH.
THE PLUMS POPPED INTO THEIR MOUTHS!!
HM?!
HM?!
HUH?!
SOOUUR!!
THEY WOKE UP!!

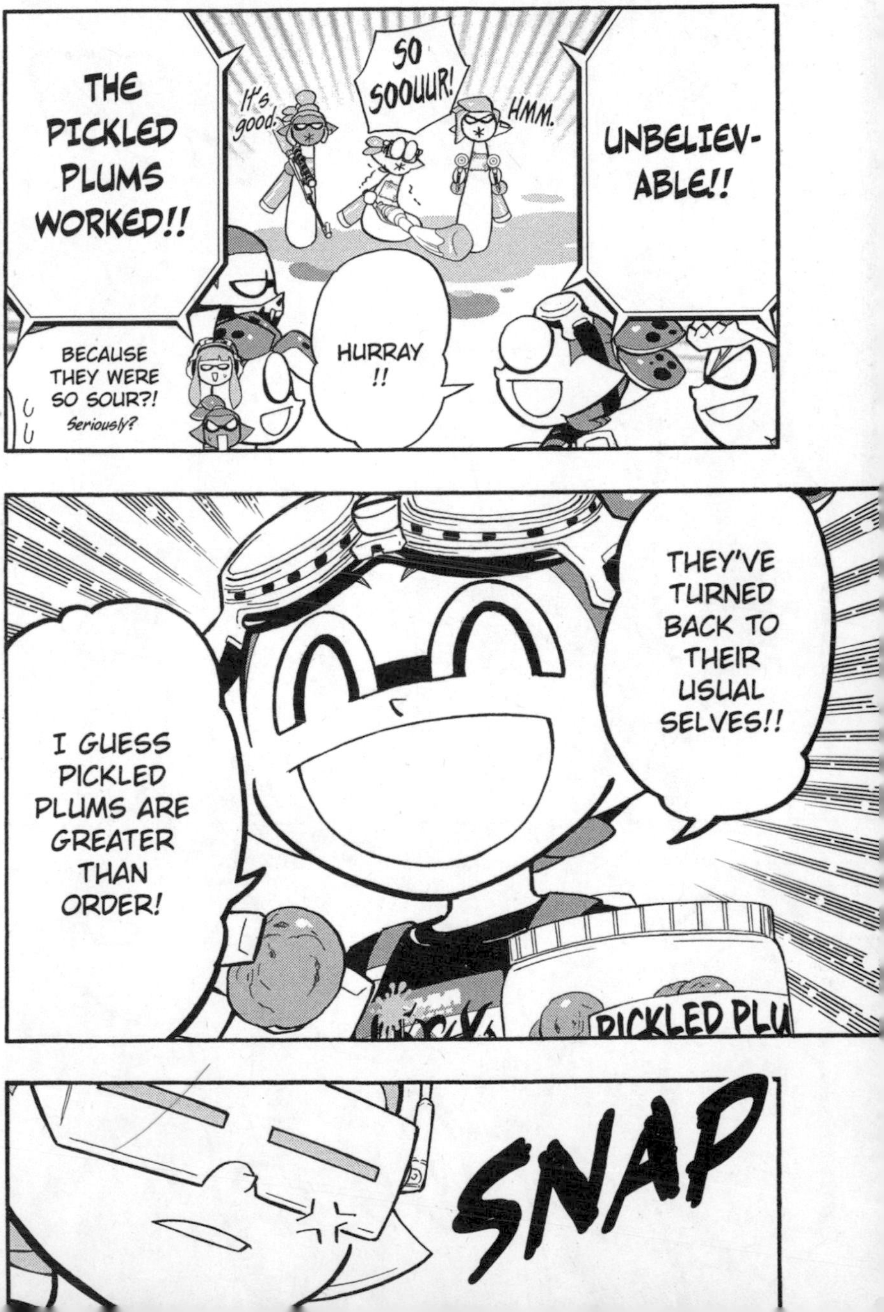
UNBELIEV-ABLE!!
HMM.
SO SOOUUR!
It's good.
THE PICKLED PLUMS WORKED!!
HURRAY !!
BECAUSE THEY WERE SO SOUR?!
Seriously?
THEY'VE TURNED BACK TO THEIR USUAL SELVES!!
I GUESS PICKLED PLUMS ARE GREATER THAN ORDER!
PICKLED PLU
SNAP

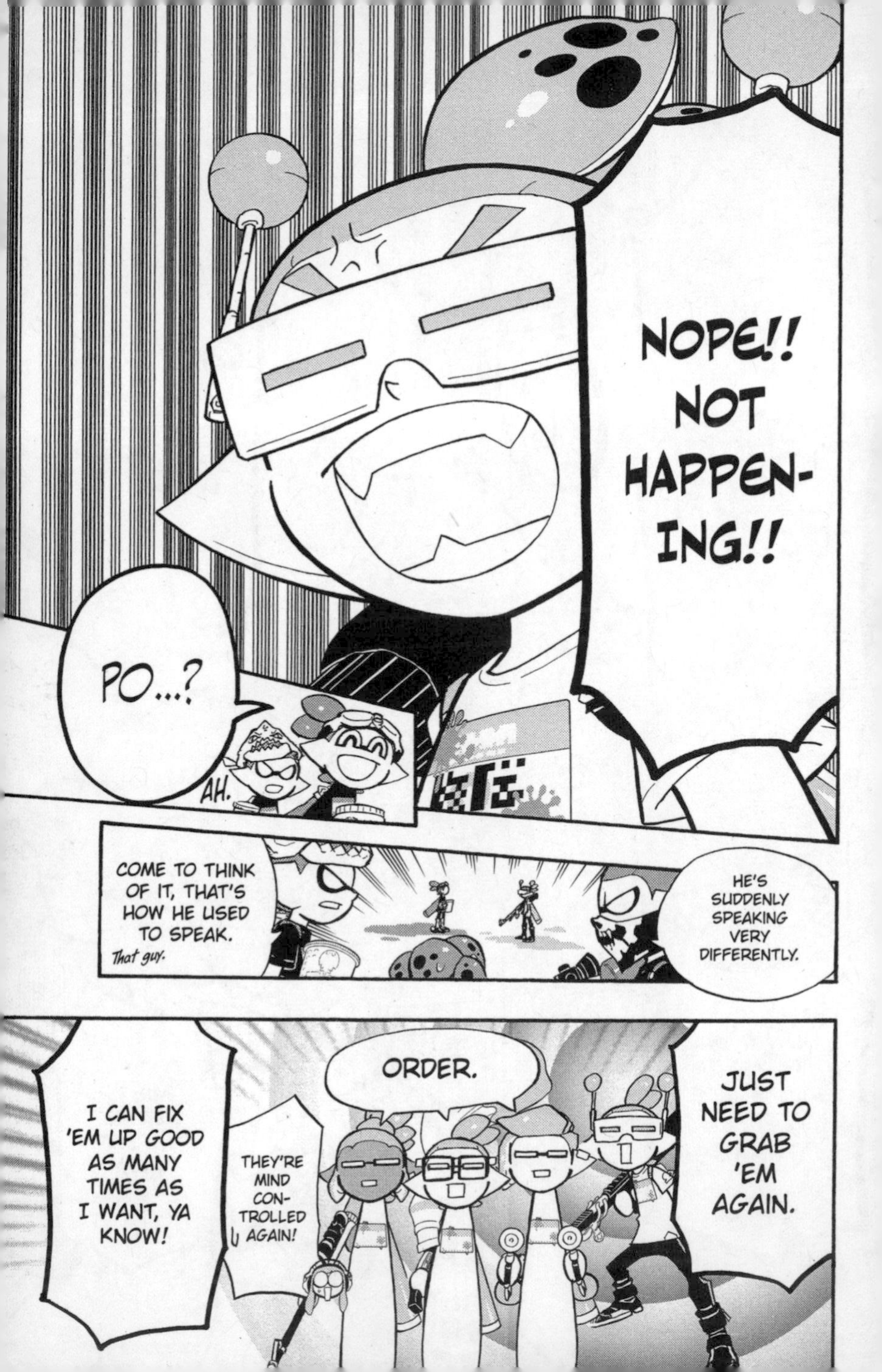
NOPE!! NOT HAPPEN-ING!!
PO...?
AH.
HE'S SUDDENLY SPEAKING VERY DIFFERENTLY.
COME TO THINK OF IT, THAT'S HOW HE USED TO SPEAK.
That guy.
JUST NEED TO GRAB 'EM AGAIN.
ORDER.
THEY'RE MIND CON-TROLLED AGAIN!
I CAN FIX 'EM UP GOOD AS MANY TIMES AS I WANT, YA KNOW!

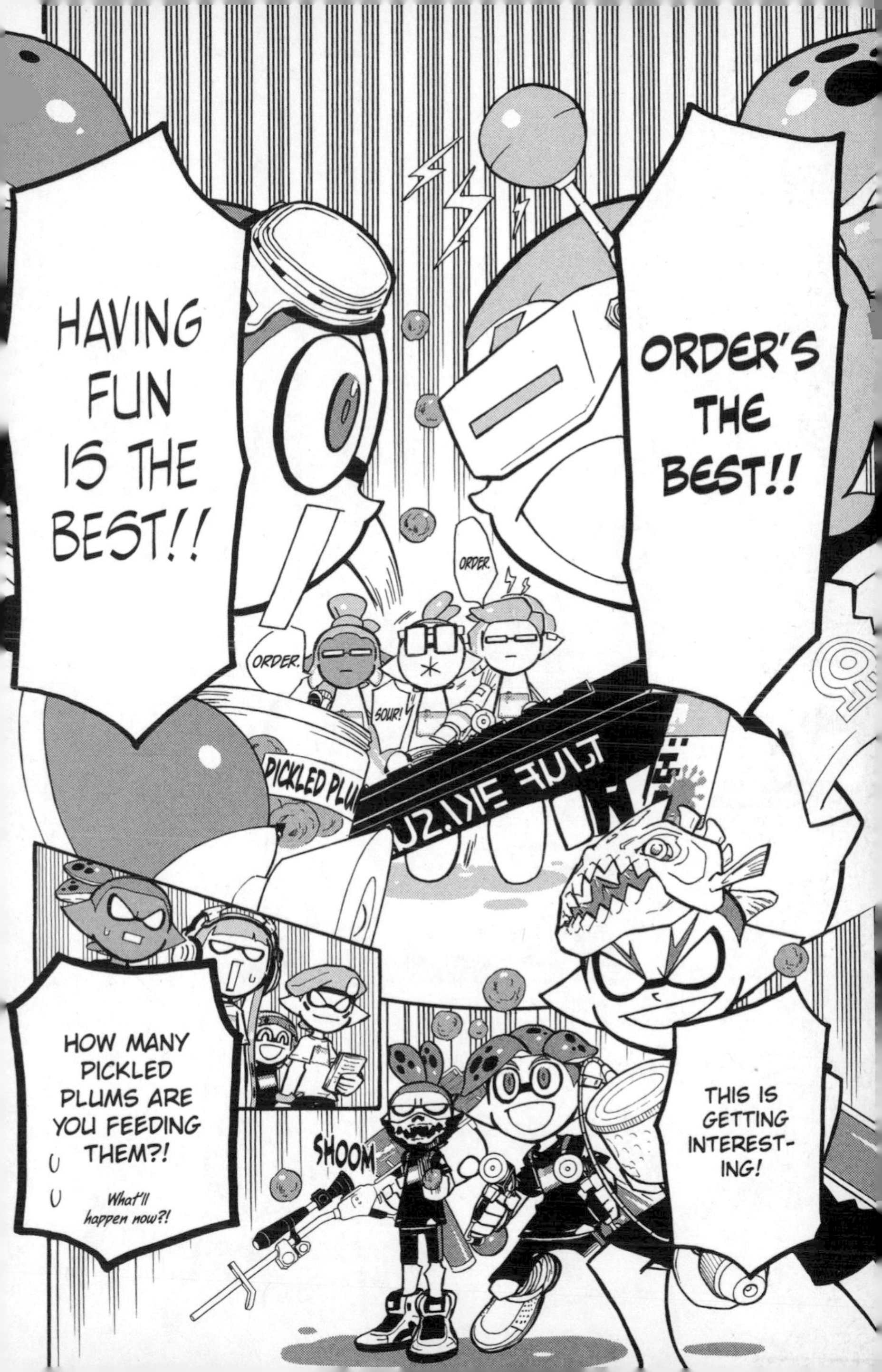
ORDER'S THE BEST!!
HAVING FUN IS THE BEST!!
ORDER.
SOUR!
ORDER.
PICKLED PLU
THIS IS GETTING INTEREST-ING!
SHOOM
HOW MANY PICKLED PLUMS ARE YOU FEEDING THEM?!
What'll happen now?!

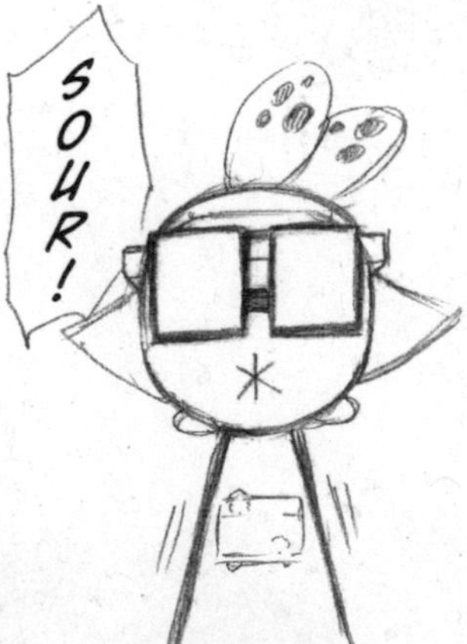
SOUR!

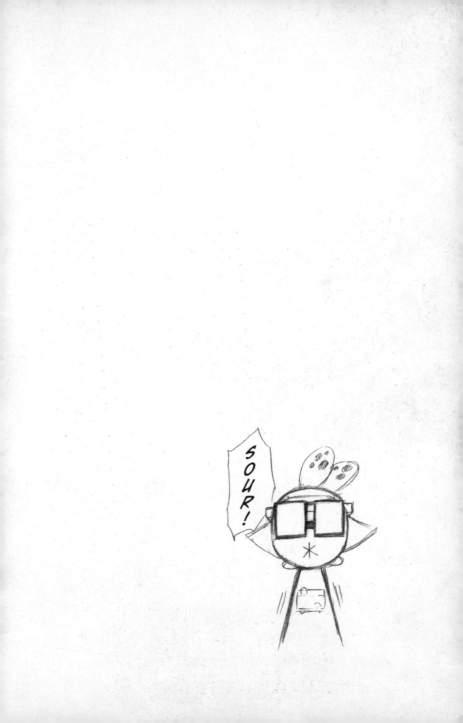

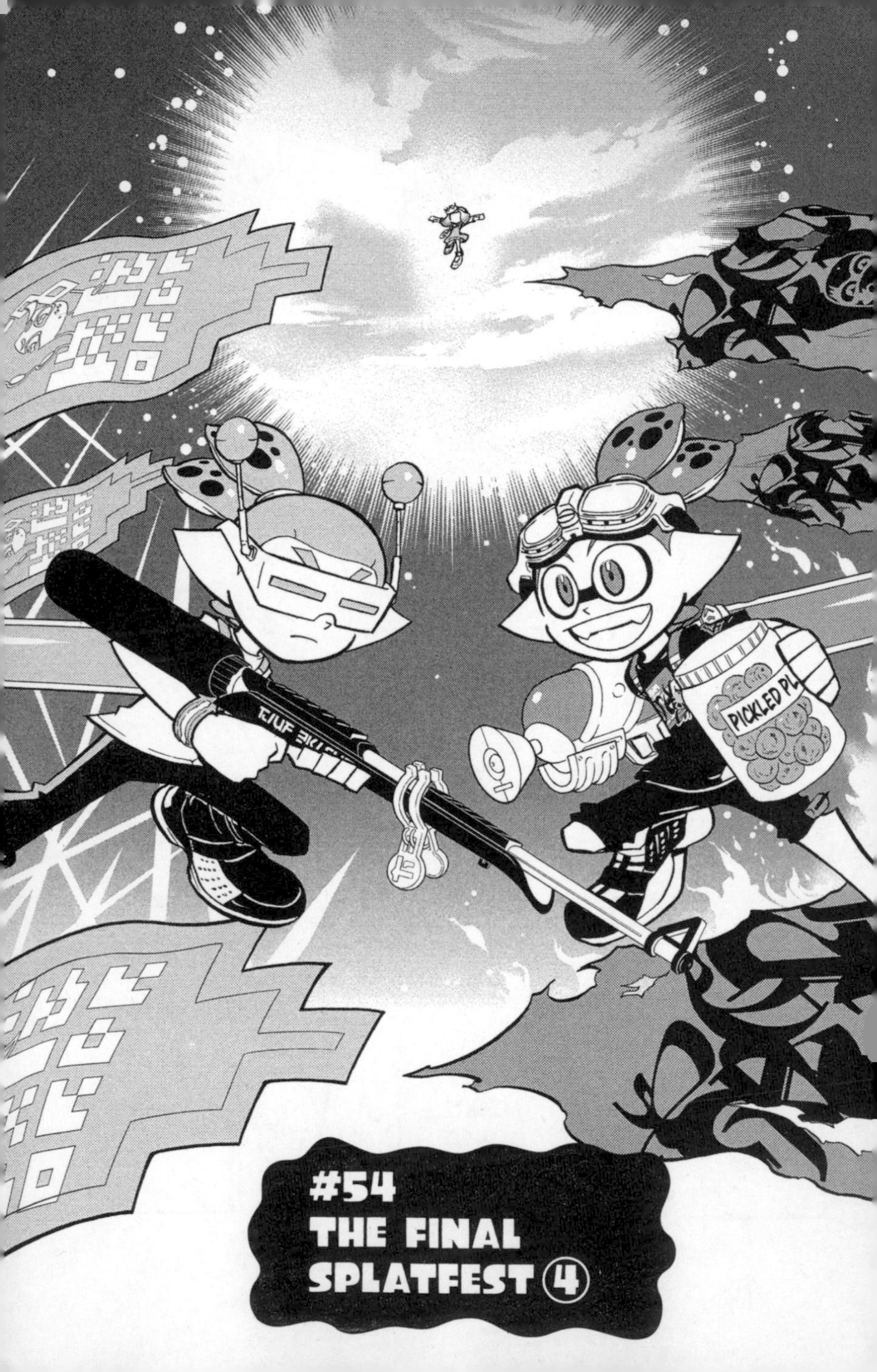
PICKLED PL
#54
THE FINAL
SPLATFEST ④

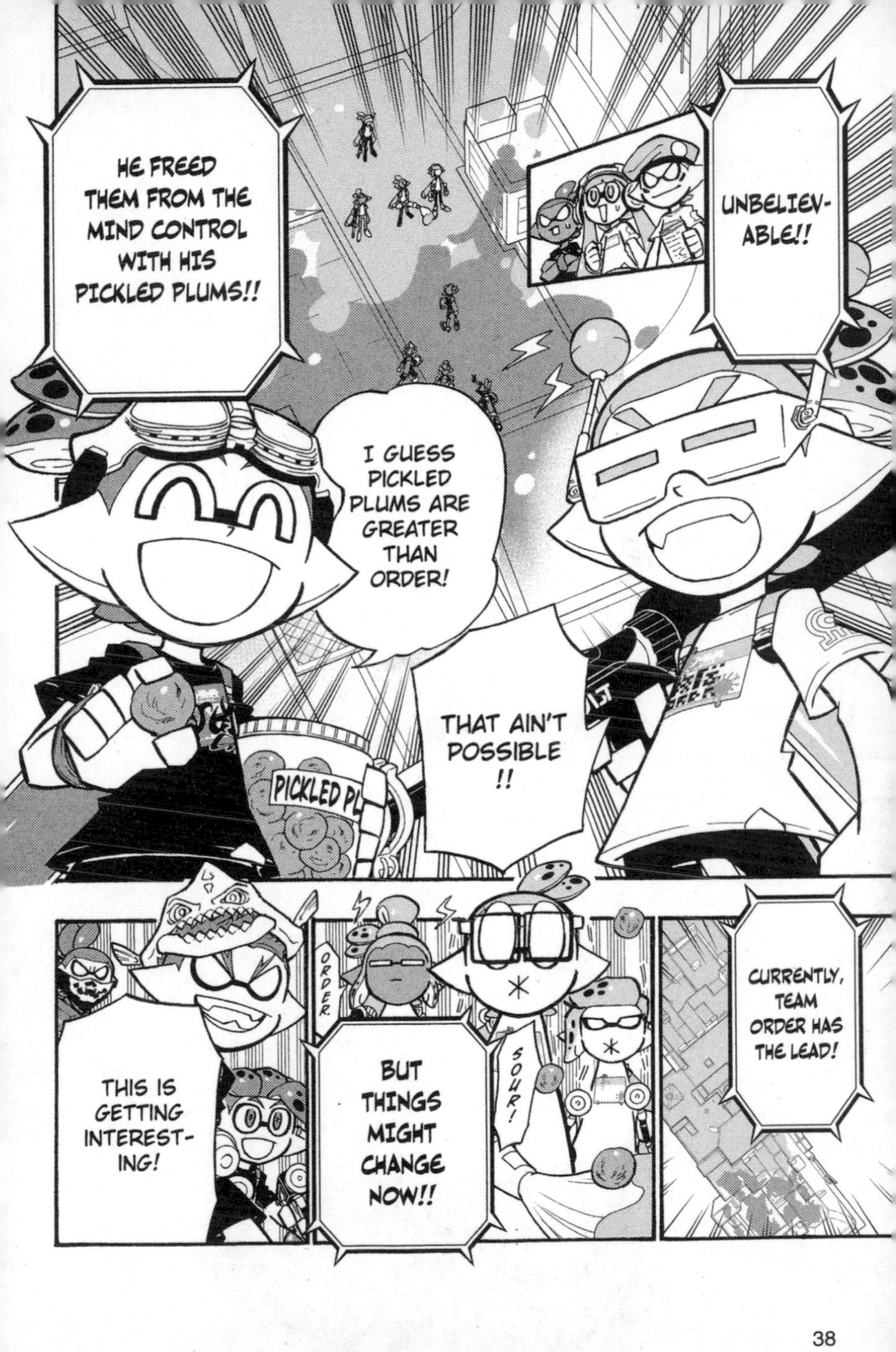
UNBELIEV-ABLE!!
HE FREED THEM FROM THE MIND CONTROL WITH HIS PICKLED PLUMS!!
I GUESS PICKLED PLUMS ARE GREATER THAN ORDER!
THAT AIN'T POSSIBLE!!
PICKLED PL
CURRENTLY, TEAM ORDER HAS THE LEAD!
ORDER.
SOUR!
BUT THINGS MIGHT CHANGE NOW!!
THIS IS GETTING INTEREST-ING!

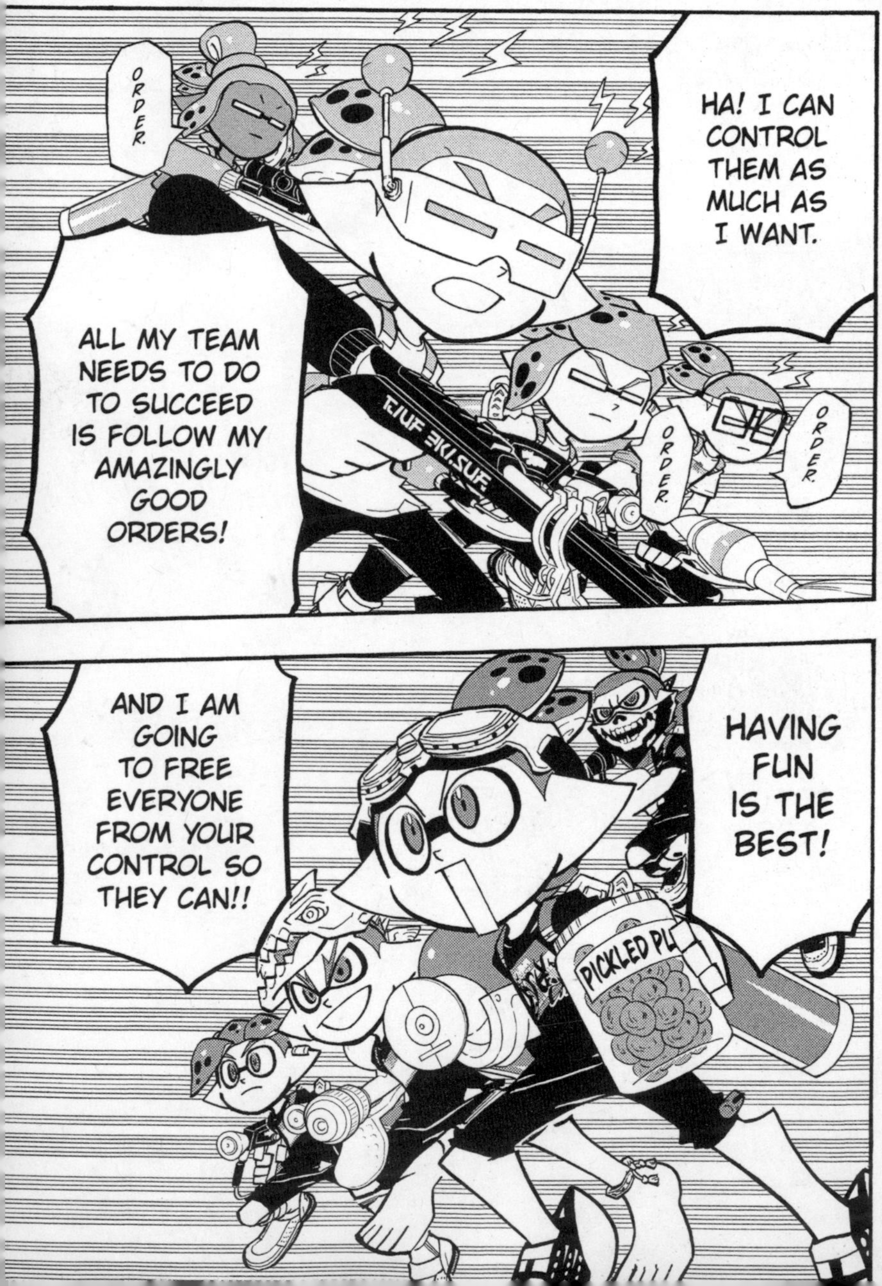
HA! I CAN CONTROL THEM AS MUCH AS I WANT.
ORDER.
ALL MY TEAM NEEDS TO DO TO SUCCEED IS FOLLOW MY AMAZINGLY GOOD ORDERS!
ORDER.
ORDER.
HAVING FUN IS THE BEST!
AND I AM GOING TO FREE EVERYONE FROM YOUR CONTROL SO THEY CAN!!
PICKLED PL

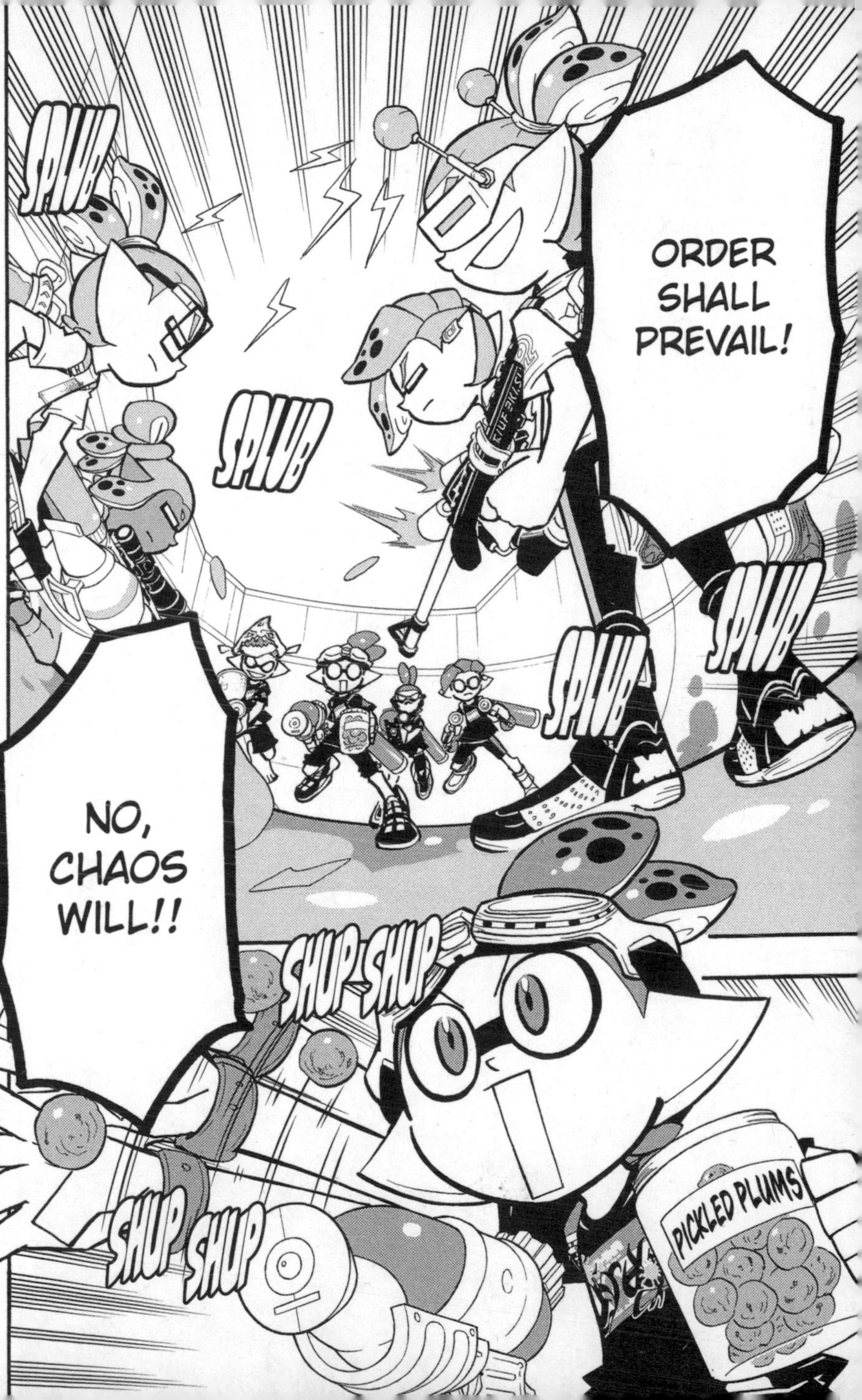
ORDER SHALL PREVAIL!
SPLUB
SPLUB
SPLUB
SPLUB
NO, CHAOS WILL!!
SHUP SHUP
PICKLED PLUMS
SHUP SHUP

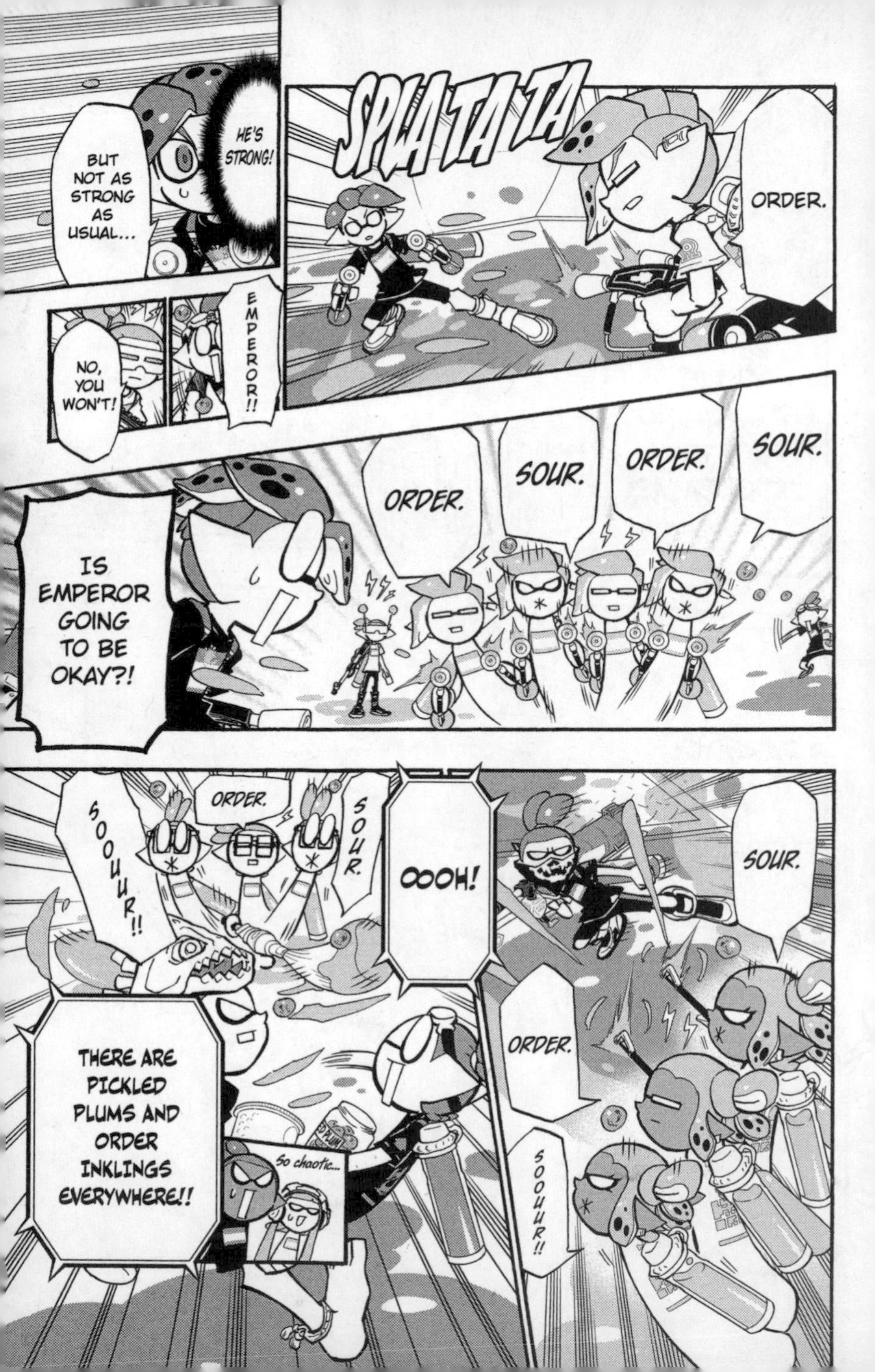
SPLATATA
ORDER.
HE'S STRONG!
BUT NOT AS STRONG AS USUAL...
EMPEROR!!
NO, YOU WON'T!
SOUR.
ORDER.
SOUR.
ORDER.
IS EMPEROR GOING TO BE OKAY?!
SOUR.
ORDER.
SOOUUR!!
OOOH!
SOUR.
ORDER.
SOOUUR!!
THERE ARE PICKLED PLUMS AND ORDER INKLINGS EVERYWHERE!!
So chaotic...

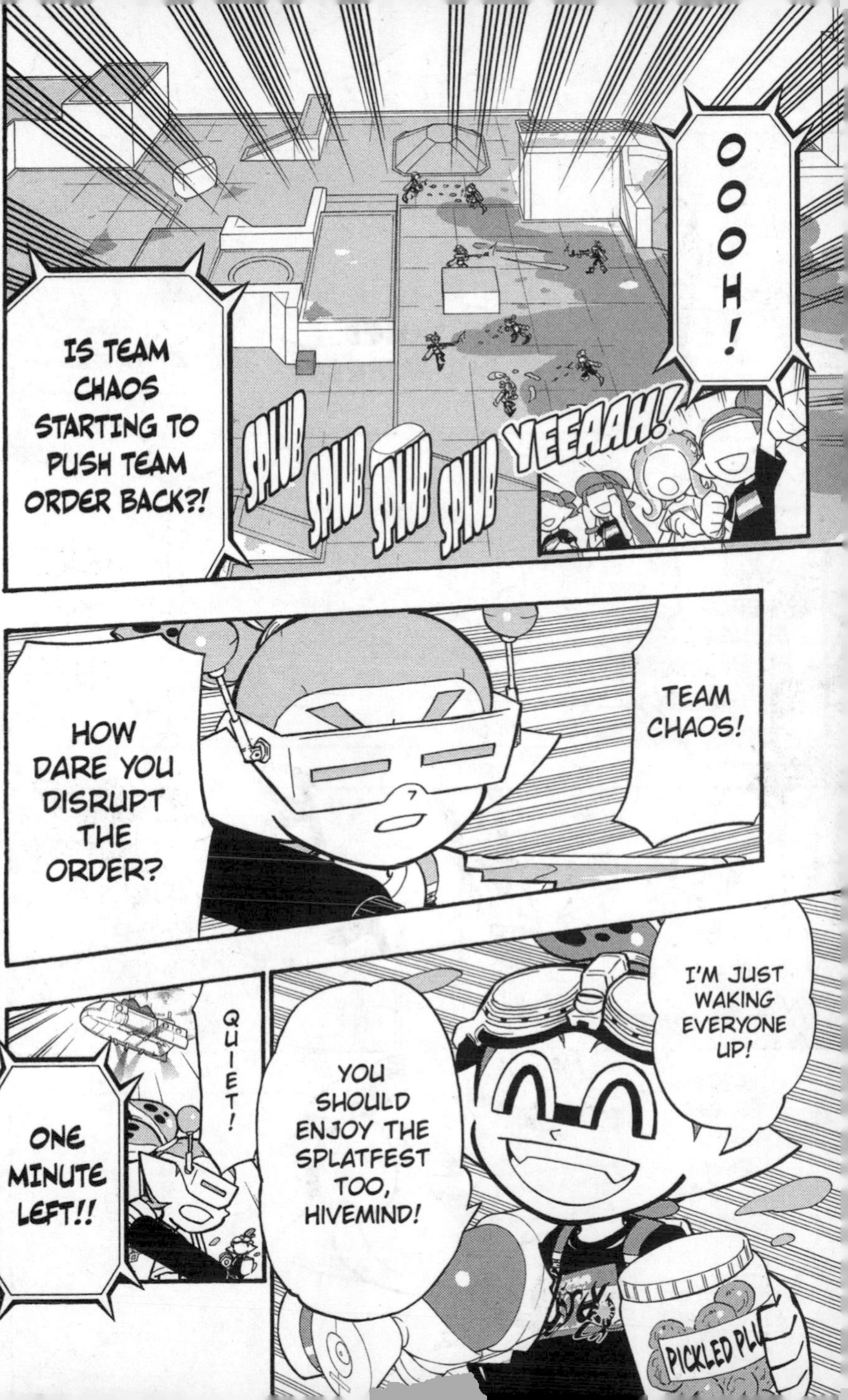

OOOH!
YEEAAH!
SPLUB SPLUB SPLUB SPLUB
IS TEAM CHAOS STARTING TO PUSH TEAM ORDER BACK?!
TEAM CHAOS!
HOW DARE YOU DISRUPT THE ORDER?
I'M JUST WAKING EVERYONE UP!
YOU SHOULD ENJOY THE SPLATFEST TOO, HIVEMIND!
PICKLED PL
QUIET!
ONE MINUTE LEFT!!

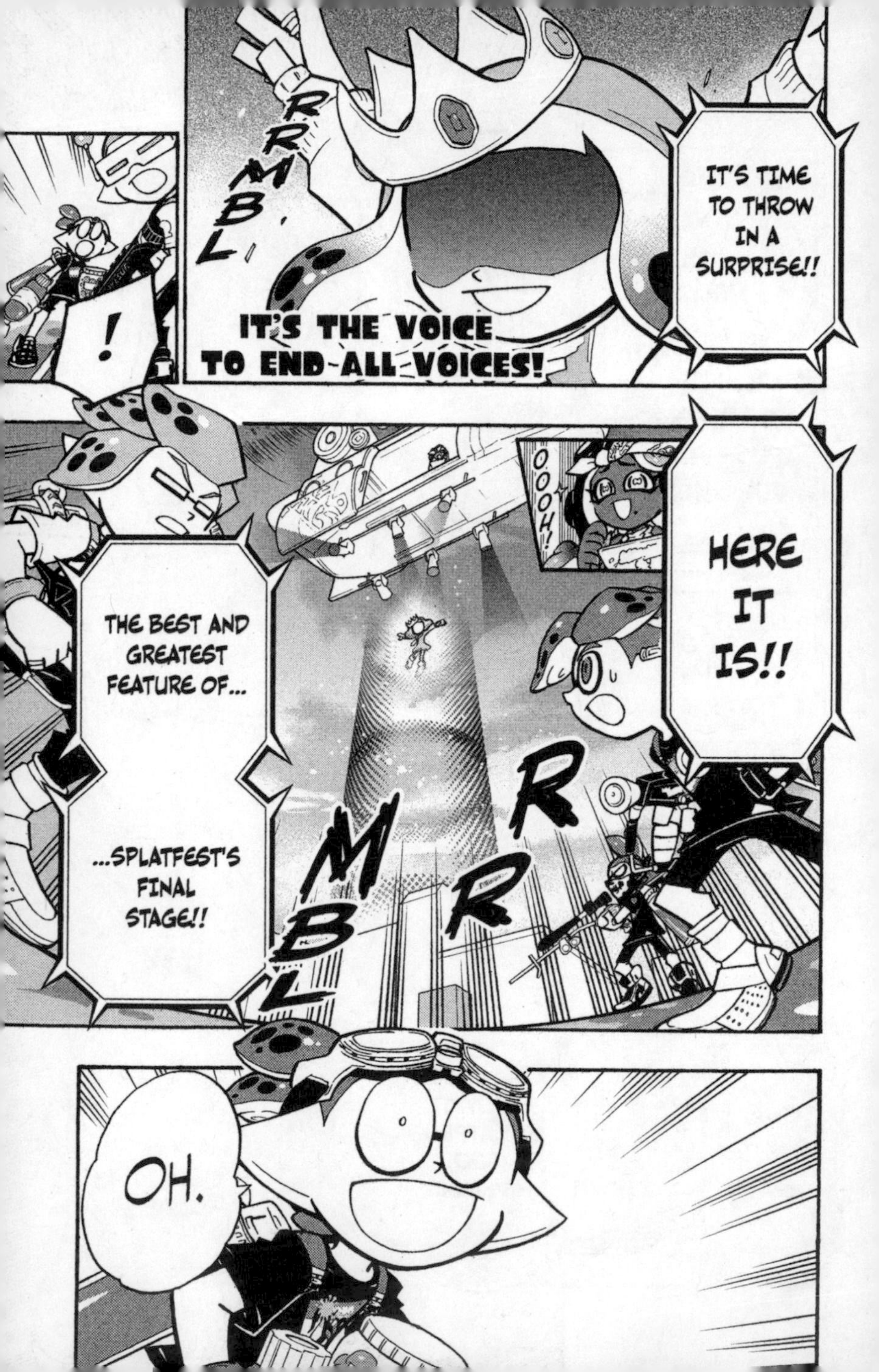
IT'S TIME TO THROW IN A SURPRISE!!
RRMBL
IT'S THE VOICE TO END ALL VOICES!
!
OOOOH!
HERE IT IS!!
THE BEST AND GREATEST FEATURE OF...
...SPLATFEST'S FINAL STAGE!!
RRMBL
OH.

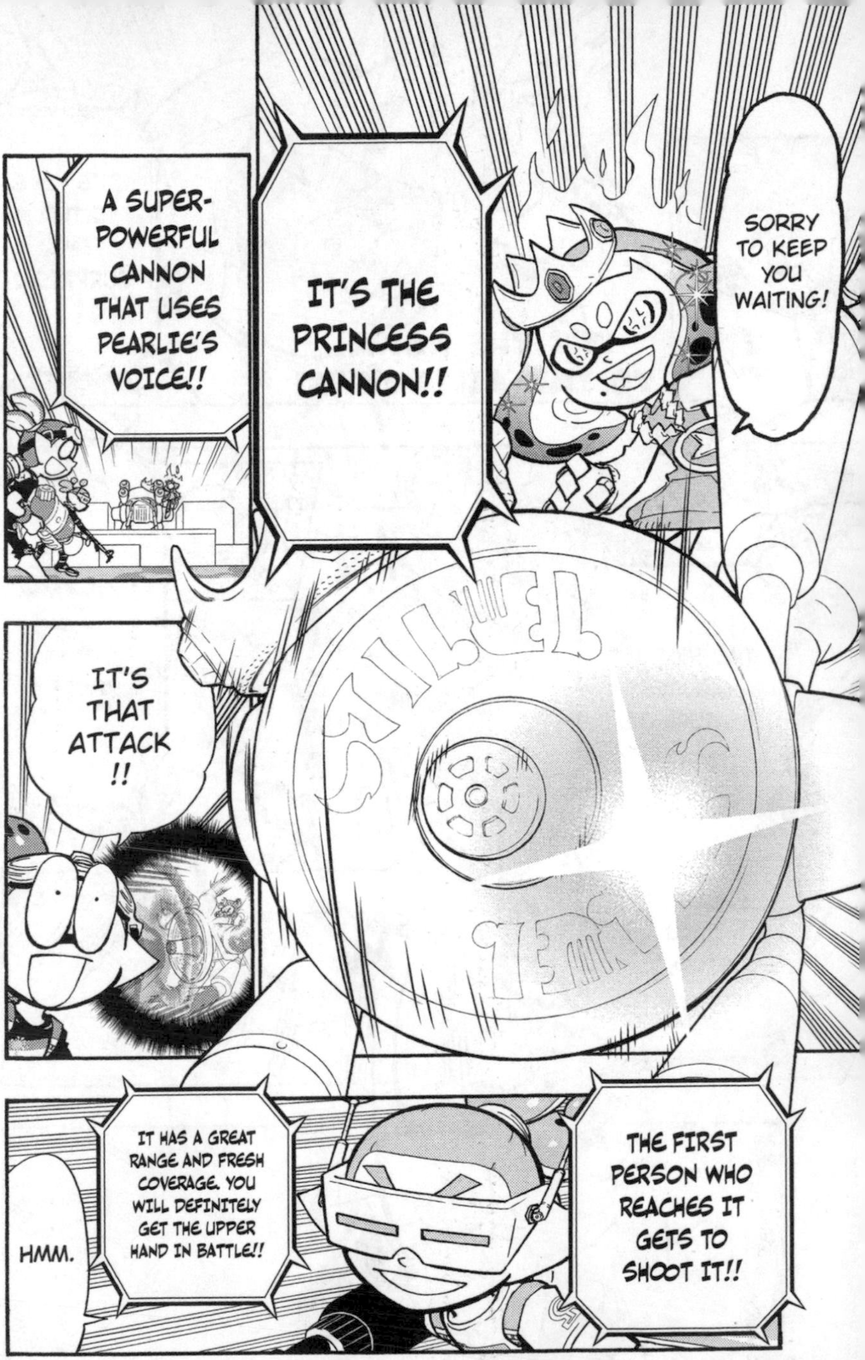
SORRY TO KEEP YOU WAITING!
IT'S THE PRINCESS CANNON!!
A SUPER-POWERFUL CANNON THAT USES PEARLIE'S VOICE!!
IT'S THAT ATTACK!!
THE FIRST PERSON WHO REACHES IT GETS TO SHOOT IT!!
IT HAS A GREAT RANGE AND FRESH COVERAGE. YOU WILL DEFINITELY GET THE UPPER HAND IN BATTLE!!
HMM.

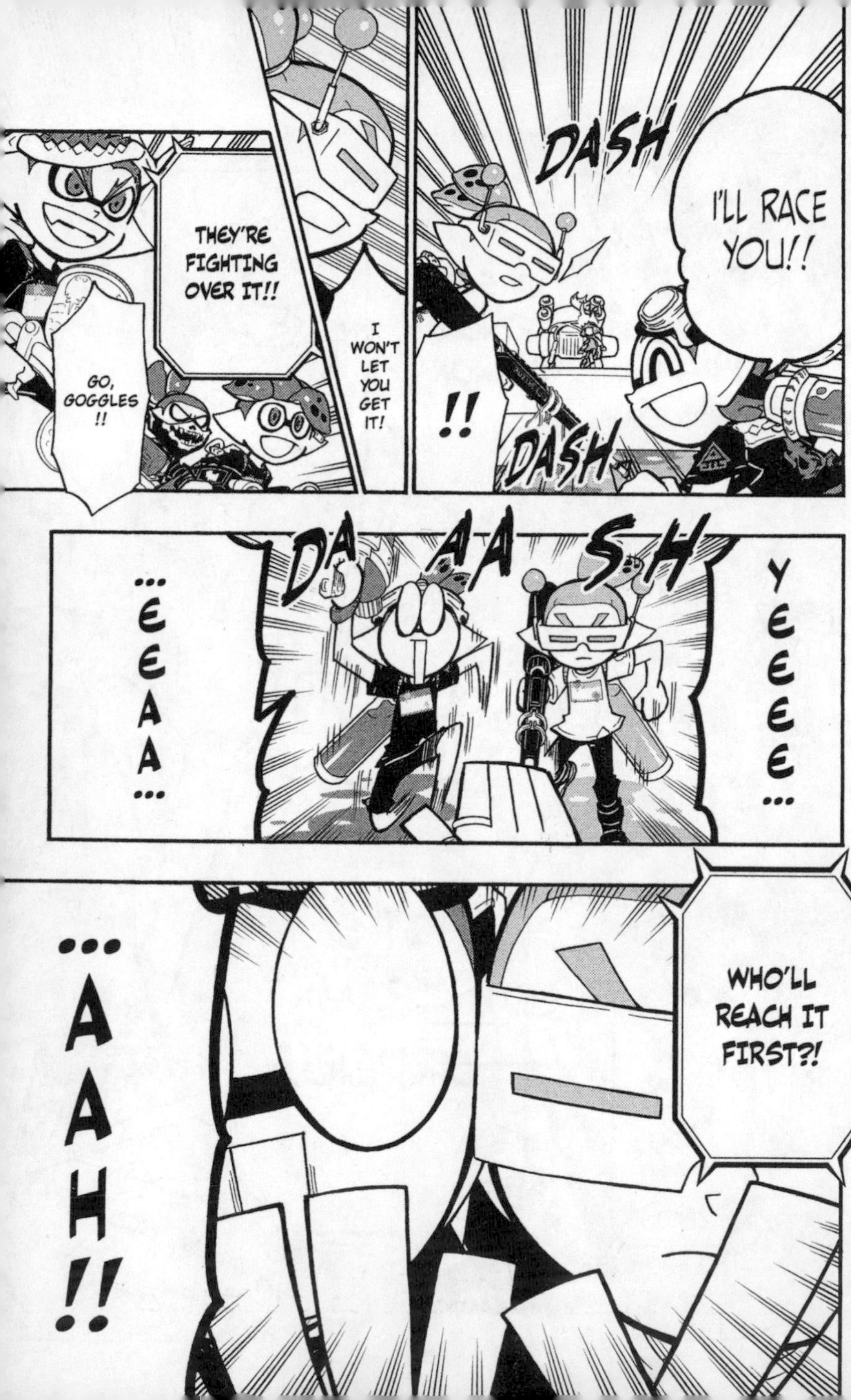
I'LL RACE YOU!!
DASH
DASH
!!
I WON'T LET YOU GET IT!
THEY'RE FIGHTING OVER IT!!
GO, GOGGLES!!
YEEEEE...
DAAASH
...EEAA...
WHO'LL REACH IT FIRST?!
...AAAH!!

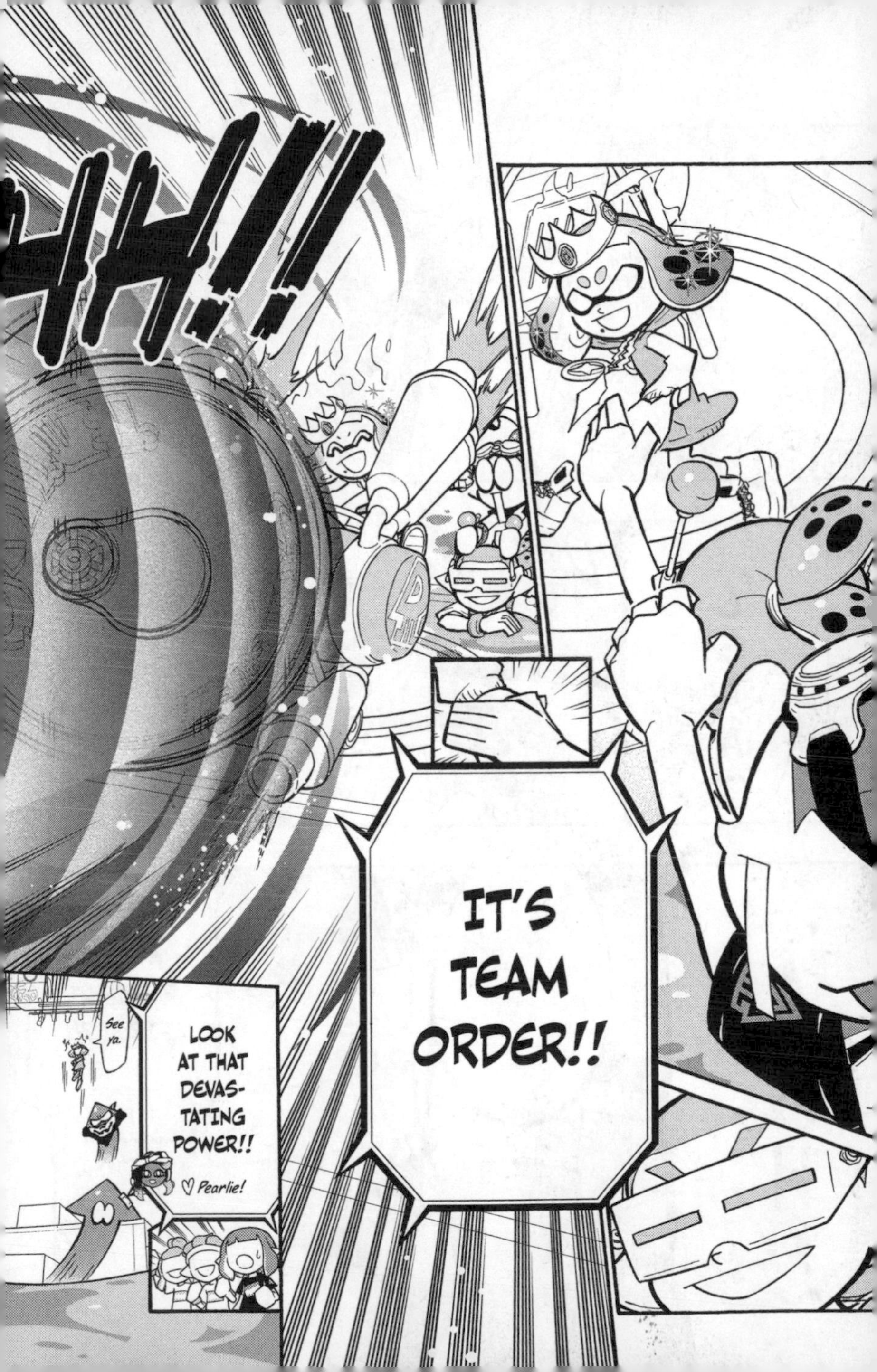
IT'S TEAM ORDER!!
LOOK AT THAT DEVAS-TATING POWER!!
♡ Pearlie!
See ya.

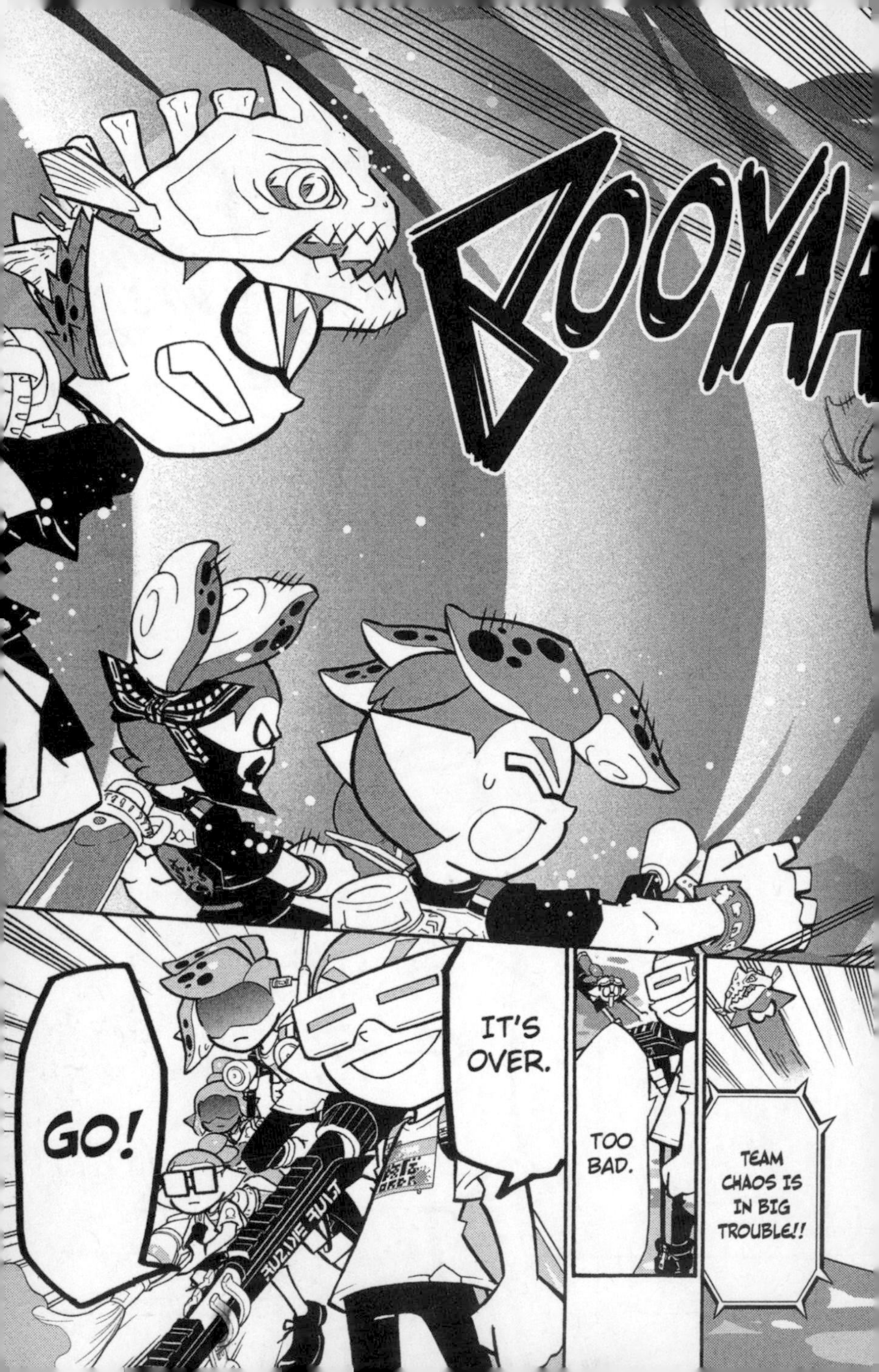
BOOYA
TEAM CHAOS IS IN BIG TROUBLE!!
TOO BAD.
IT'S OVER.
GO!

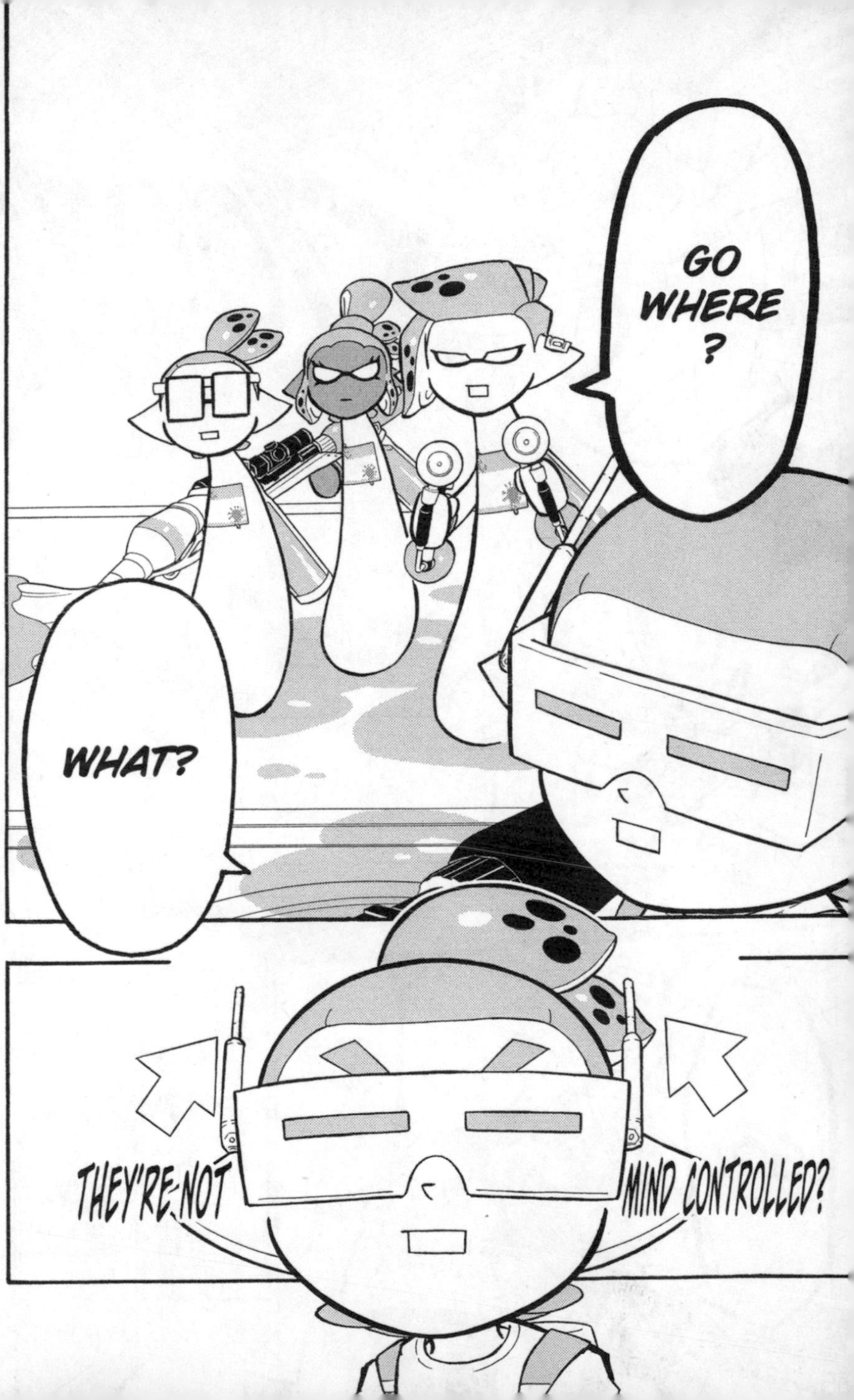
GO WHERE ?
WHAT?
THEY'RE NOT MIND CONTROLLED?

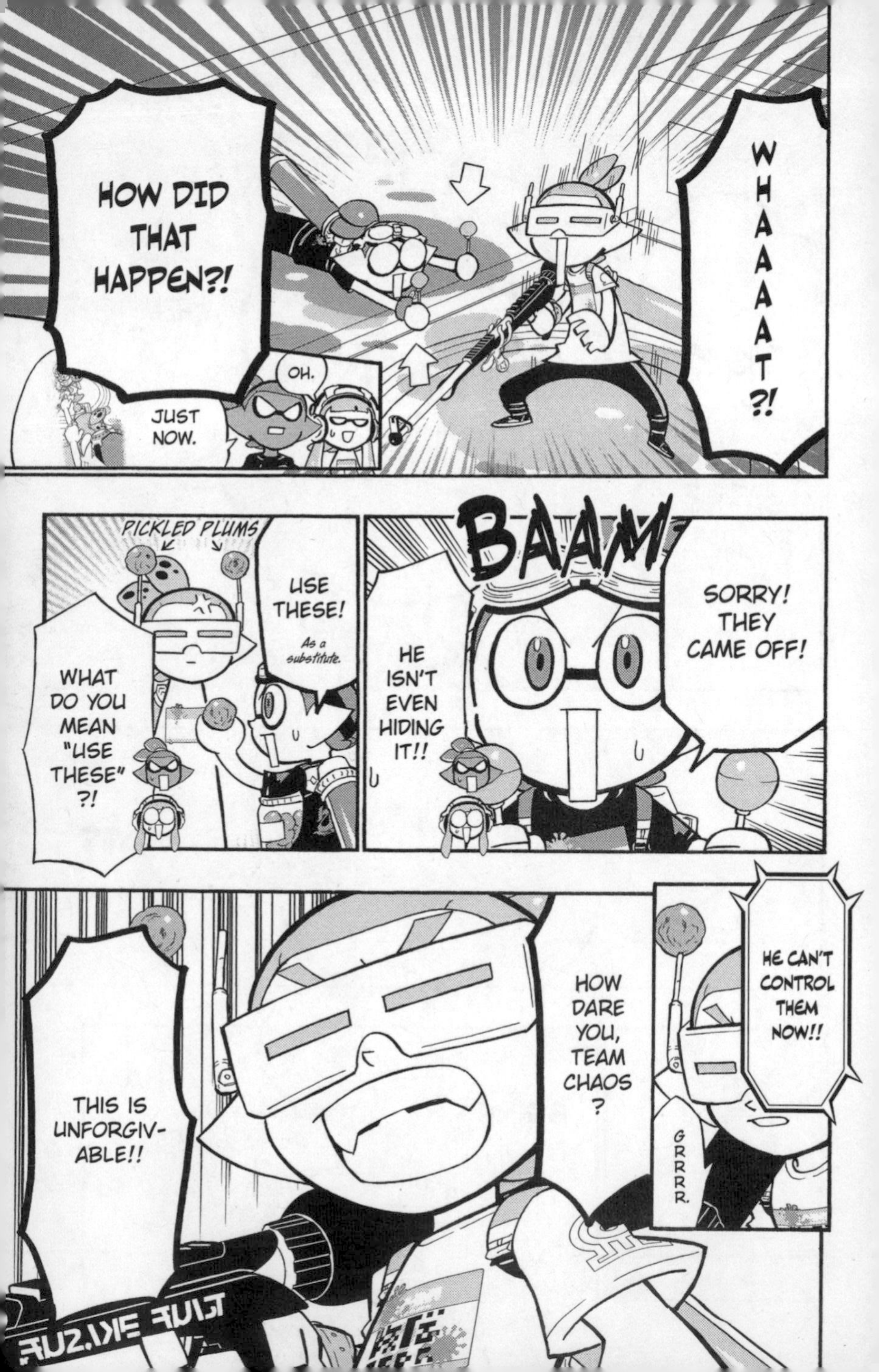
WHAAAAAT?!
HOW DID THAT HAPPEN?!
OH.
JUST NOW.
BAAM
SORRY! THEY CAME OFF!
HE ISN'T EVEN HIDING IT!!
PICKLED PLUMS
USE THESE!
As a substitute.
WHAT DO YOU MEAN "USE THESE"?!
HE CAN'T CONTROL THEM NOW!!
GRRRR.
HOW DARE YOU, TEAM CHAOS?
THIS IS UNFORGIV-ABLE!!

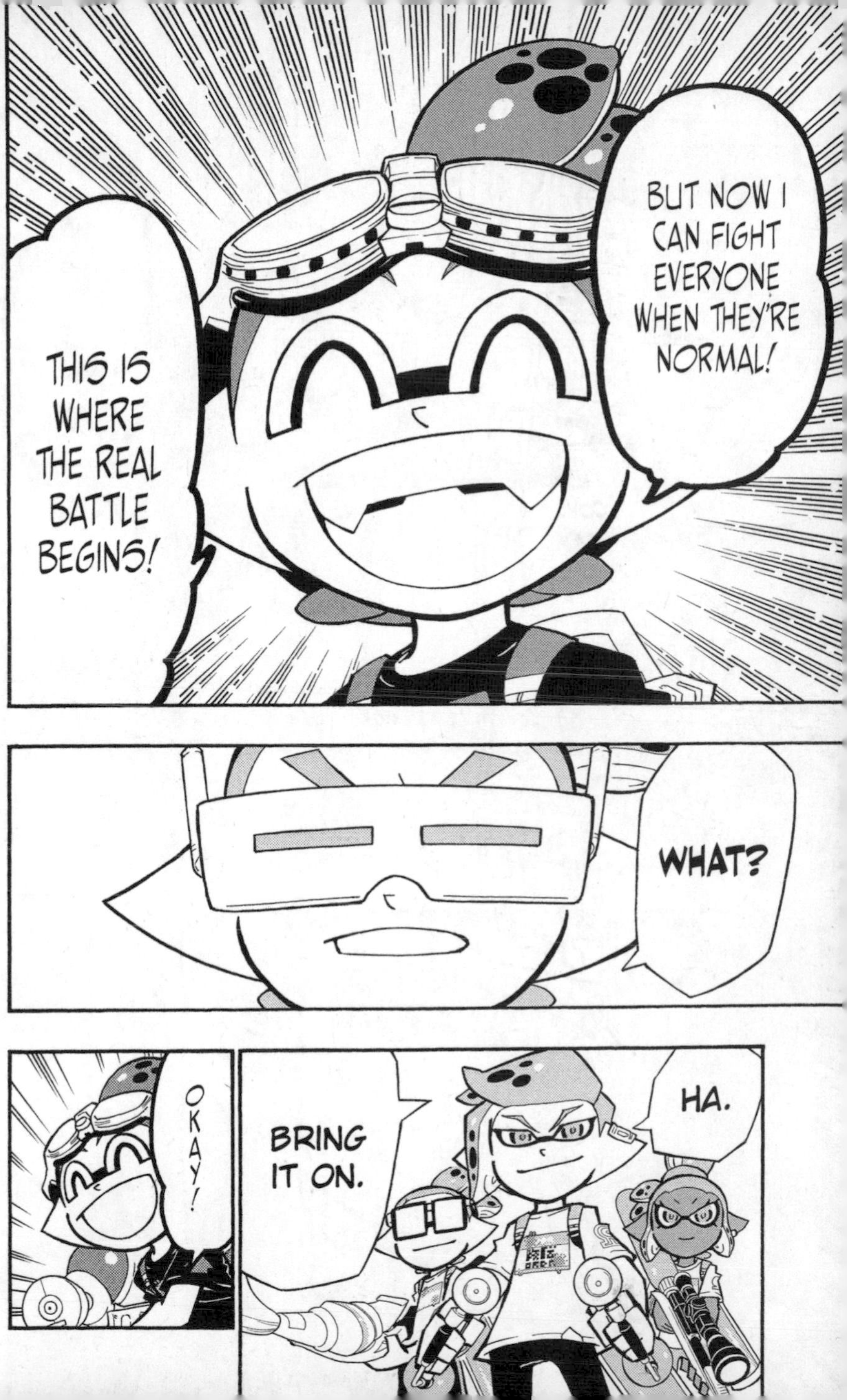
BUT NOW I CAN FIGHT EVERYONE WHEN THEY'RE NORMAL!
THIS IS WHERE THE REAL BATTLE BEGINS!
WHAT?
HA.
BRING IT ON.
OKAY!

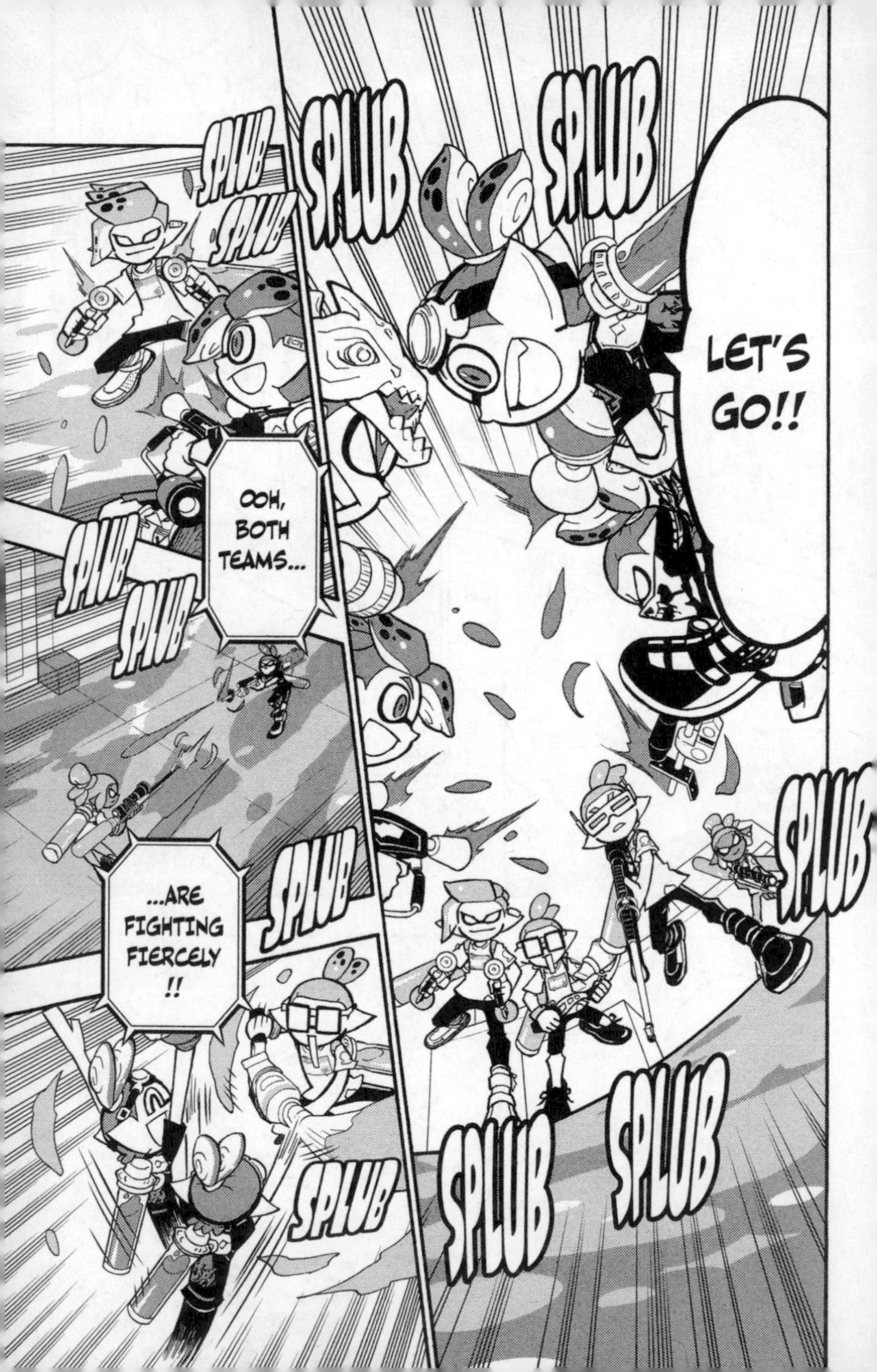
SPLUB
SPLUB
LET'S GO!!
SPLUB
SPLUB
SPLUB
SPLUB
SPLUB
SPLUB
SPLUB
OOH, BOTH TEAMS...
SPLUB
SPLUB
...ARE FIGHTING FIERCELY!!
SPLUB
SPLUB

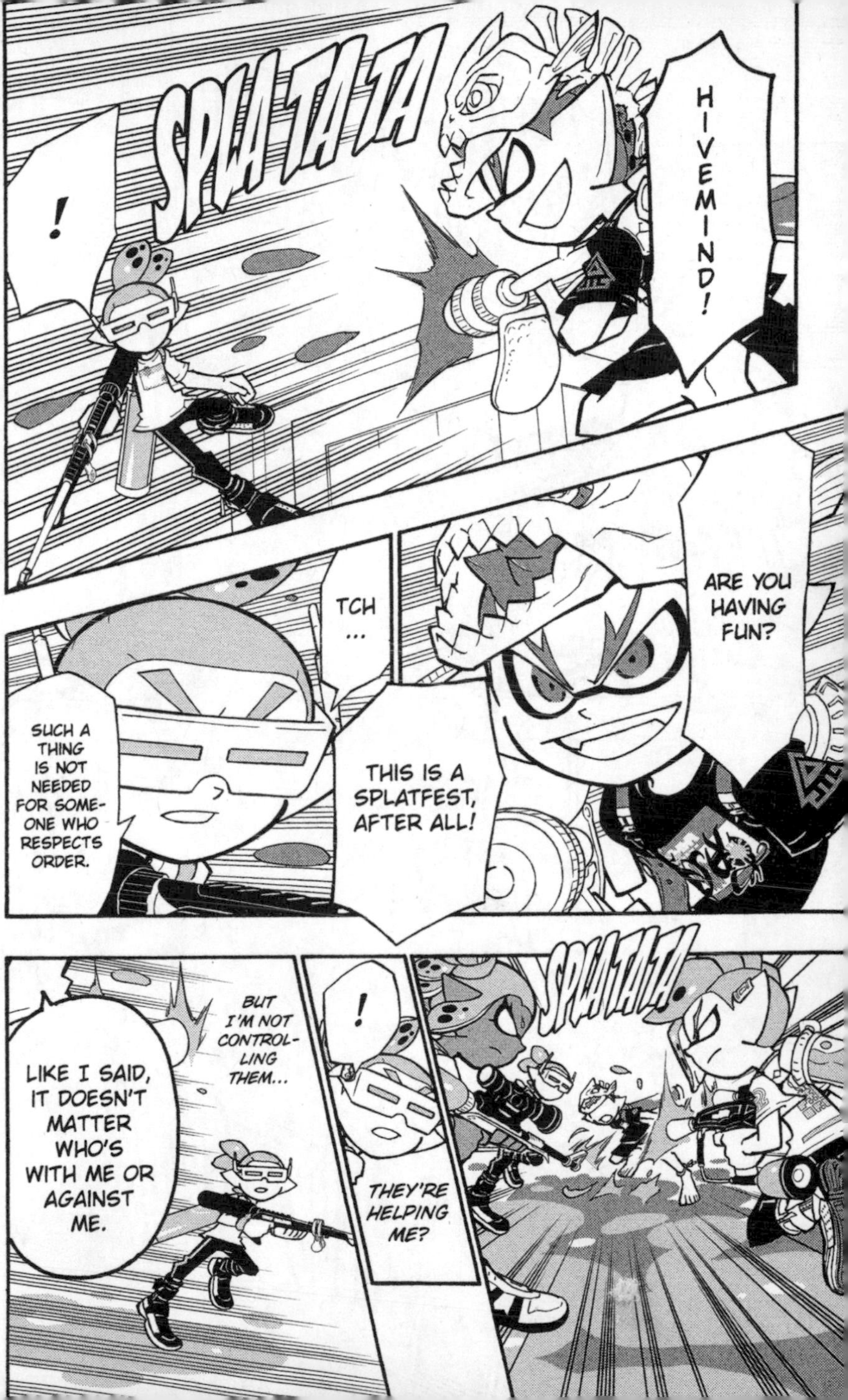
HIVEMIND!
SPLA TA TA
!
ARE YOU HAVING FUN?
THIS IS A SPLATFEST, AFTER ALL!
TCH...
SUCH A THING IS NOT NEEDED FOR SOME-ONE WHO RESPECTS ORDER.
SPLATATA
!
BUT I'M NOT CONTROL-LING THEM...
THEY'RE HELPING ME?
LIKE I SAID, IT DOESN'T MATTER WHO'S WITH ME OR AGAINST ME.

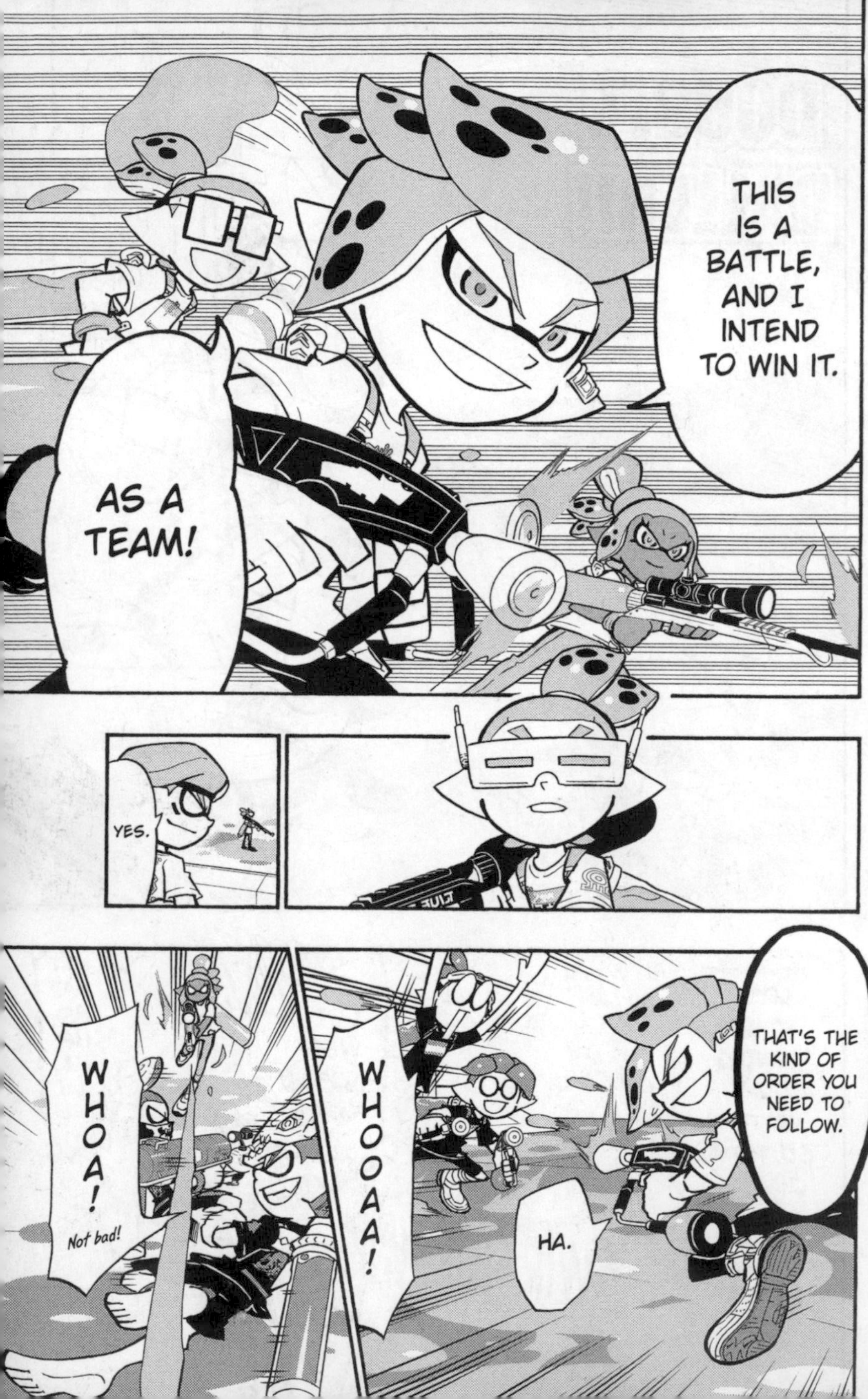
THIS IS A BATTLE, AND I INTEND TO WIN IT.
AS A TEAM!
YES.
THAT'S THE KIND OF ORDER YOU NEED TO FOLLOW.
HA.
WHOOAA!
WHOA!
Not bad!

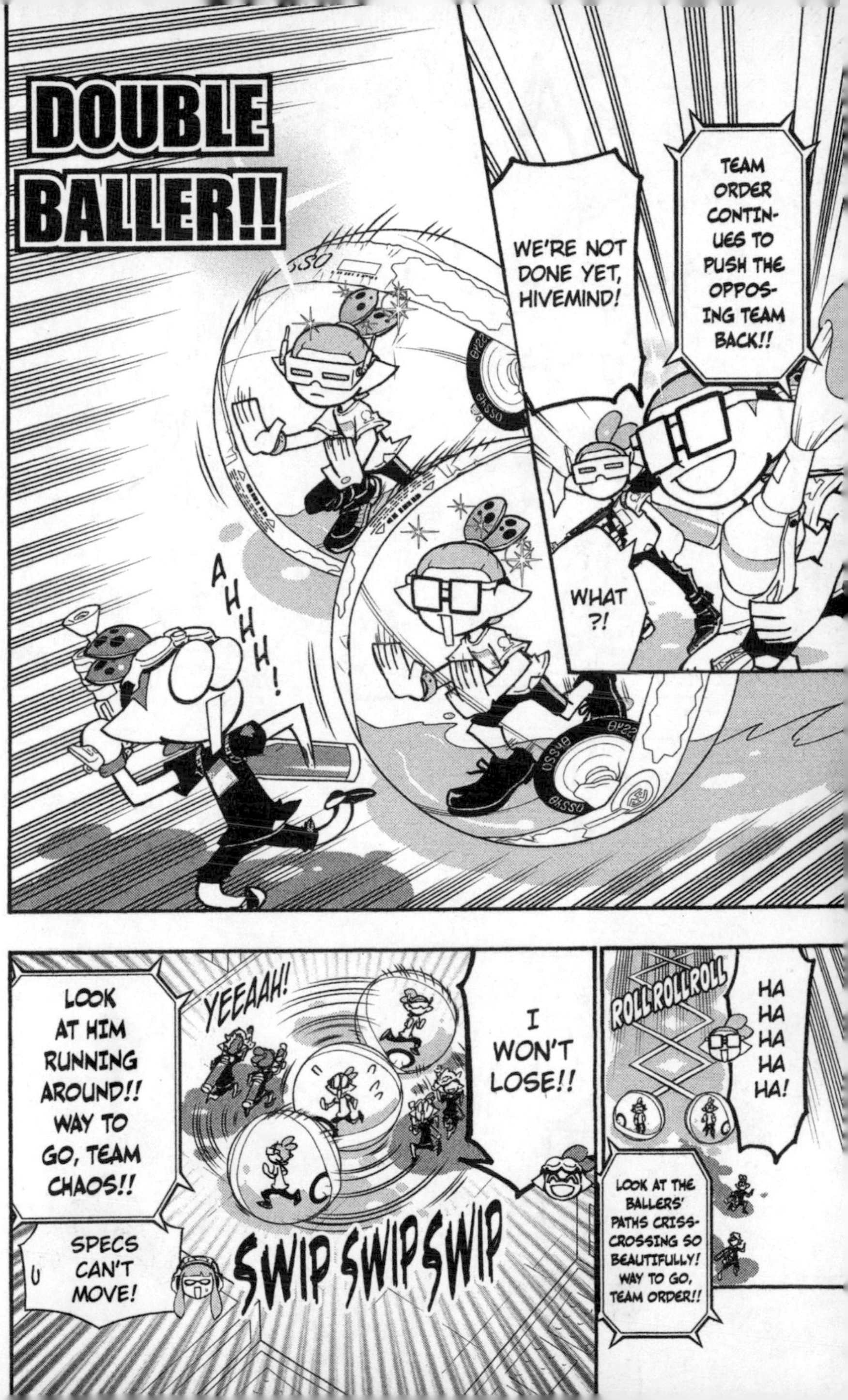
TEAM ORDER CONTINUES TO PUSH THE OPPOSING TEAM BACK!!
WE'RE NOT DONE YET, HIVEMIND!
WHAT?!
DOUBLE BALLER!!
AHHHH!
ROLL ROLL ROLL
HA HA HA HA HA HA!
LOOK AT THE BALLERS' PATHS CRISSCROSSING SO BEAUTIFULLY! WAY TO GO, TEAM ORDER!!
I WON'T LOSE!!
YEEAAH!
LOOK AT HIM RUNNING AROUND!! WAY TO GO, TEAM CHAOS!!
SPECS CAN'T MOVE!
SWIP SWIP SWIP

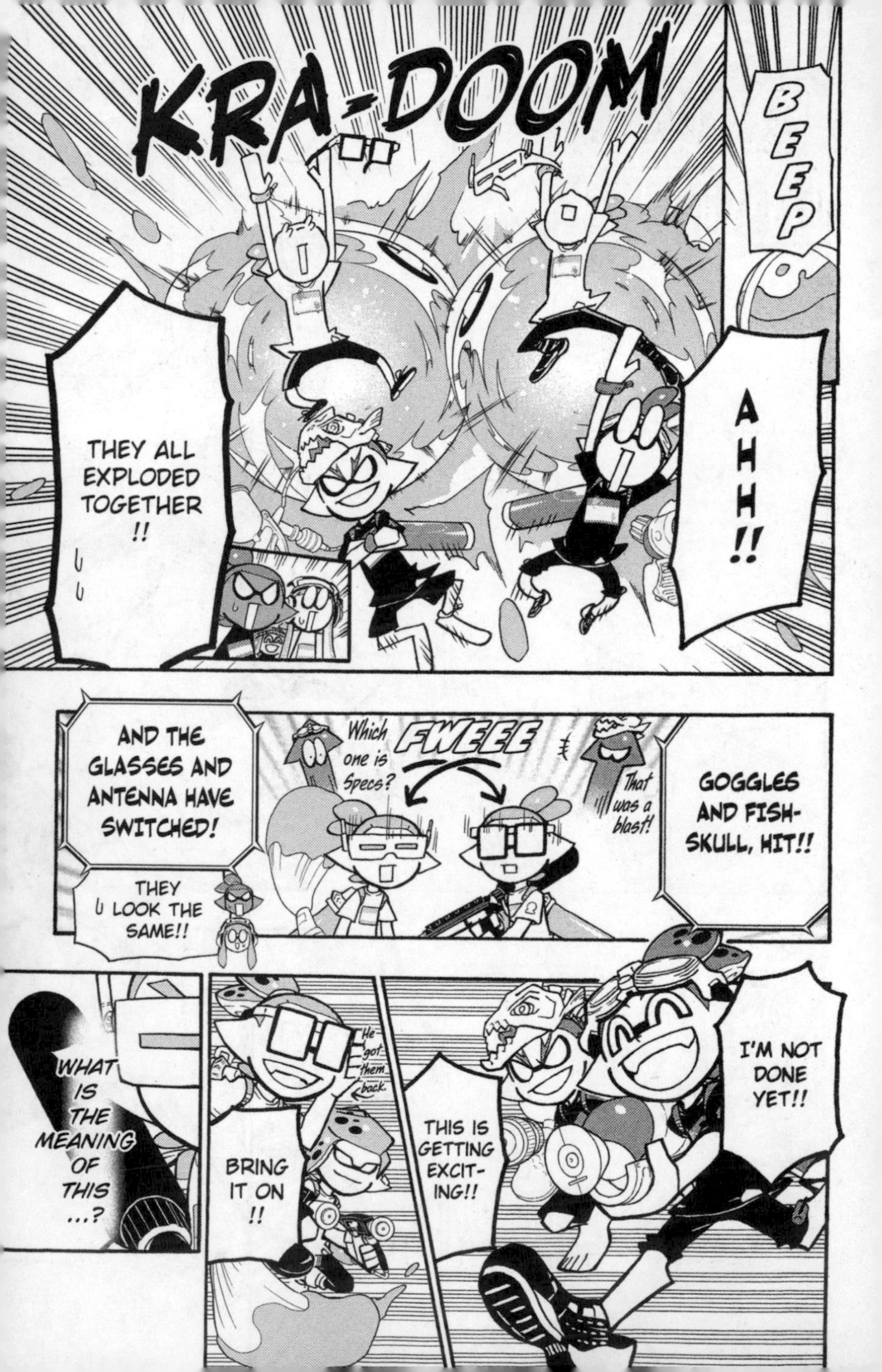
BEEP
KRA-DOOM
AHH!!
THEY ALL EXPLODED TOGETHER!!
GOGGLES AND FISH-SKULL, HIT!!
That was a blast!
FWEEE
Which one is Specs?
AND THE GLASSES AND ANTENNA HAVE SWITCHED!
THEY LOOK THE SAME!!
I'M NOT DONE YET!!
THIS IS GETTING EXCIT-ING!!
He got them back
BRING IT ON!!
WHAT IS THE MEANING OF THIS...?

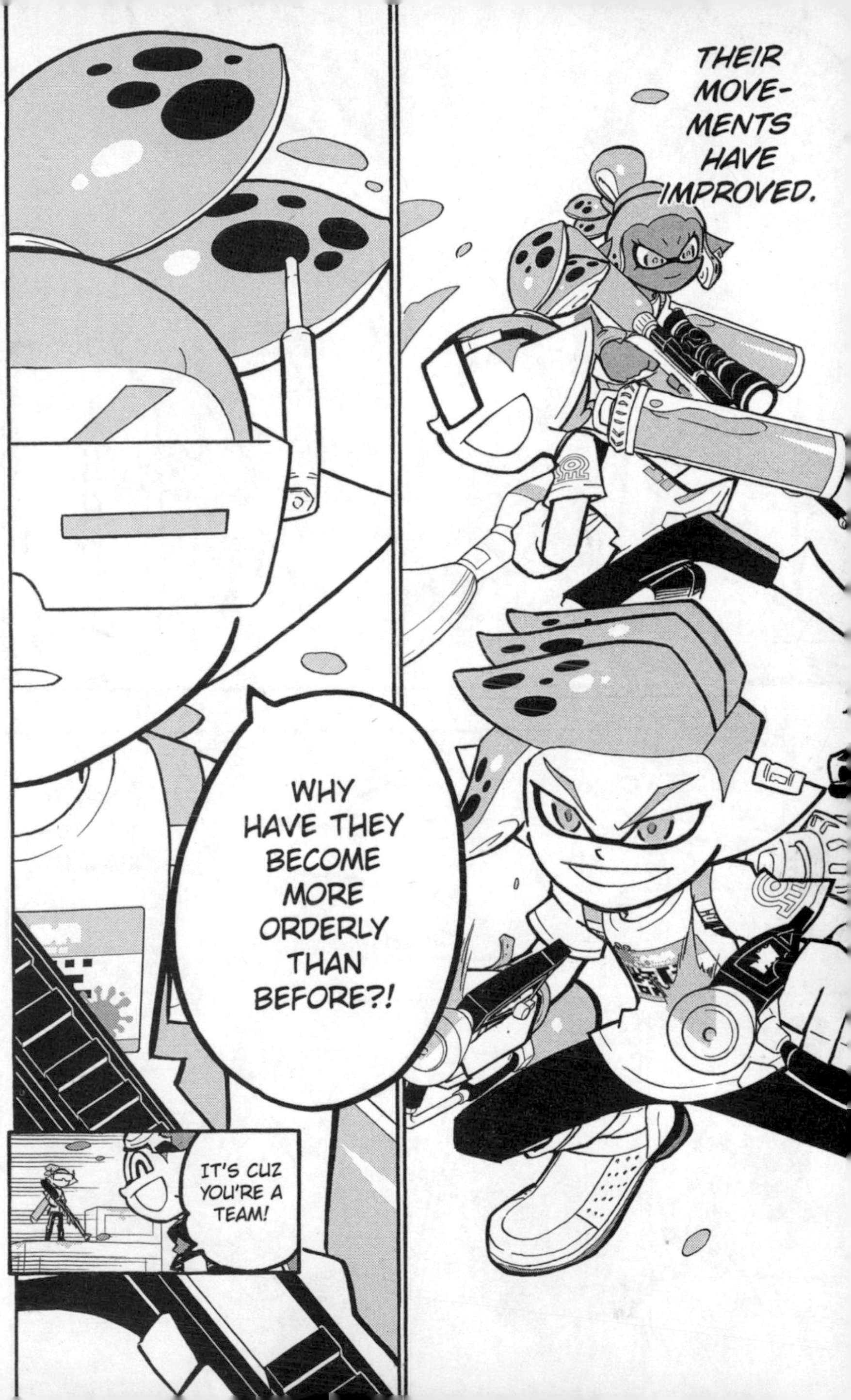
THEIR MOVE-MENTS HAVE IMPROVED.
WHY HAVE THEY BECOME MORE ORDERLY THAN BEFORE?!
IT'S CUZ YOU'RE A TEAM!

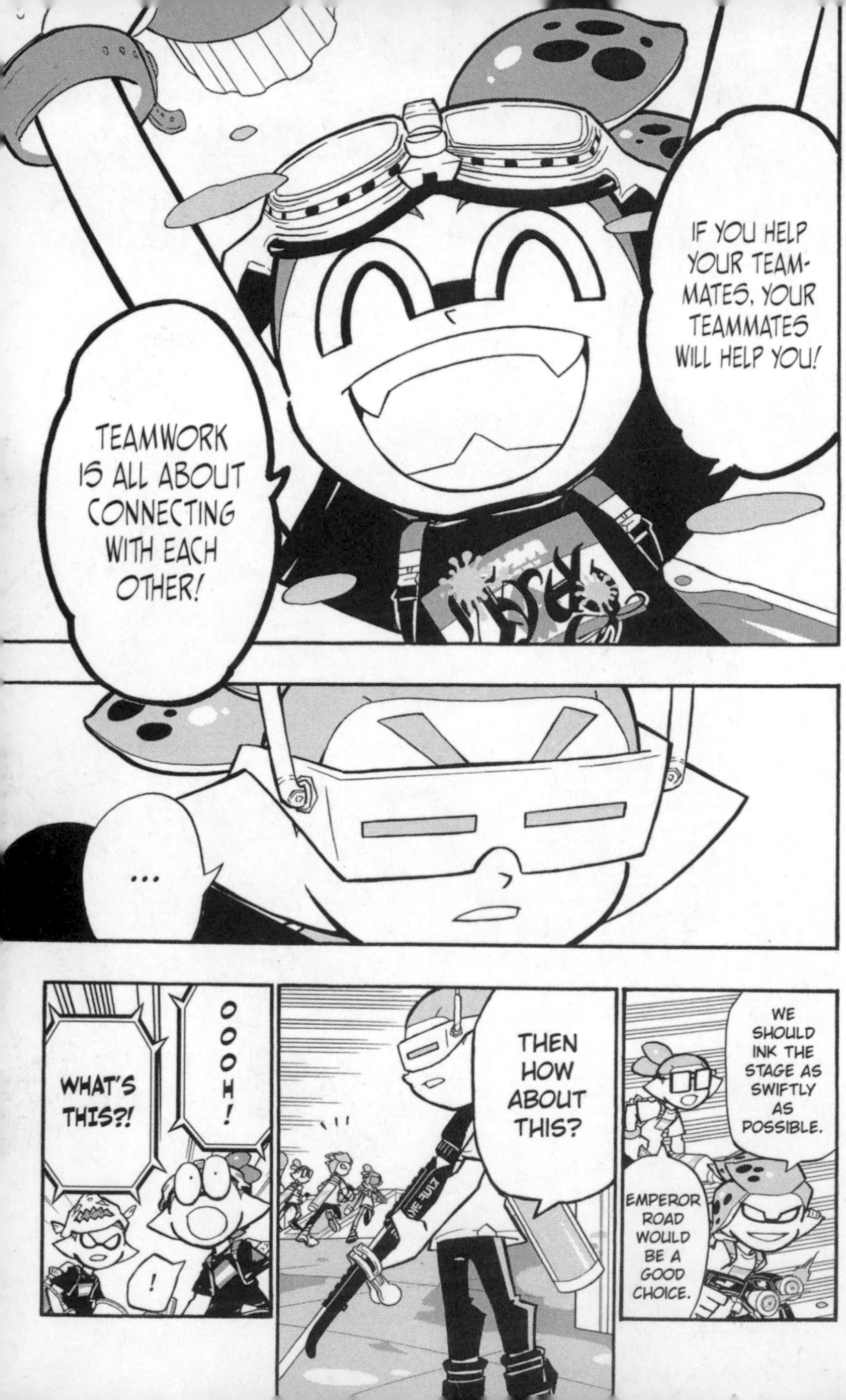
IF YOU HELP YOUR TEAM-MATES, YOUR TEAMMATES WILL HELP YOU!
TEAMWORK IS ALL ABOUT CONNECTING WITH EACH OTHER!
...
WE SHOULD INK THE STAGE AS SWIFTLY AS POSSIBLE.
EMPEROR ROAD WOULD BE A GOOD CHOICE.
THEN HOW ABOUT THIS?
OOOH!
WHAT'S THIS?!
!

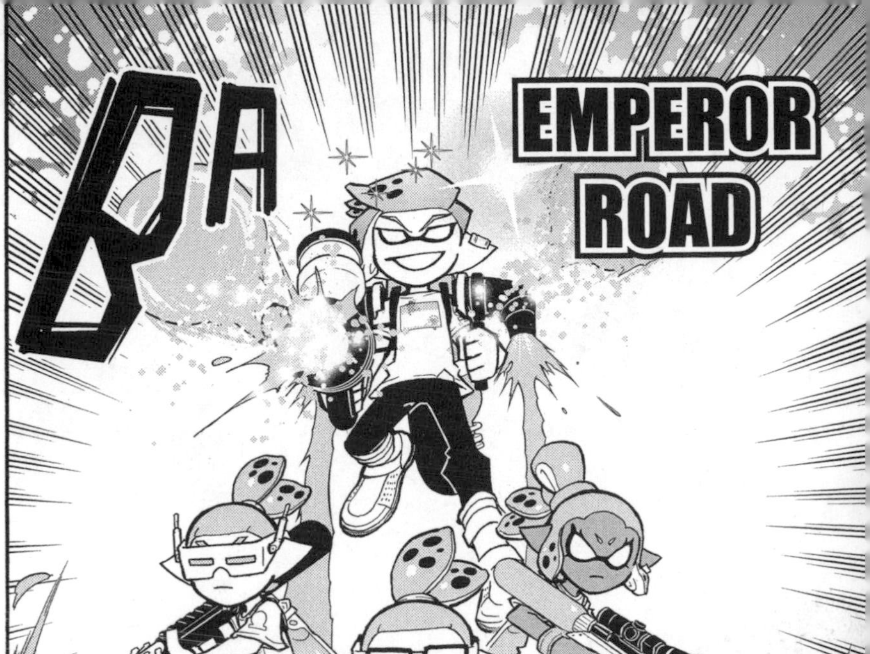
EMPEROR ROAD
BA
AM
TEAM ORDER VERSION!!

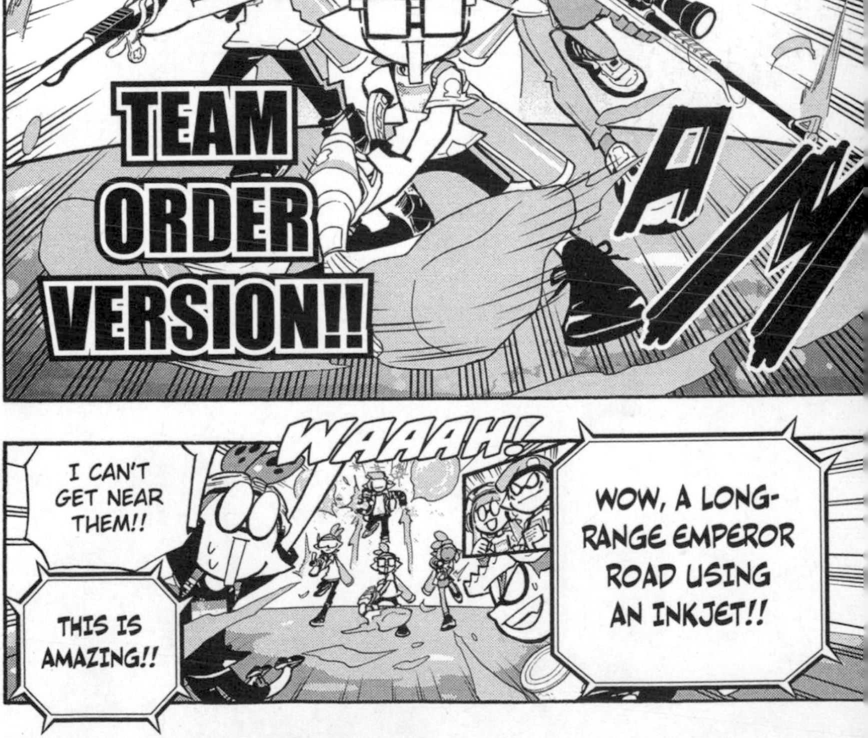
WOW, A LONG-RANGE EMPEROR ROAD USING AN INKJET!!
WAAAH!
I CAN'T GET NEAR THEM!!
THIS IS AMAZING!!

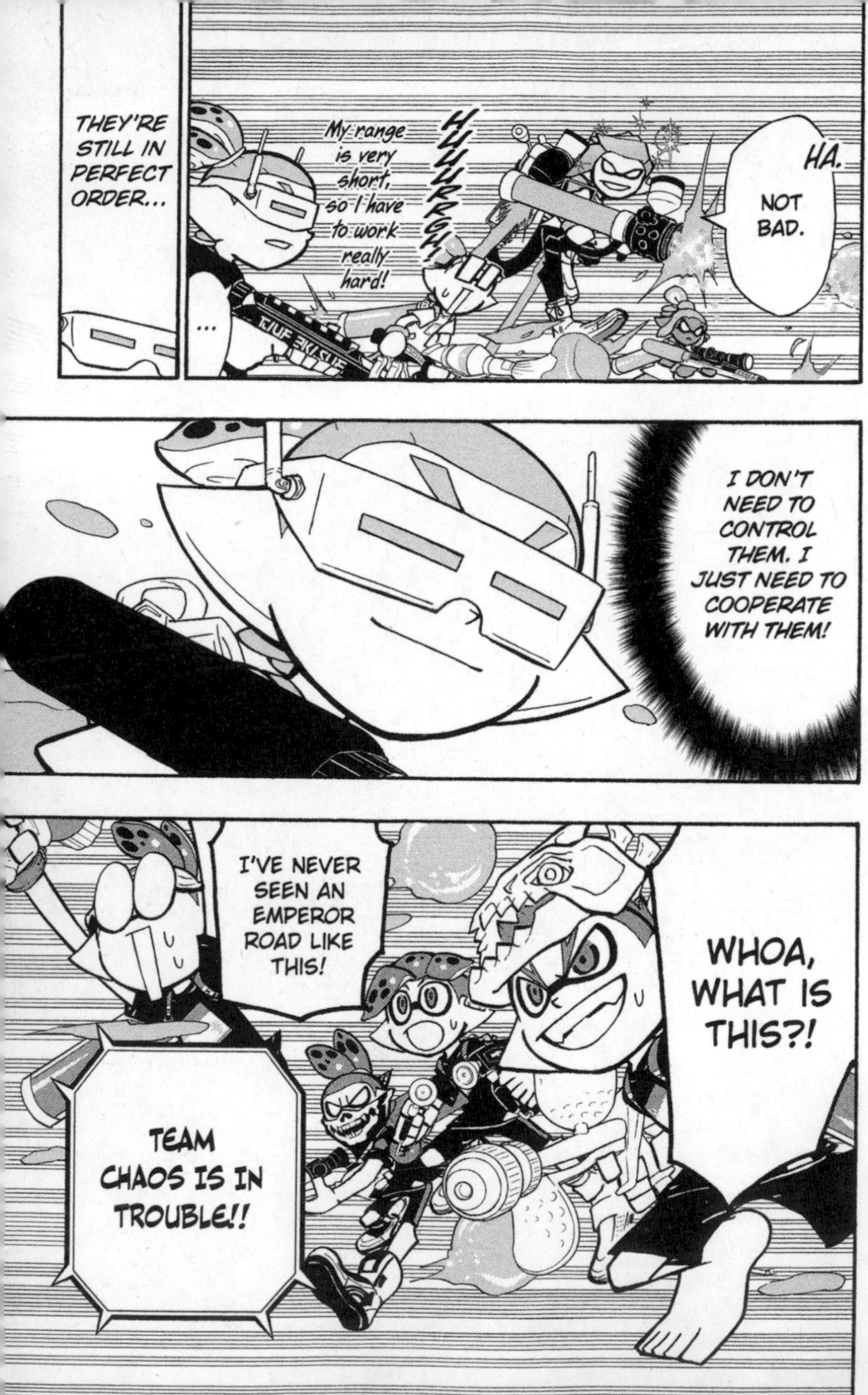
HA.
NOT BAD.
HUUURRGH!
My range is very short, so I have to work really hard!
...
THEY'RE STILL IN PERFECT ORDER...
I DON'T NEED TO CONTROL THEM. I JUST NEED TO COOPERATE WITH THEM!
WHOA, WHAT IS THIS?!
I'VE NEVER SEEN AN EMPEROR ROAD LIKE THIS!
TEAM CHAOS IS IN TROUBLE!!

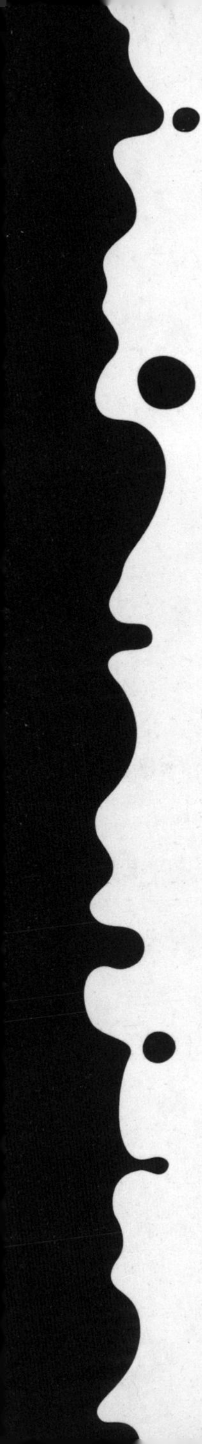

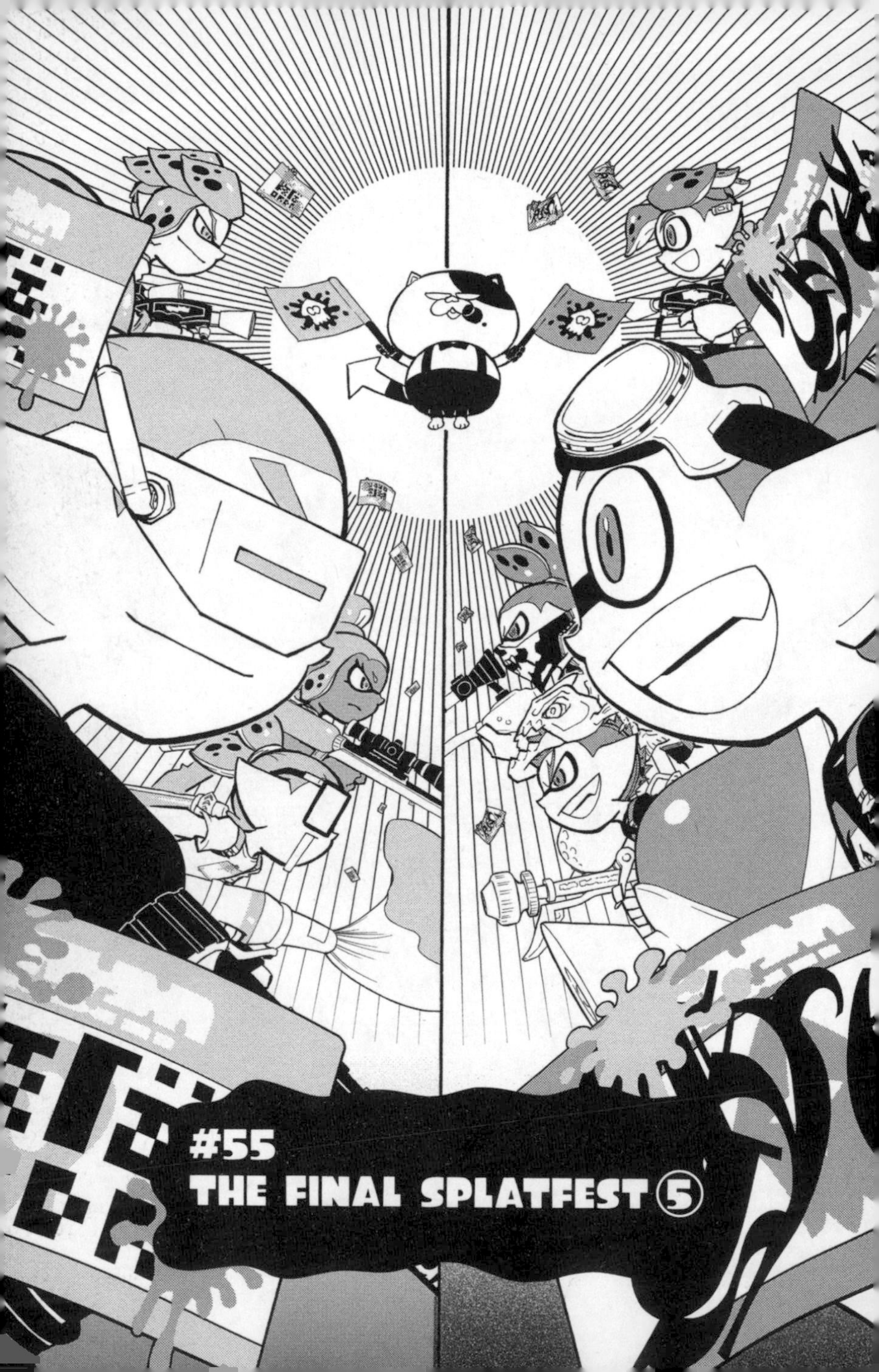
#55
THE FINAL SPLATFEST ⑤

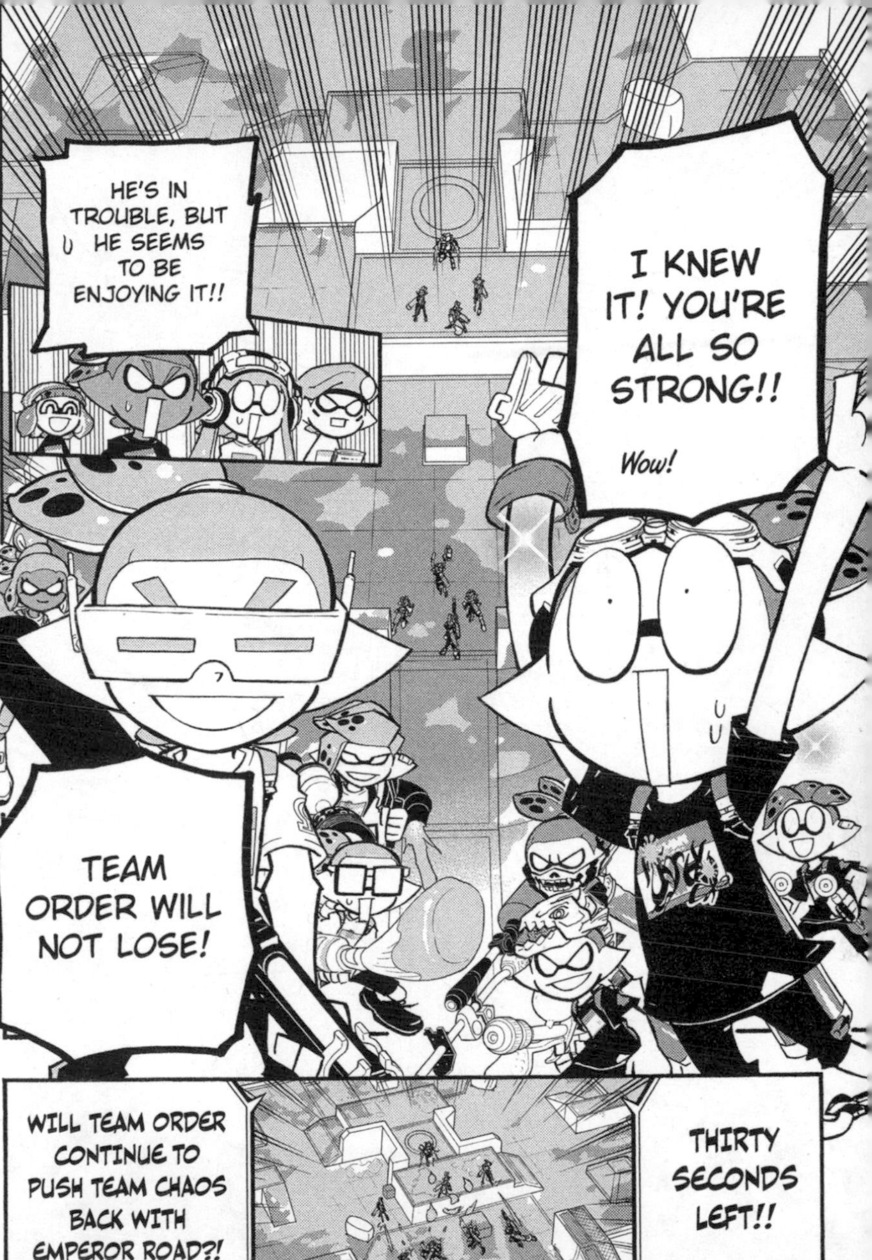
I KNEW IT! YOU'RE ALL SO STRONG!!
Wow!
HE'S IN TROUBLE, BUT HE SEEMS TO BE ENJOYING IT!!
TEAM ORDER WILL NOT LOSE!
THIRTY SECONDS LEFT!!
WILL TEAM ORDER CONTINUE TO PUSH TEAM CHAOS BACK WITH EMPEROR ROAD?!

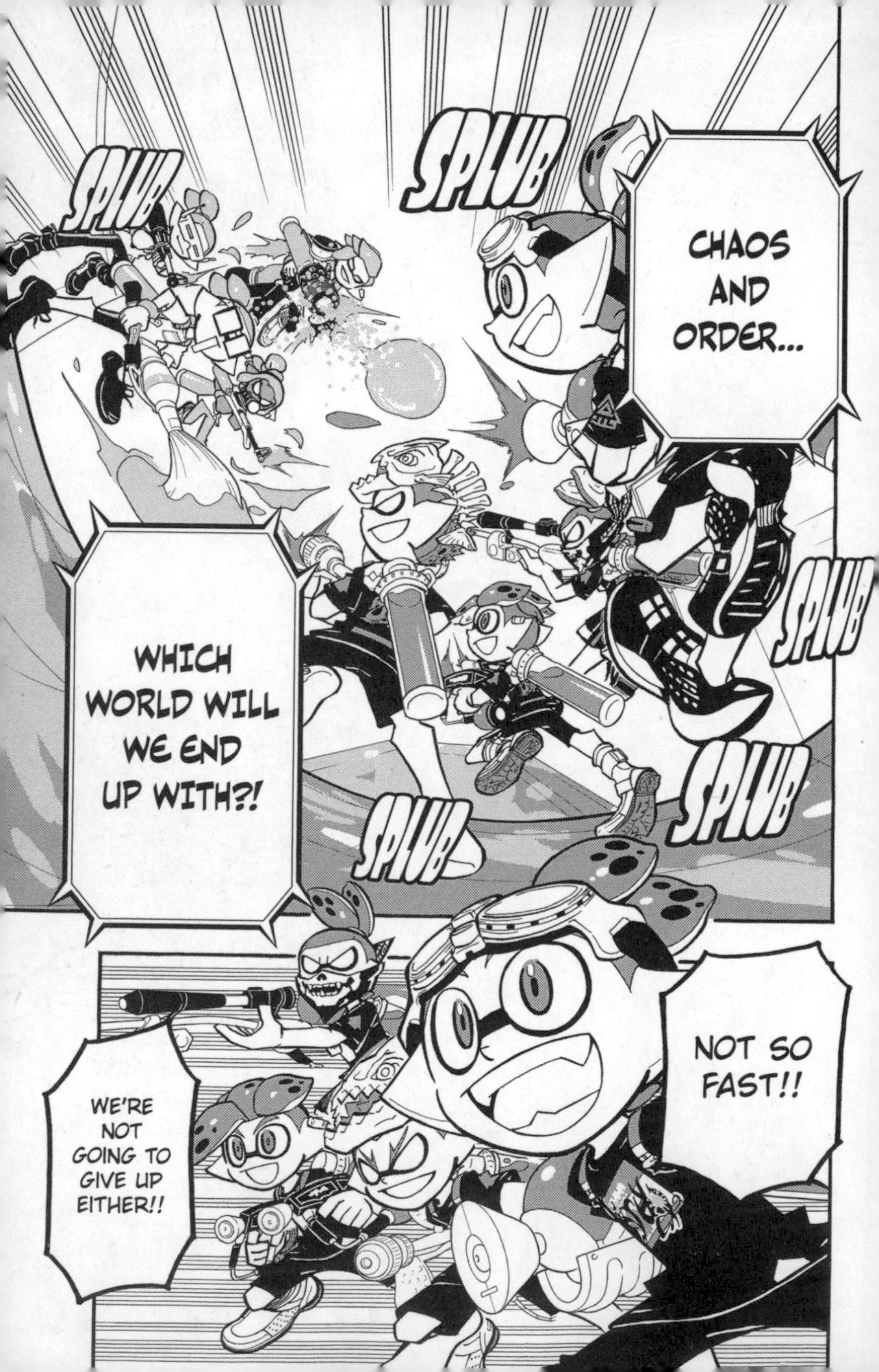
SPLUB
CHAOS AND ORDER...
SPLUB
SPLUB
SPLUB
SPLUB
WHICH WORLD WILL WE END UP WITH?!
NOT SO FAST!!
WE'RE NOT GOING TO GIVE UP EITHER!!

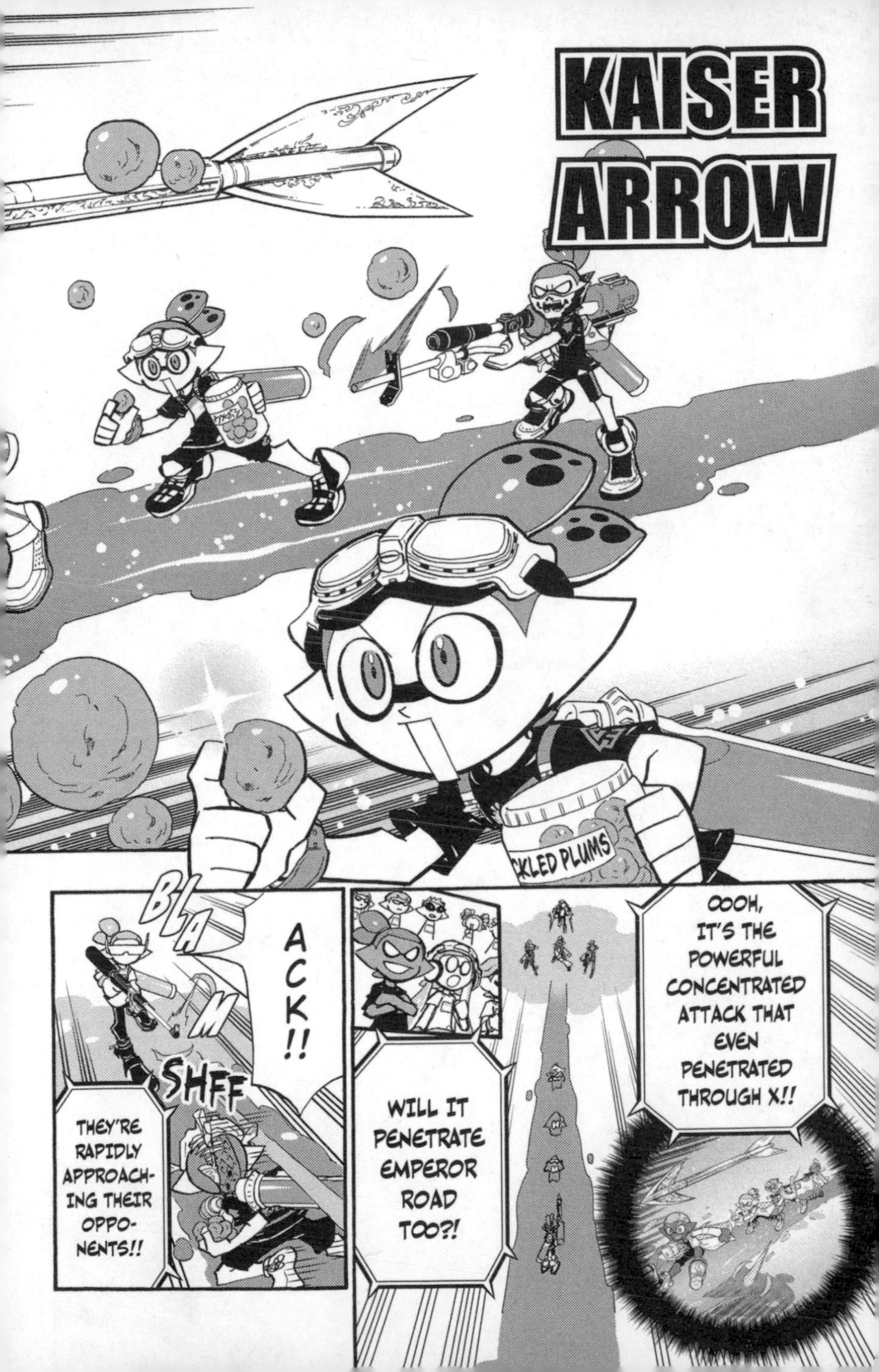
KAISER ARROW
CKLED PLUMS
OOOH, IT'S THE POWERFUL CONCENTRATED ATTACK THAT EVEN PENETRATED THROUGH X!!
WILL IT PENETRATE EMPEROR ROAD TOO?!
ACK!!
BLAM
SHFF
THEY'RE RAPIDLY APPROACH-ING THEIR OPPO-NENTS!!

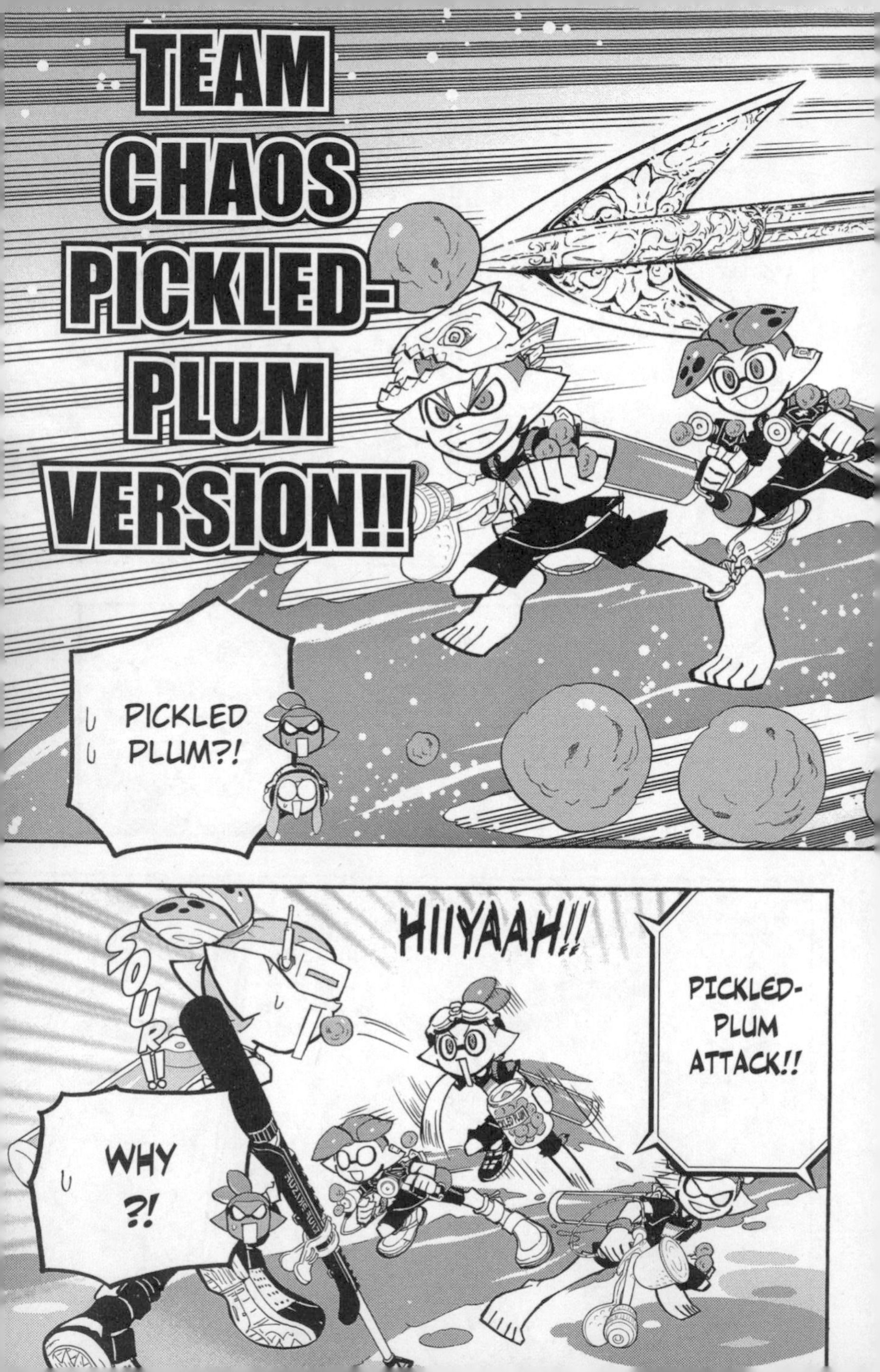
TEAM CHAOS PICKLED-PLUM VERSION!!
PICKLED PLUM?!
PICKLED-PLUM ATTACK!!
HIIYAAH!!
SOUR!!
WHY ?!

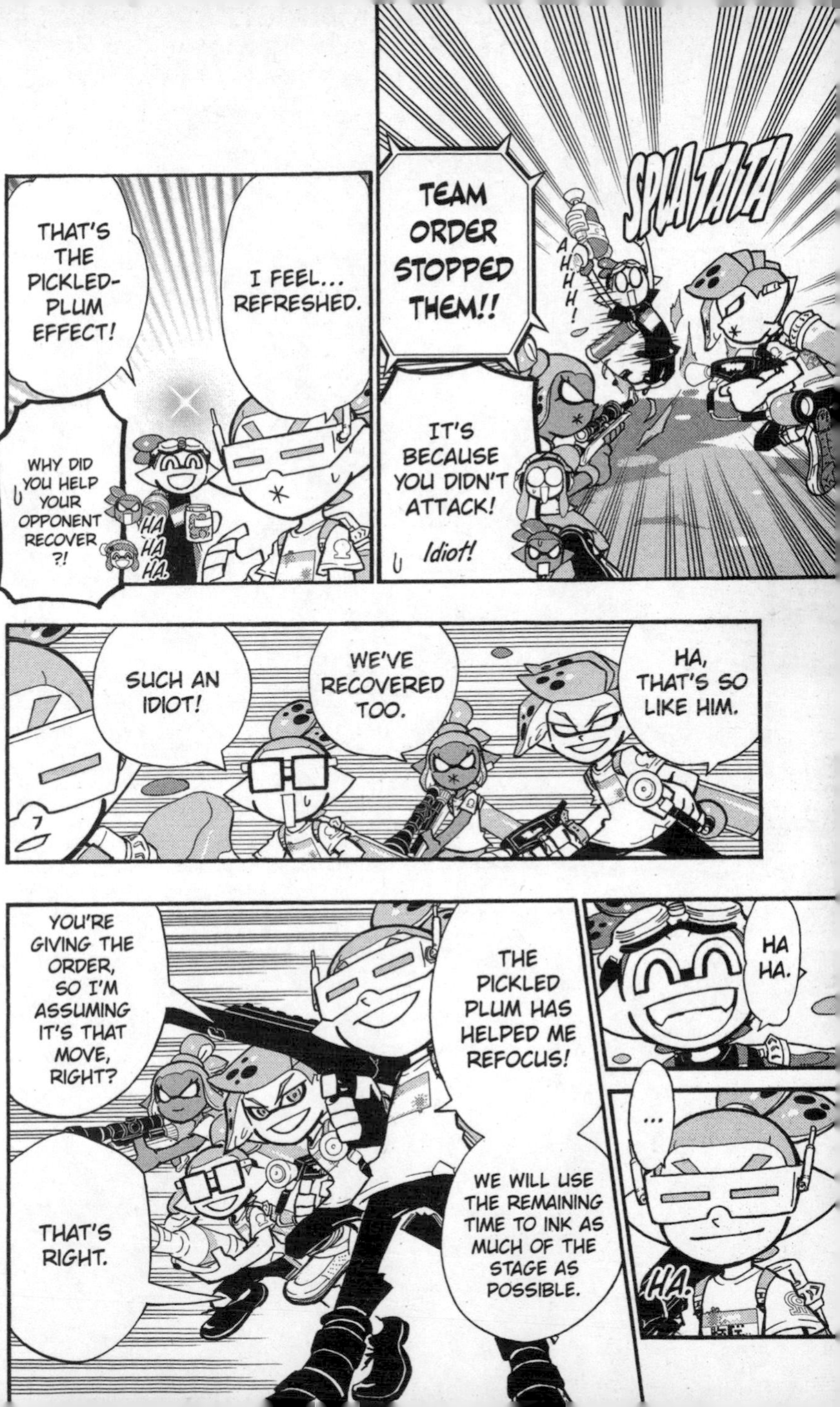
SPLATATA
AHHHH!
TEAM ORDER STOPPED THEM!!
IT'S BECAUSE YOU DIDN'T ATTACK!
Idiot!
I FEEL... REFRESHED.
THAT'S THE PICKLED-PLUM EFFECT!
HA HA HA.
WHY DID YOU HELP YOUR OPPONENT RECOVER?!
HA, THAT'S SO LIKE HIM.
WE'VE RECOVERED TOO.
SUCH AN IDIOT!
HA HA.
...
HA.
THE PICKLED PLUM HAS HELPED ME REFOCUS!
YOU'RE GIVING THE ORDER, SO I'M ASSUMING IT'S THAT MOVE, RIGHT?
WE WILL USE THE REMAINING TIME TO INK AS MUCH OF THE STAGE AS POSSIBLE.
THAT'S RIGHT.

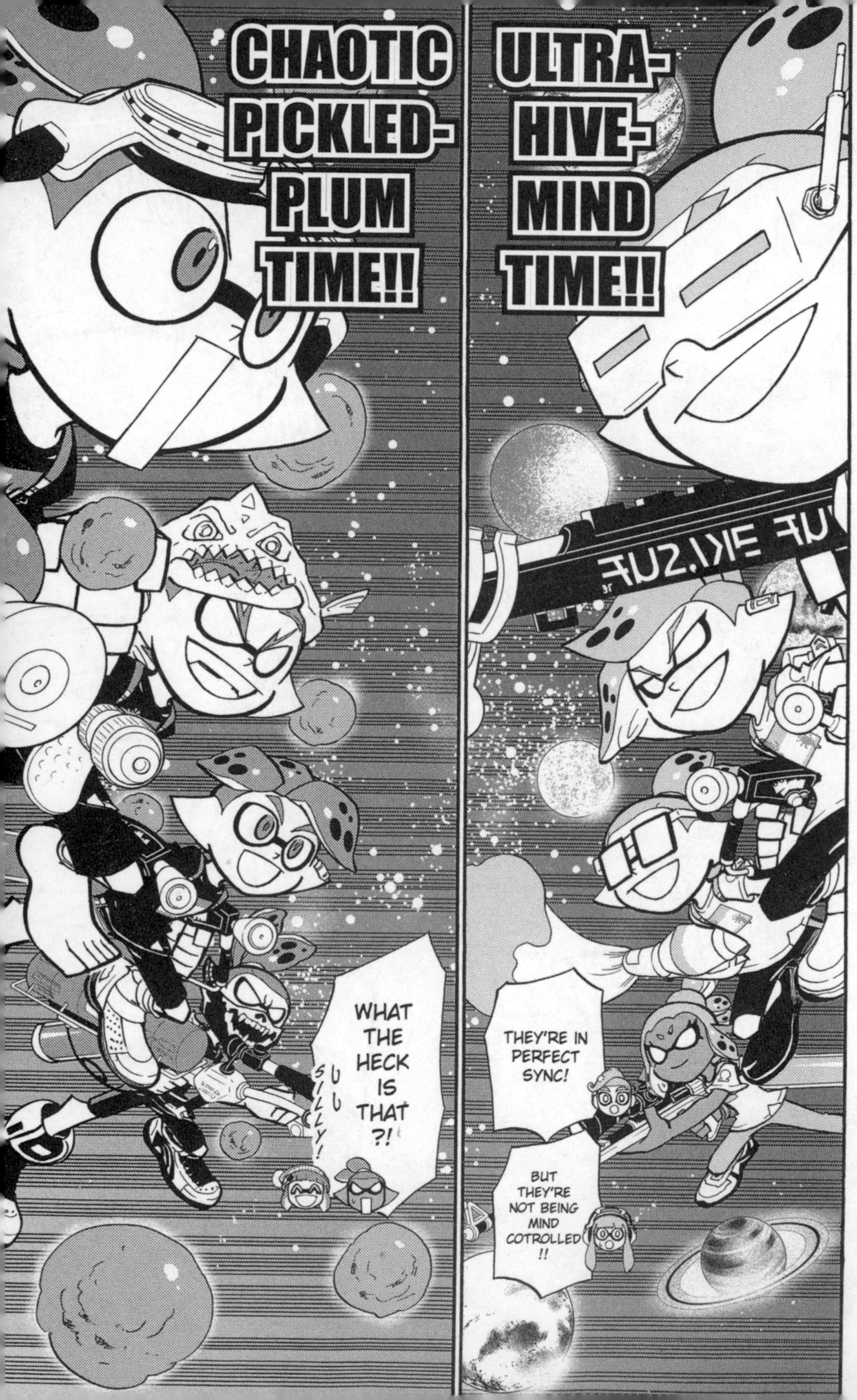
ULTRA-HIVE-MIND TIME!!
THEY'RE IN PERFECT SYNC!
BUT THEY'RE NOT BEING MIND COTROLLED!!
CHAOTIC PICKLED-PLUM TIME!!
WHAT THE HECK IS THAT?!
SILLY!

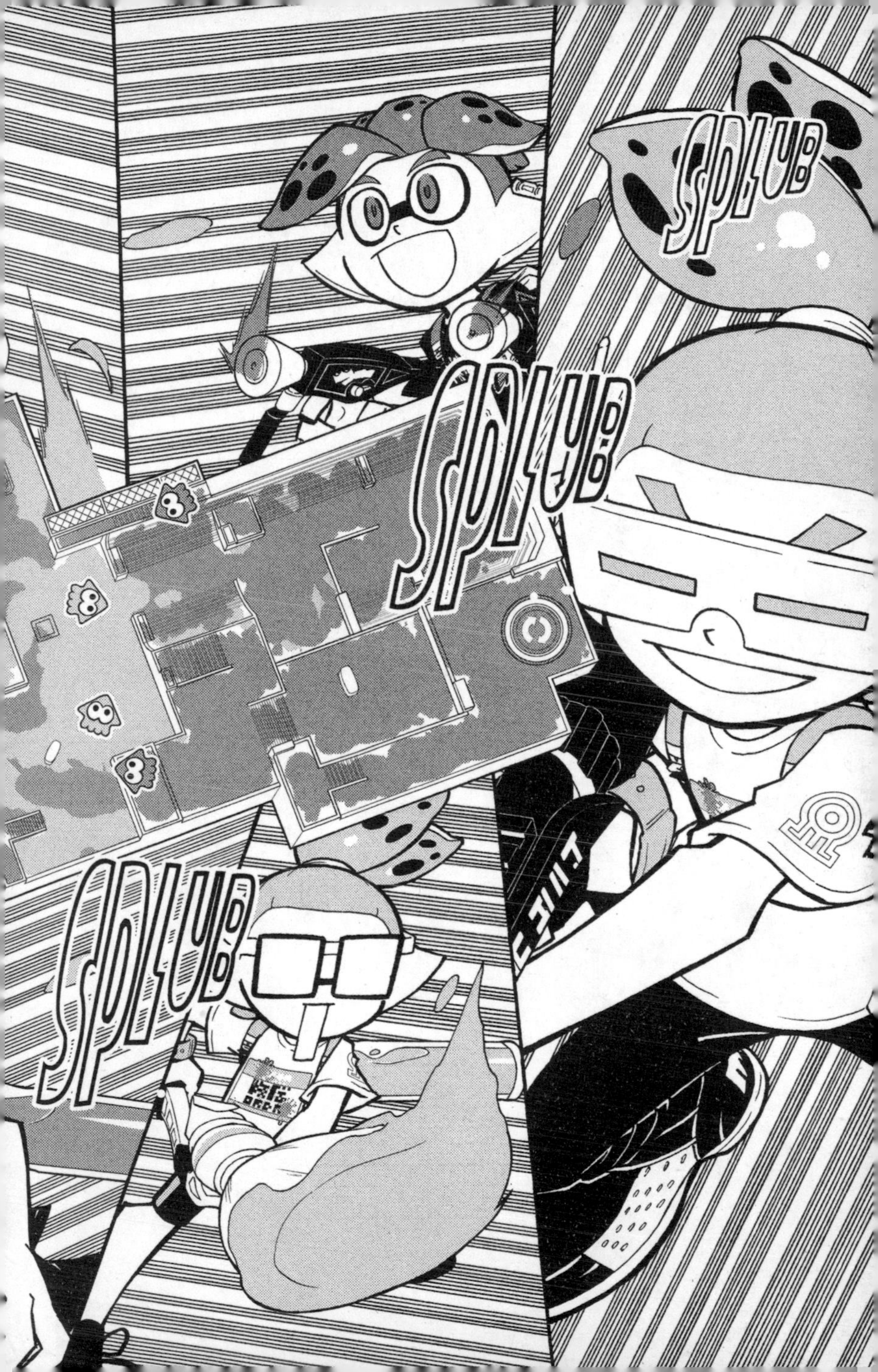
SPLUB
SPLUB
SPLUB

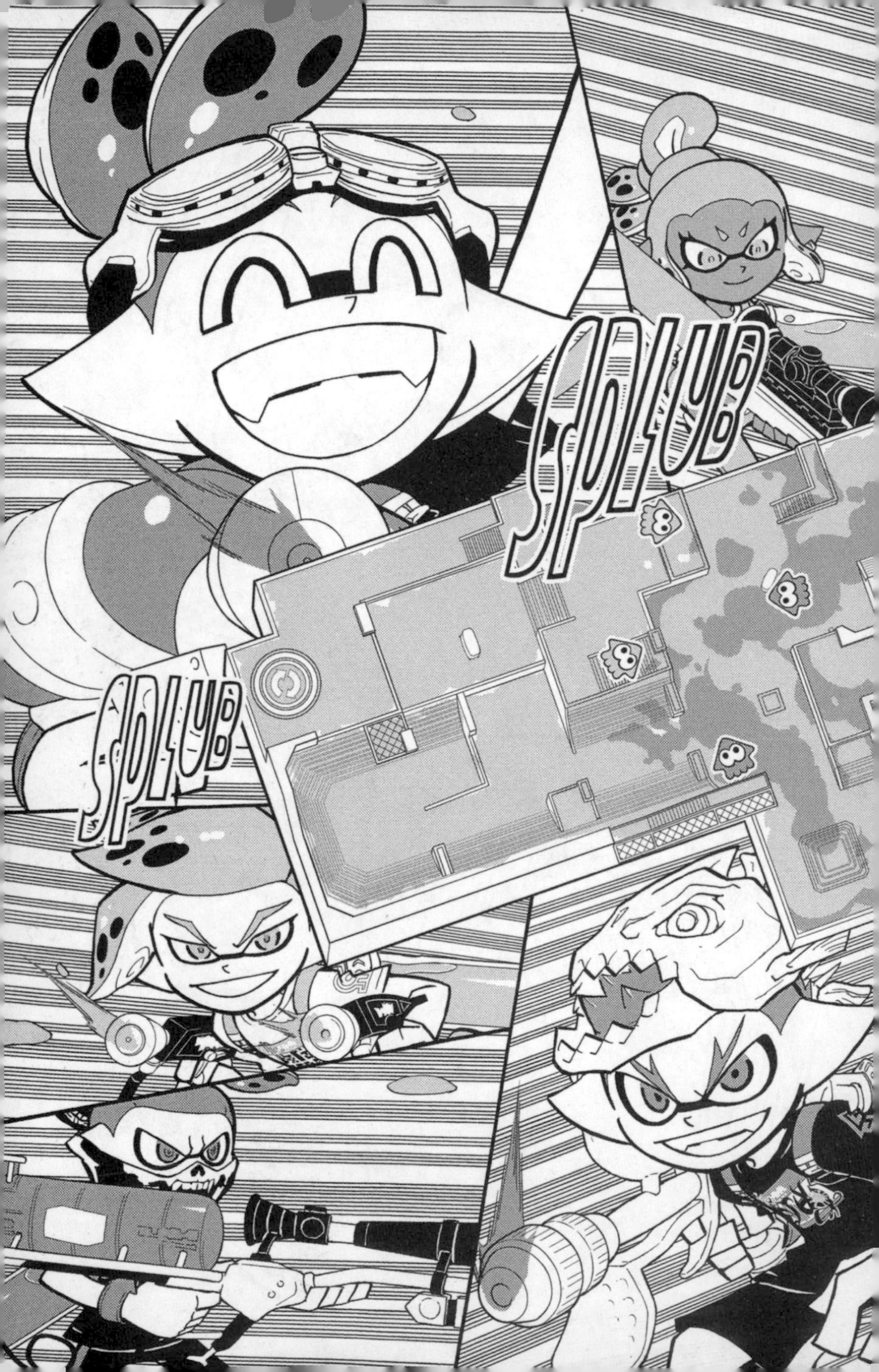
SPLUB
SPLUB

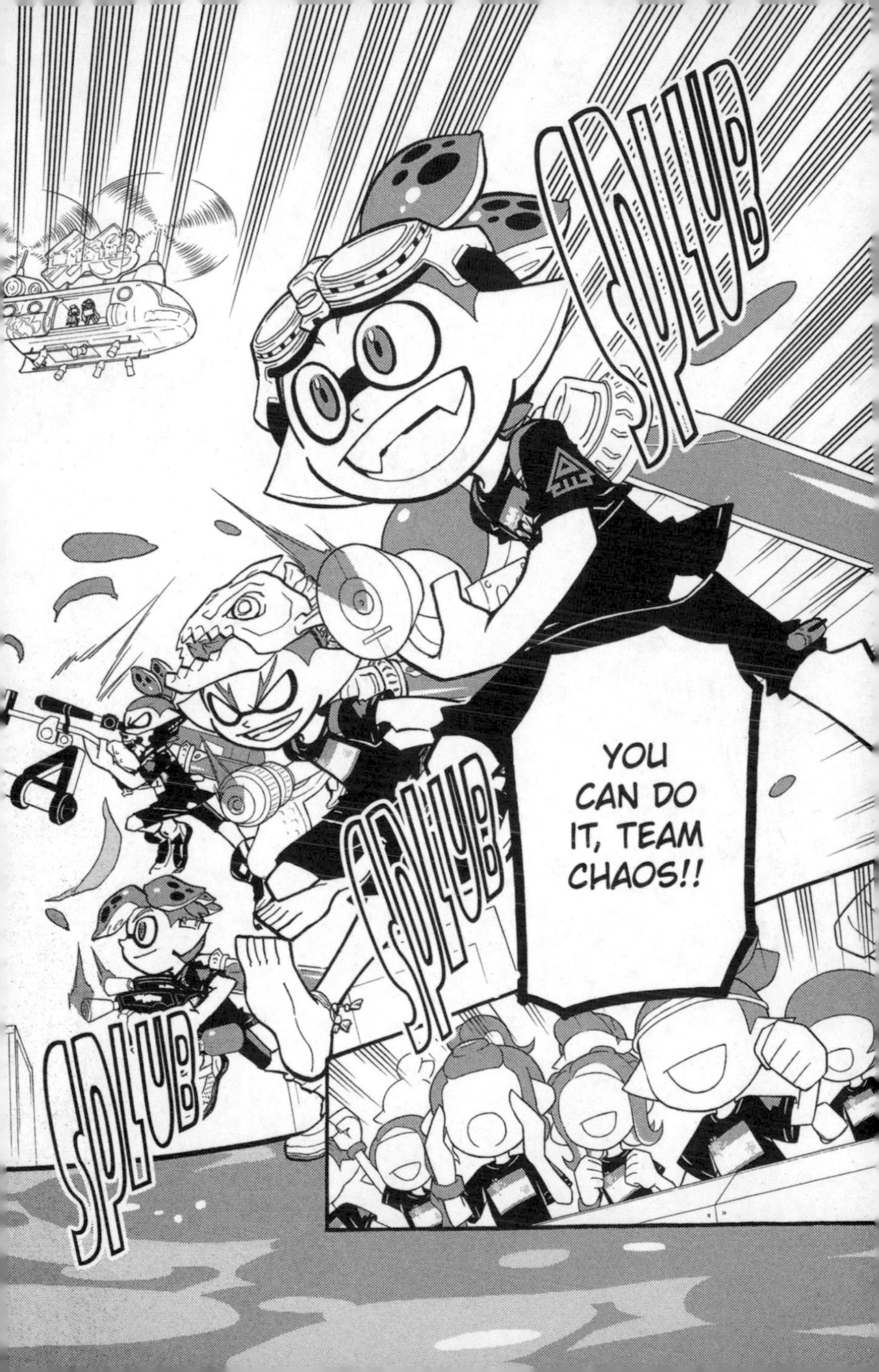
SPLUB
SPLUB
YOU CAN DO IT, TEAM CHAOS!!
SPLUB

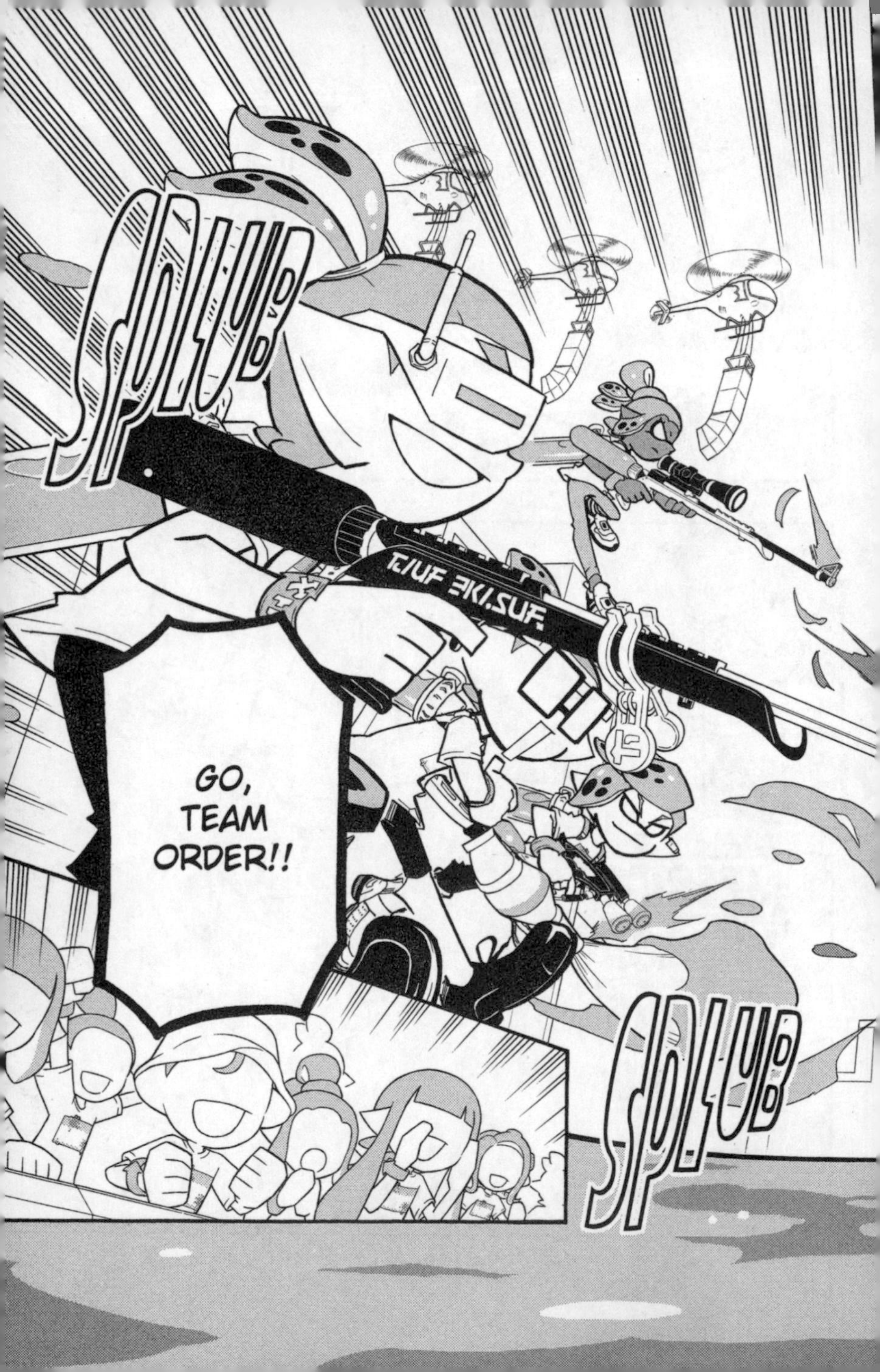
SPLUB
GO, TEAM ORDER!!
SPLUB

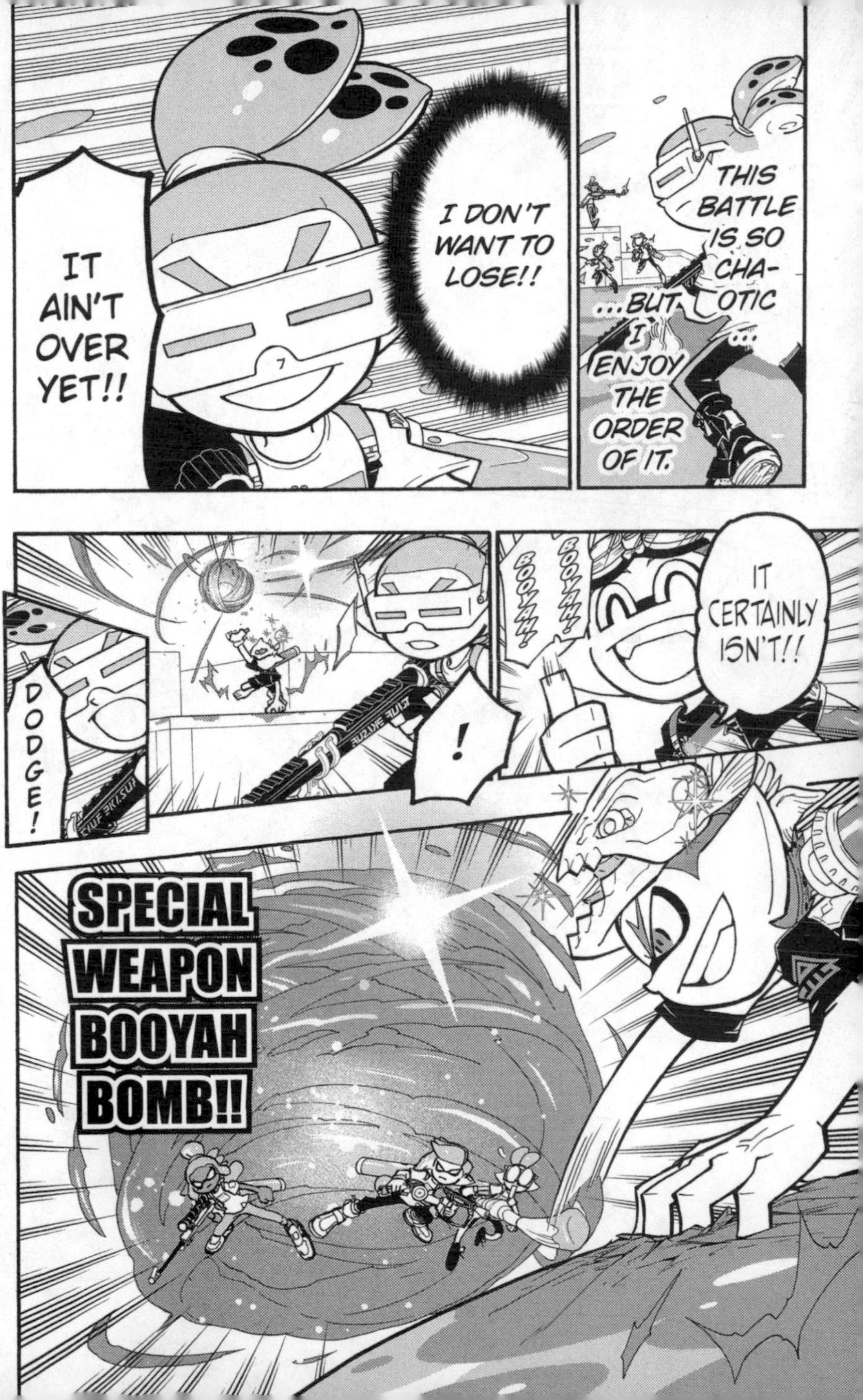
THIS BATTLE IS SO CHAOTIC...
...BUT I ENJOY THE ORDER OF IT.
I DON'T WANT TO LOSE!!
IT AIN'T OVER YET!!
BOOYAH! BOOYAH!
IT CERTAINLY ISN'T!!
!
DODGE!
SPECIAL WEAPON BOOYAH BOMB!!

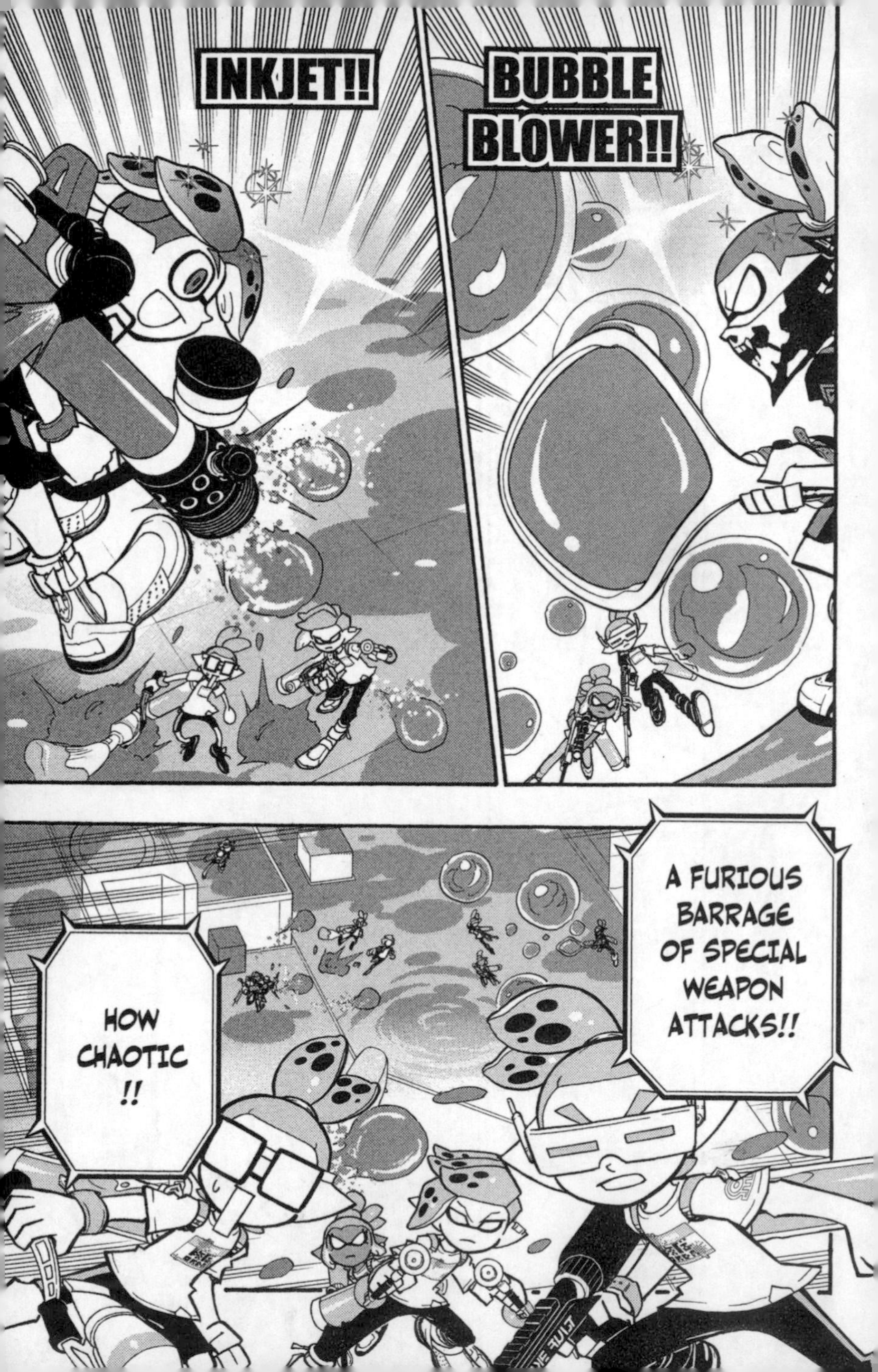
BUBBLE BLOWER!!
INKJET!!
A FURIOUS BARRAGE OF SPECIAL WEAPON ATTACKS!!
HOW CHAOTIC !!

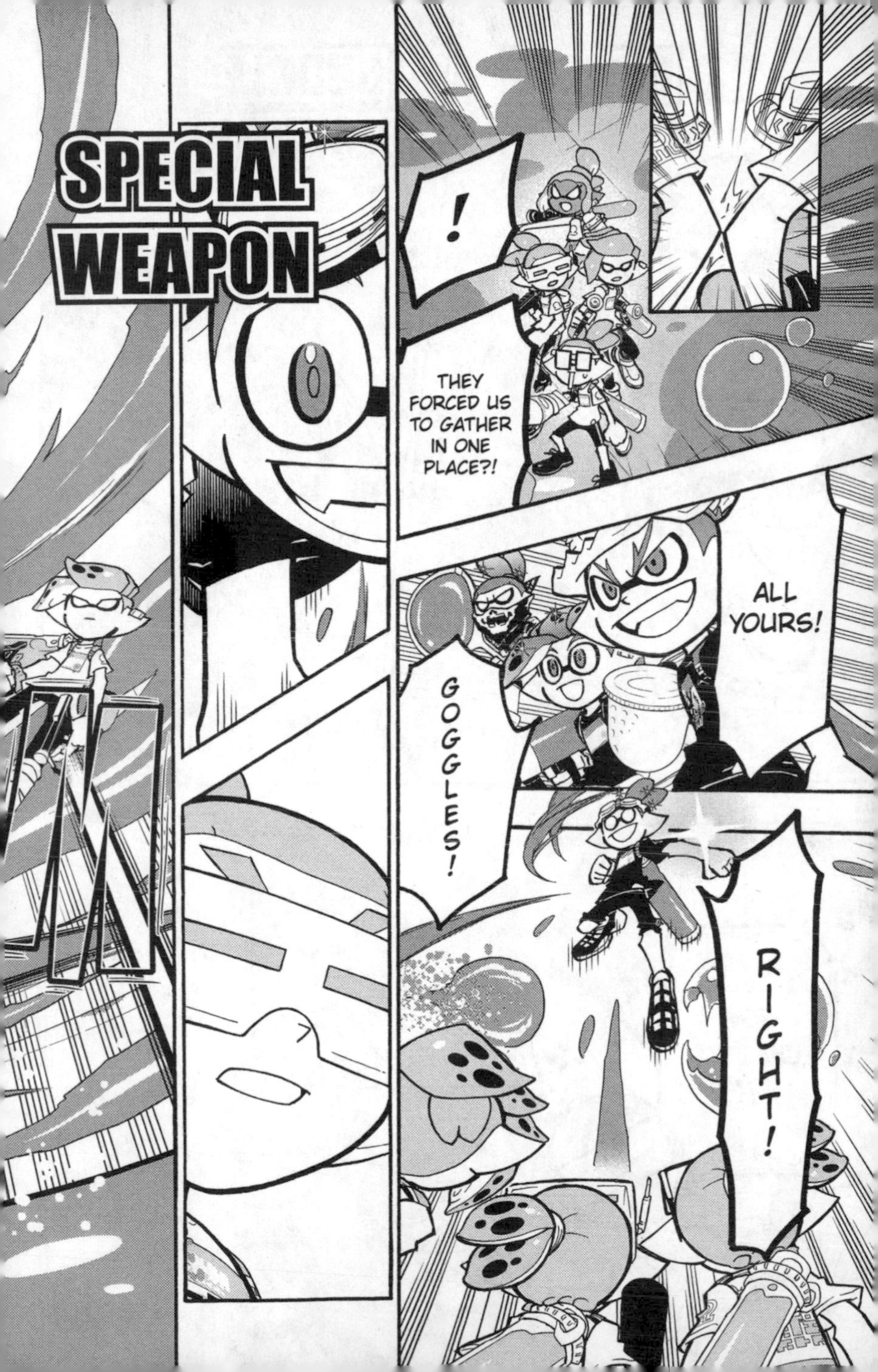
!
THEY FORCED US TO GATHER IN ONE PLACE?!
ALL YOURS!
GOGGLES!
RIGHT!
SPECIAL WEAPON

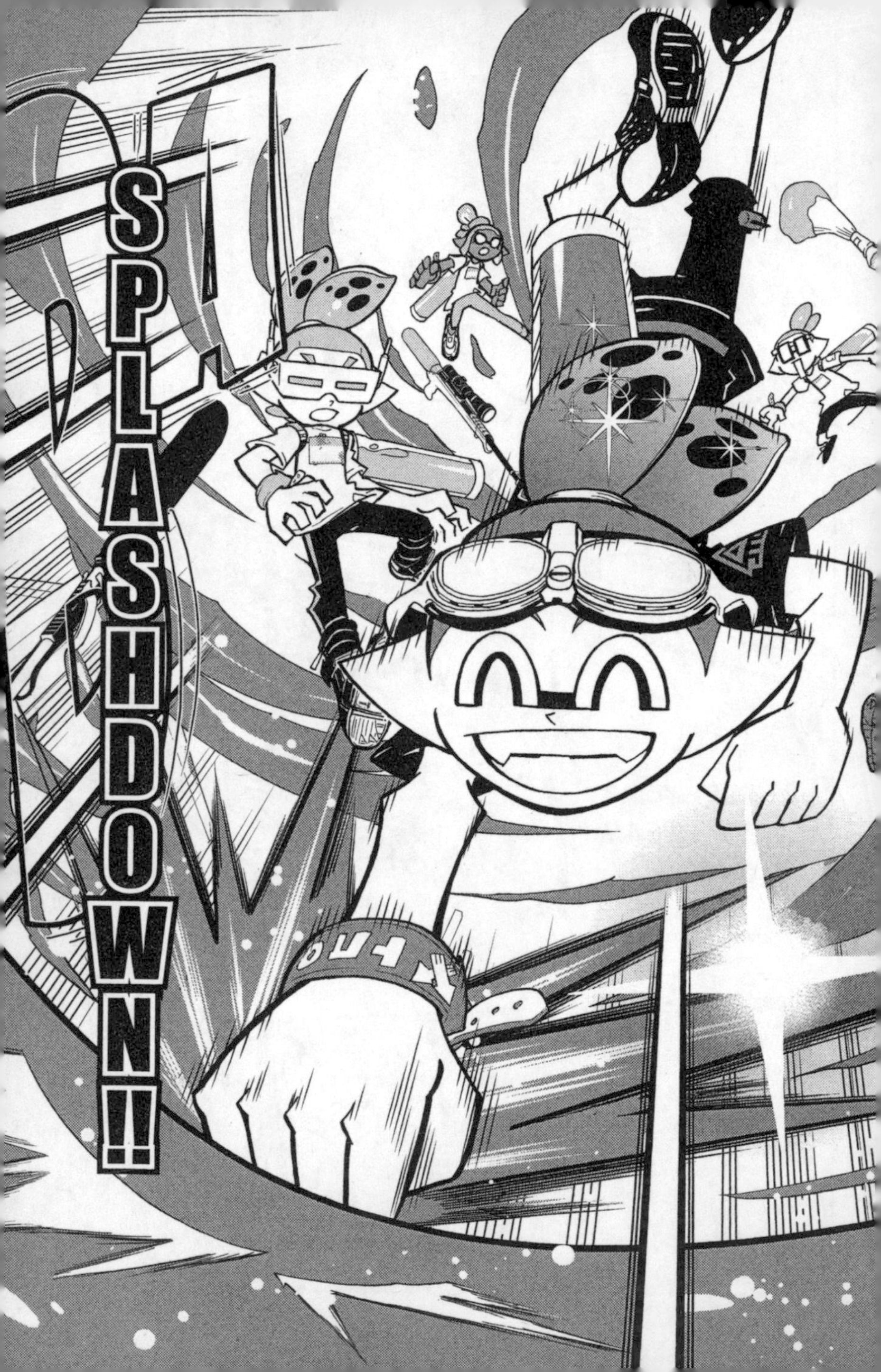
SPLASHDOWN!!

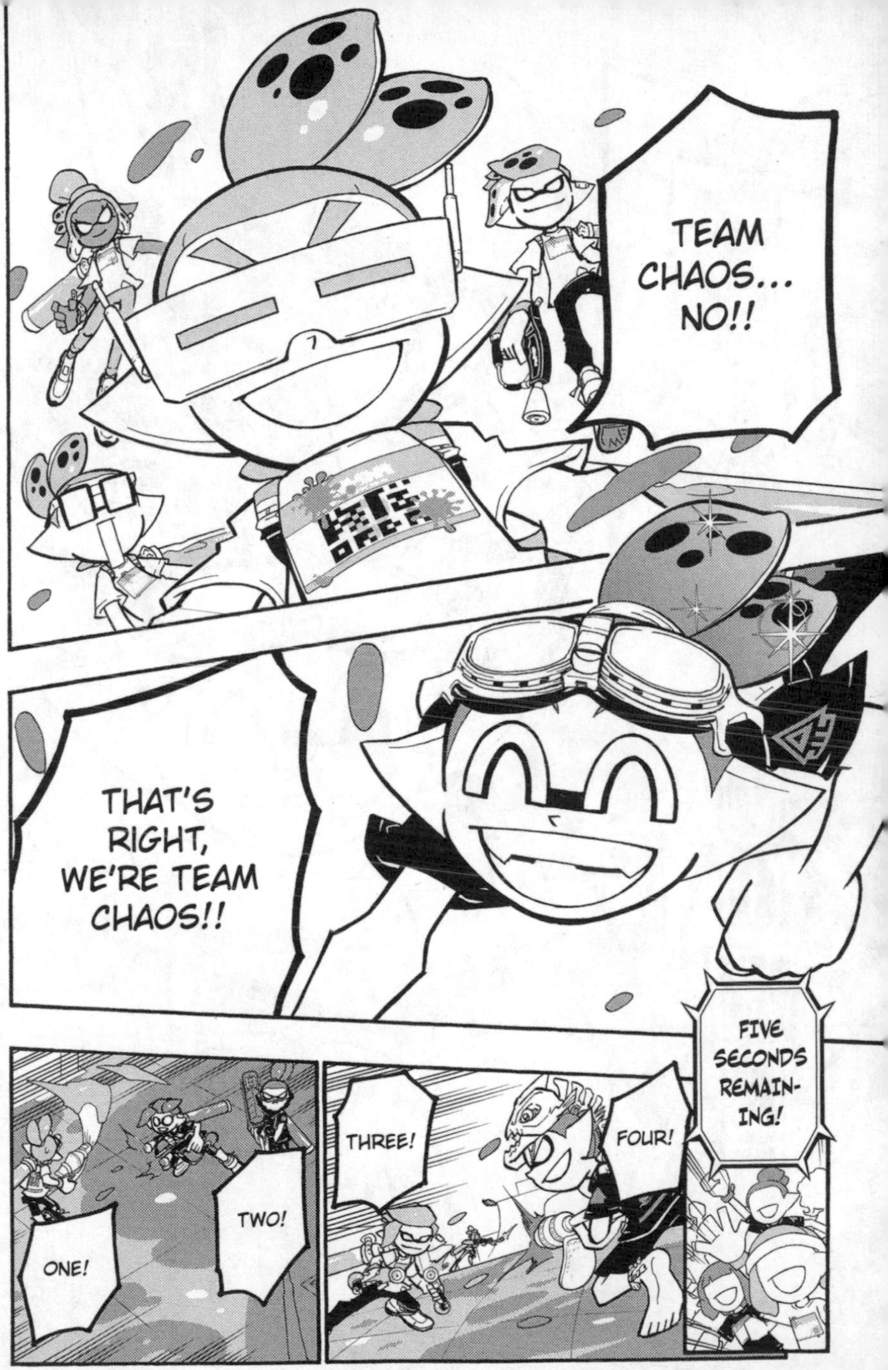
TEAM CHAOS... NO!!
THAT'S RIGHT, WE'RE TEAM CHAOS!!
FIVE SECONDS REMAINING!
FOUR!
THREE!
TWO!
ONE!

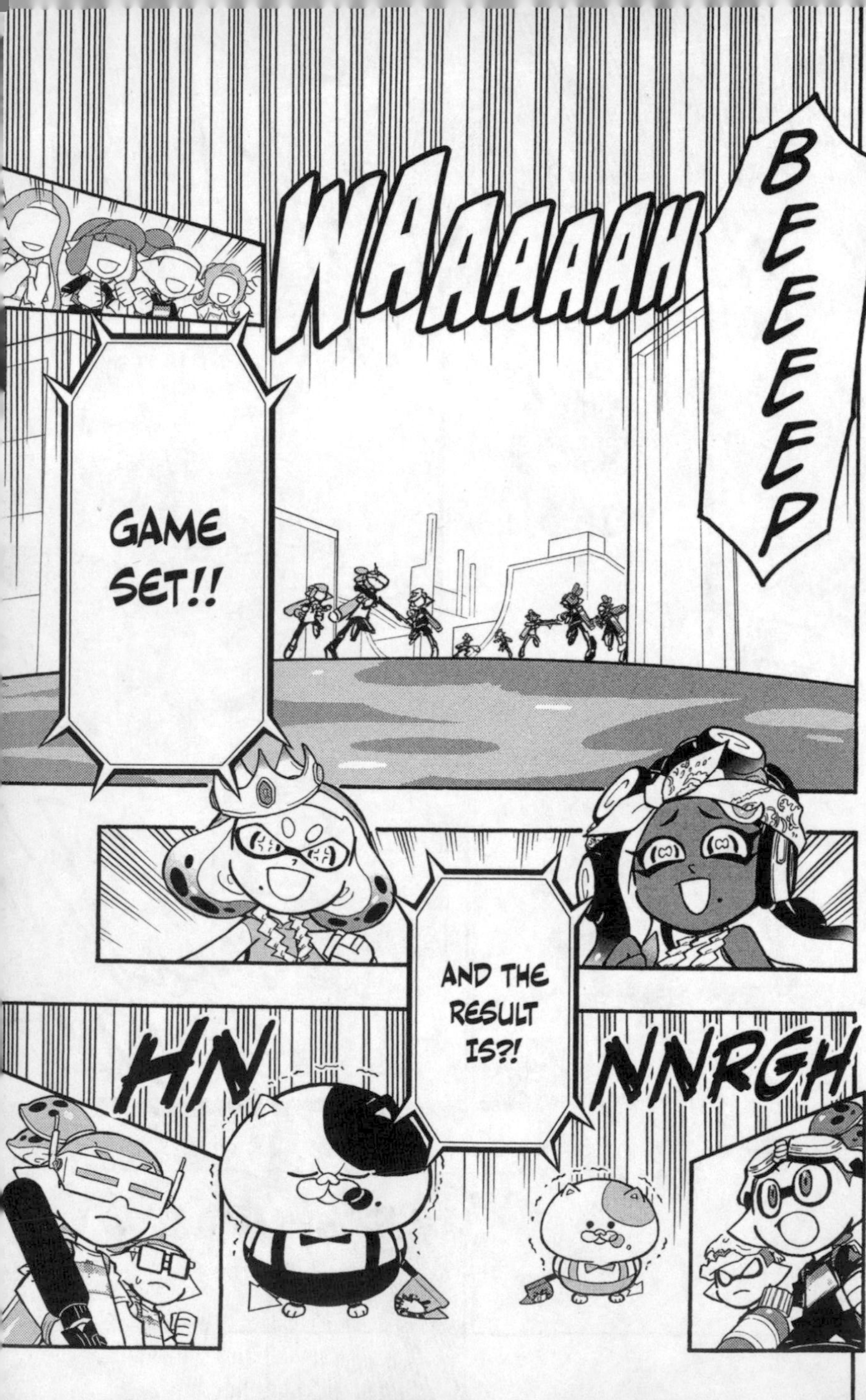
BEEEEEP
WAAAAAH
GAME SET!!
AND THE RESULT IS?!
NNRGH
HN

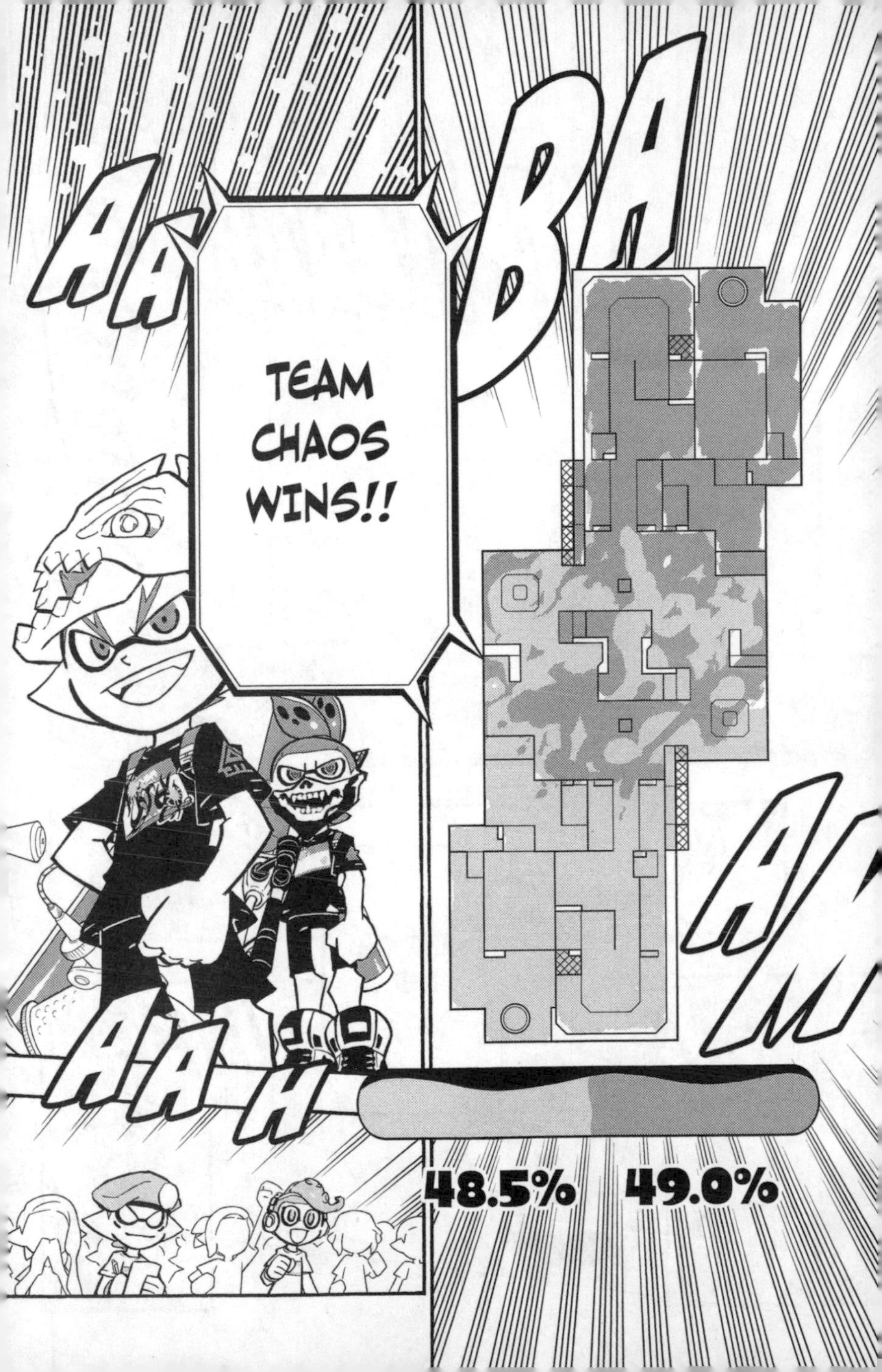
BA
AA
AA
TEAM CHAOS WINS!!
AAH
48.5%
49.0%

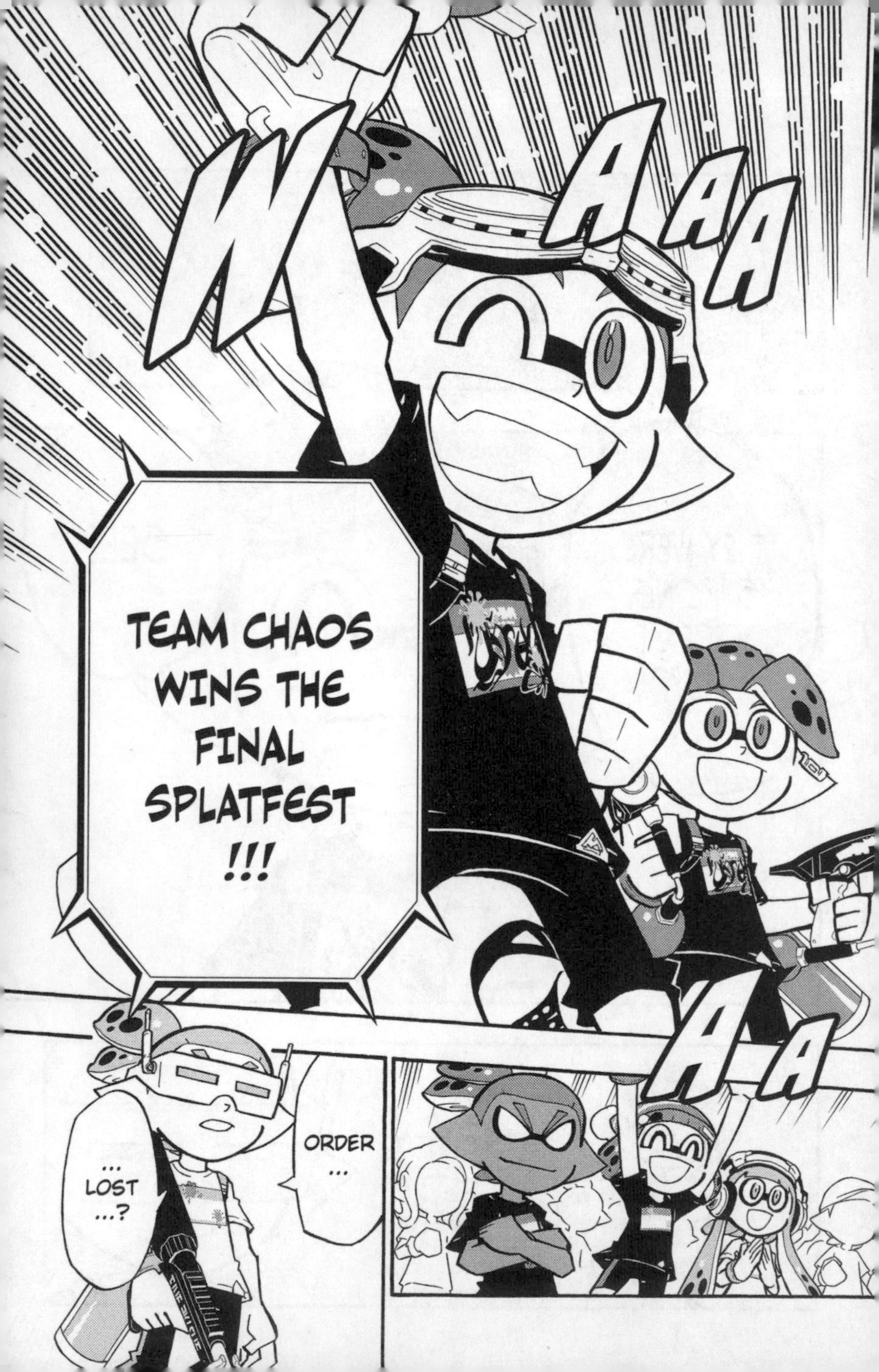
WAAA
TEAM CHAOS WINS THE FINAL SPLATFEST !!!
AA
ORDER ...
... LOST ...?

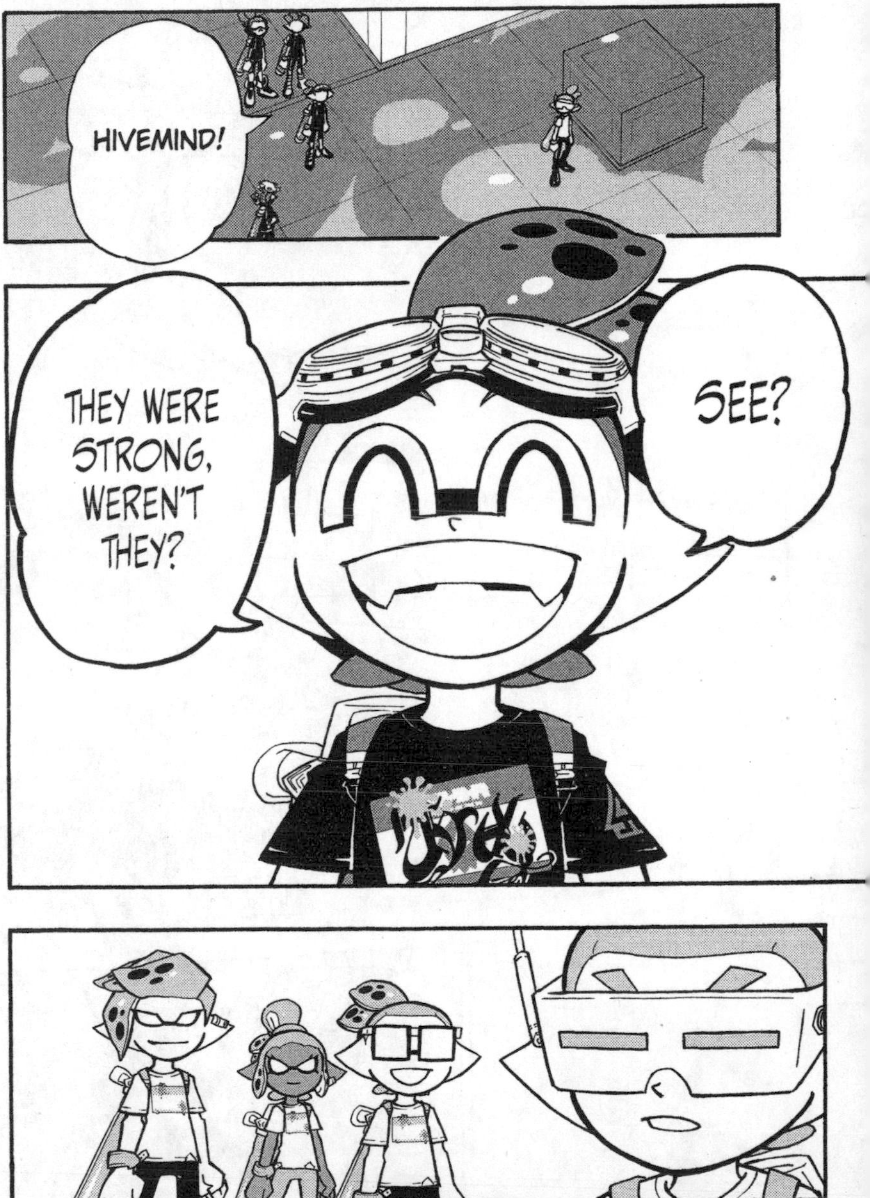
HIVEMIND!
SEE?
THEY WERE STRONG, WEREN'T THEY?

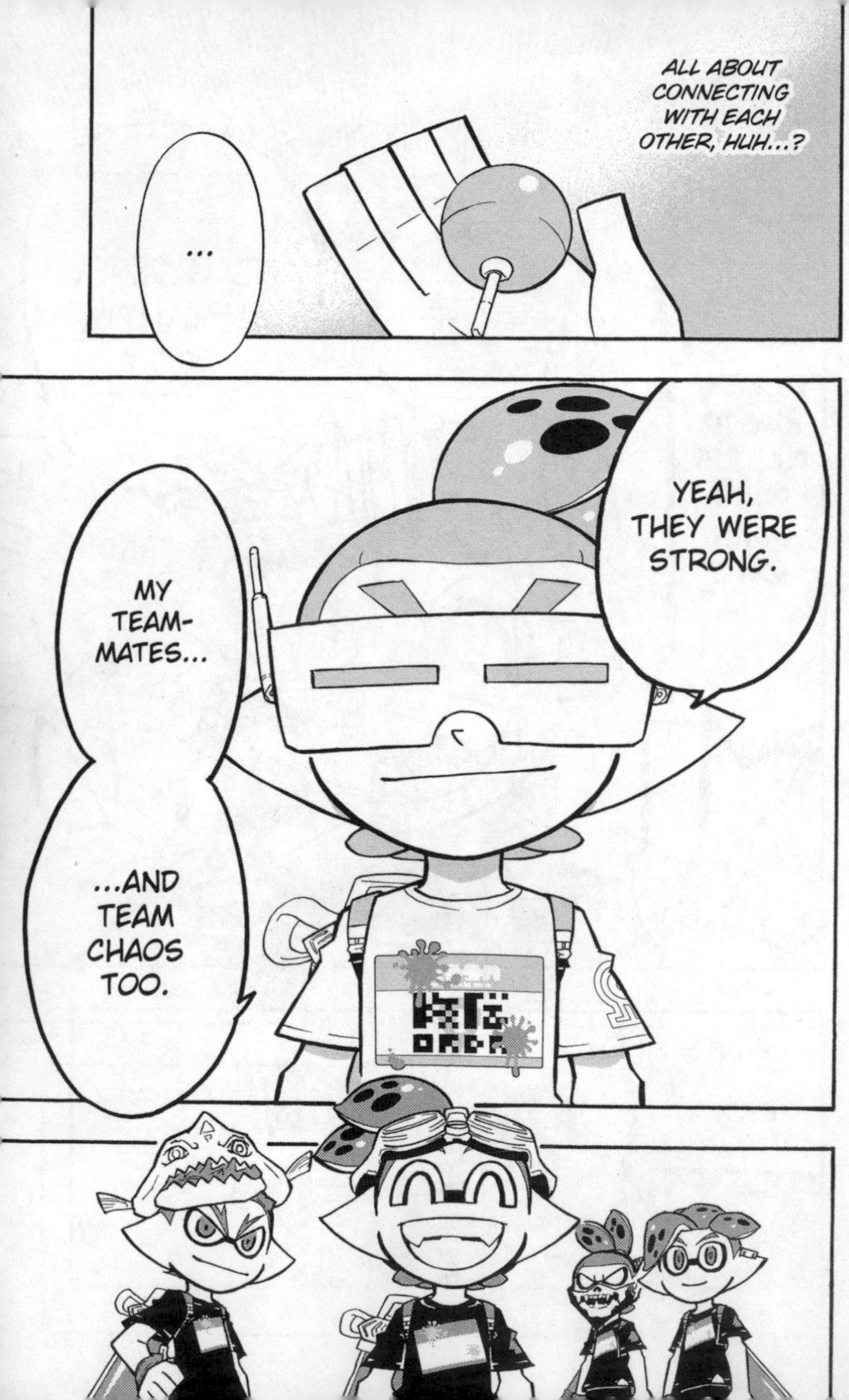
ALL ABOUT CONNECTING WITH EACH OTHER, HUH...?
...
YEAH, THEY WERE STRONG.
MY TEAM-MATES...
...AND TEAM CHAOS TOO.

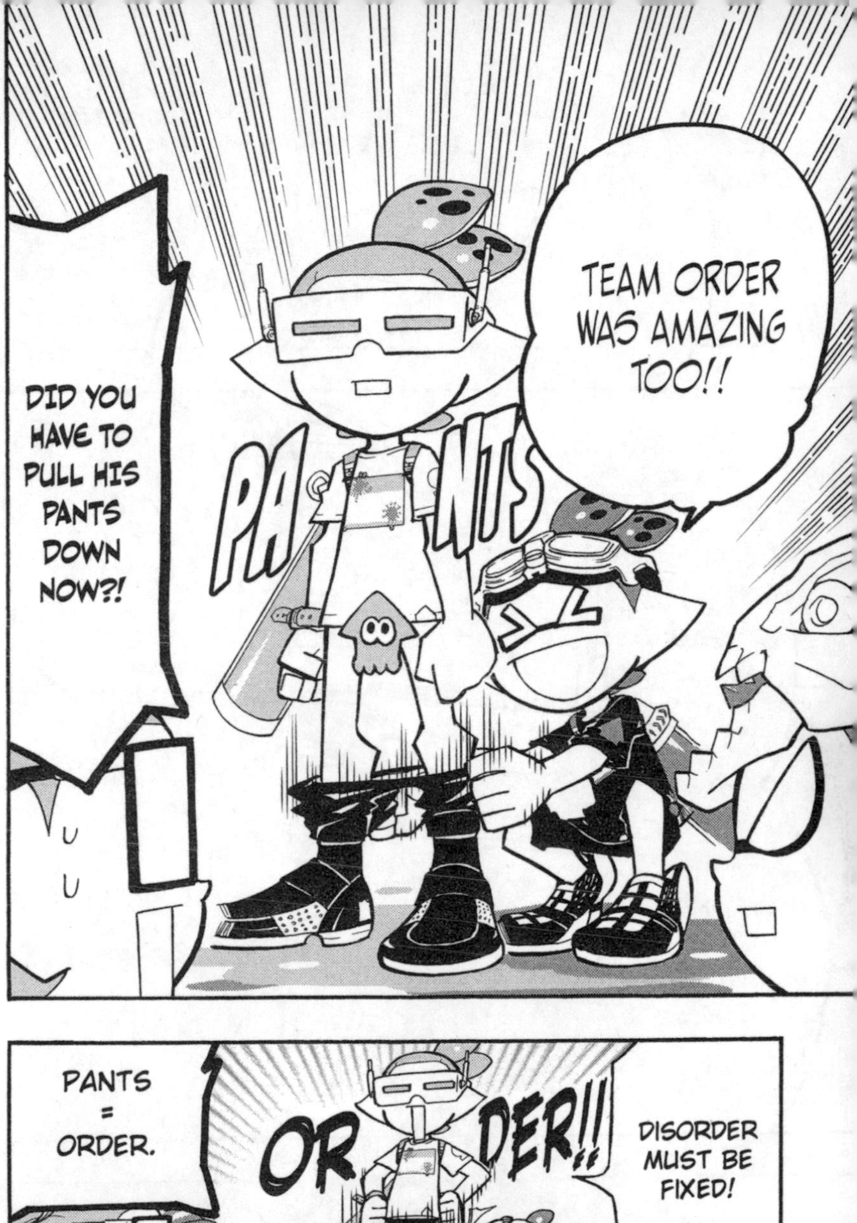
TEAM ORDER WAS AMAZING TOO!!
PANTS
DID YOU HAVE TO PULL HIS PANTS DOWN NOW?!
DISORDER MUST BE FIXED!
ORDER!!
PANTS = ORDER.
There... that's better!

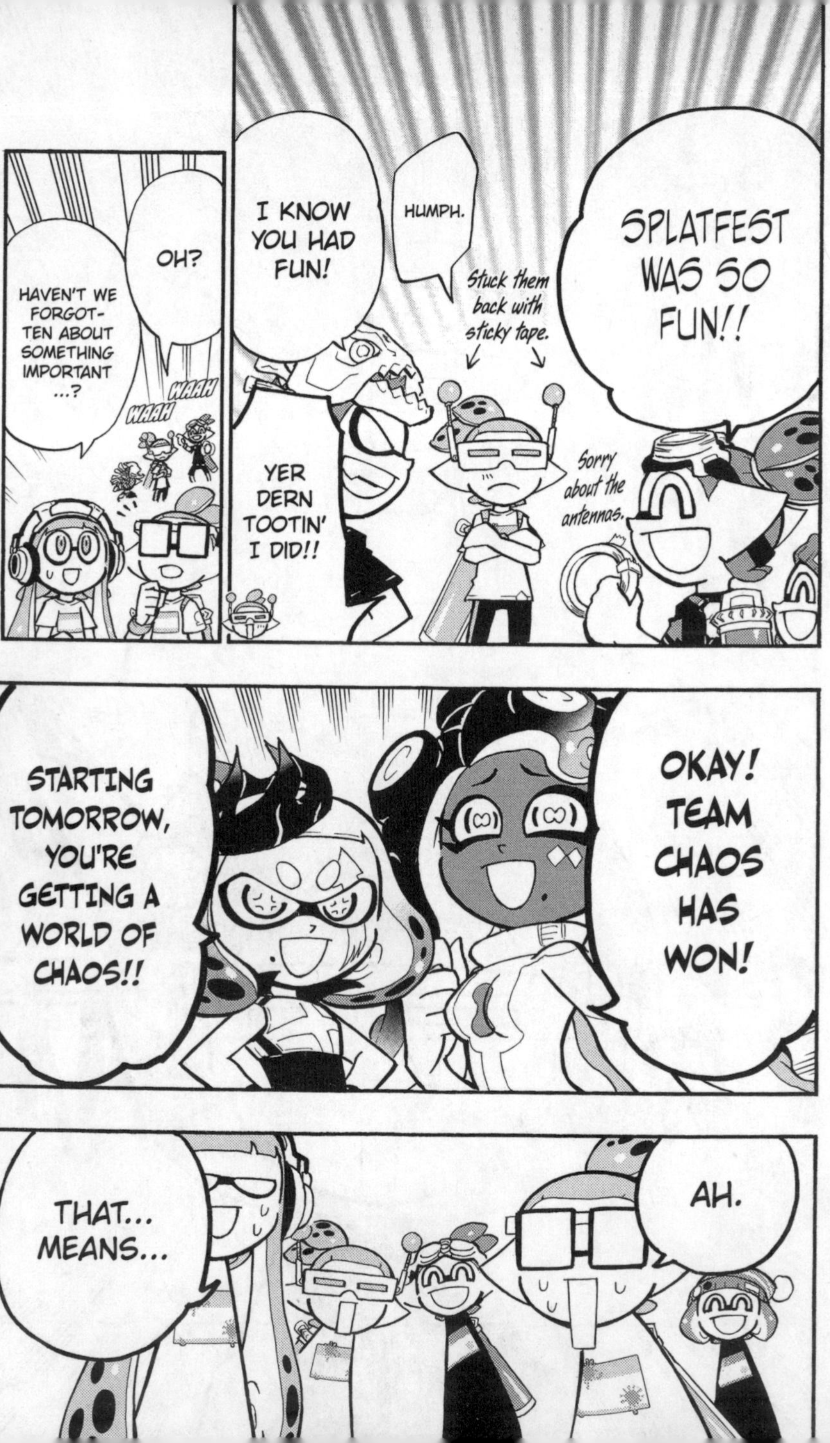
SPLATFEST WAS SO FUN!!
Sorry about the antennas.
Stuck them back with sticky tape.
HUMPH.
I KNOW YOU HAD FUN!
YER DERN TOOTIN' I DID!!
OH?
WAAH
WAAH
HAVEN'T WE FORGOT-TEN ABOUT SOMETHING IMPORTANT ...?
OKAY! TEAM CHAOS HAS WON!
STARTING TOMORROW, YOU'RE GETTING A WORLD OF CHAOS!!
AH.
THAT... MEANS...

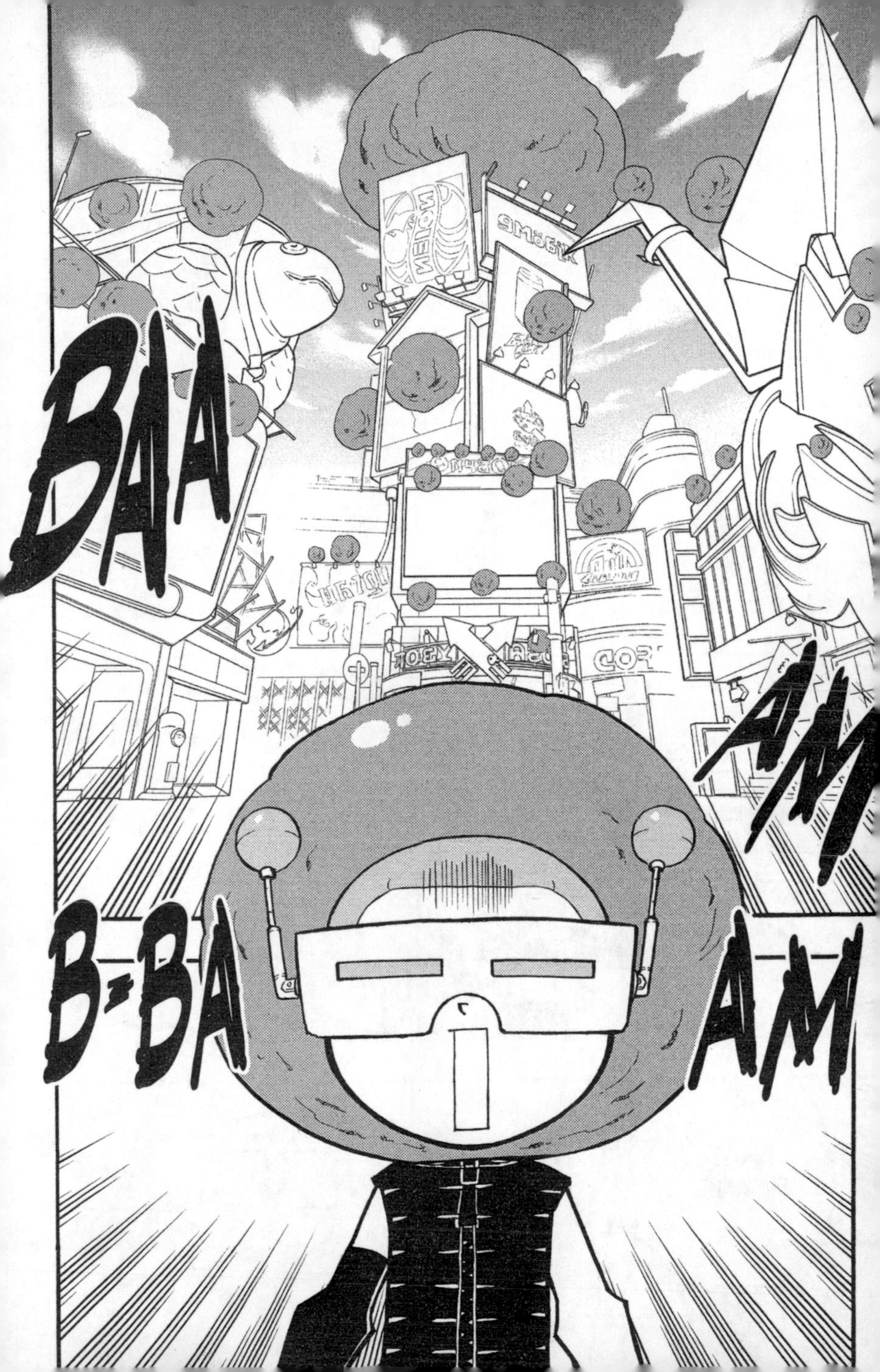
BAA AM
B-BA AM

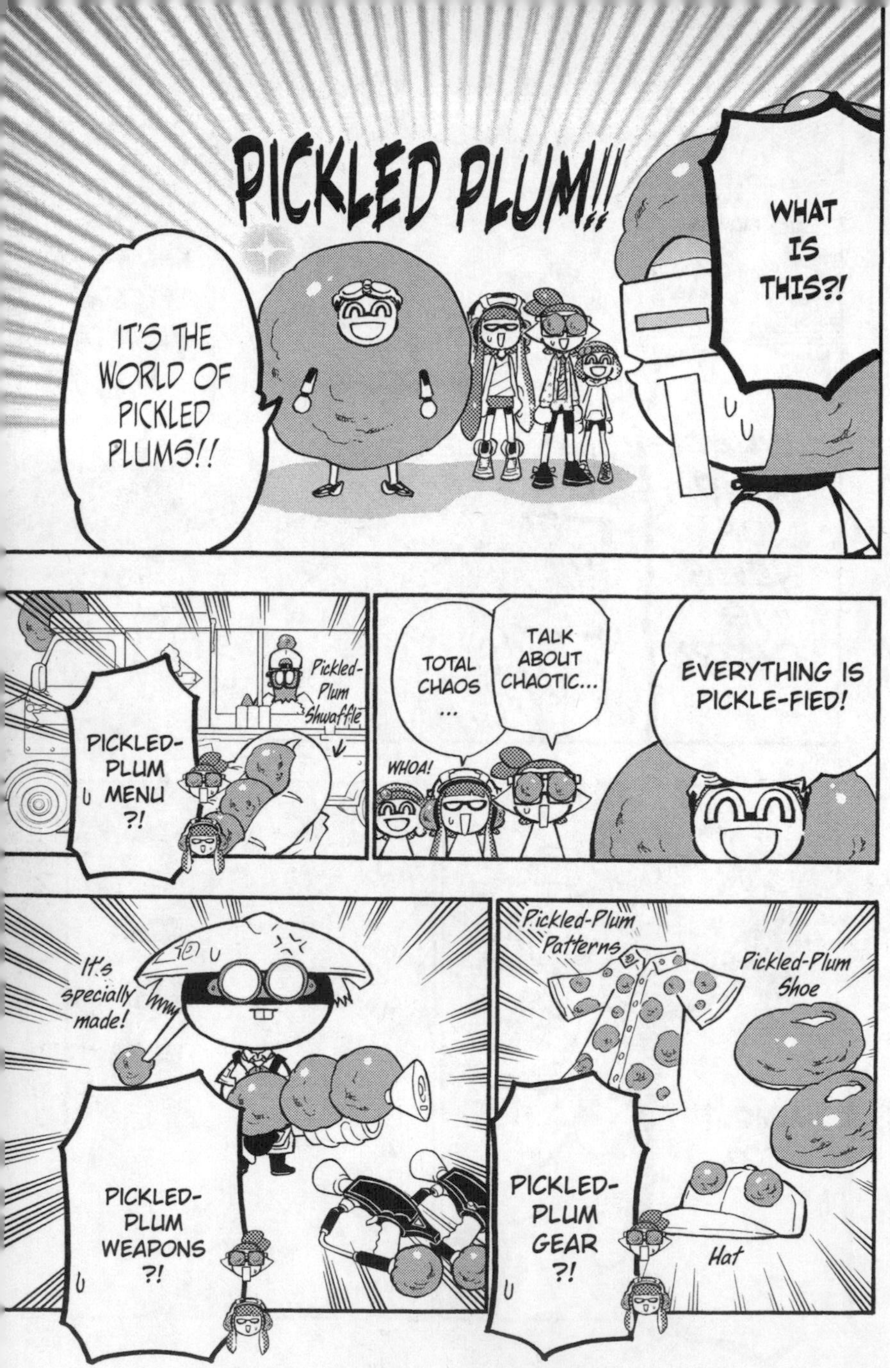
WHAT IS THIS?!
PICKLED PLUM!!
IT'S THE WORLD OF PICKLED PLUMS!!
EVERYTHING IS PICKLE-FIED!
TALK ABOUT CHAOTIC...
TOTAL CHAOS ...
WHOA!
Pickled-Plum Shwaffle
PICKLED-PLUM MENU ?!
Pickled-Plum Shoe
Pickled-Plum Patterns
Hat
PICKLED-PLUM GEAR ?!
It's specially made!
PICKLED-PLUM WEAPONS ?!

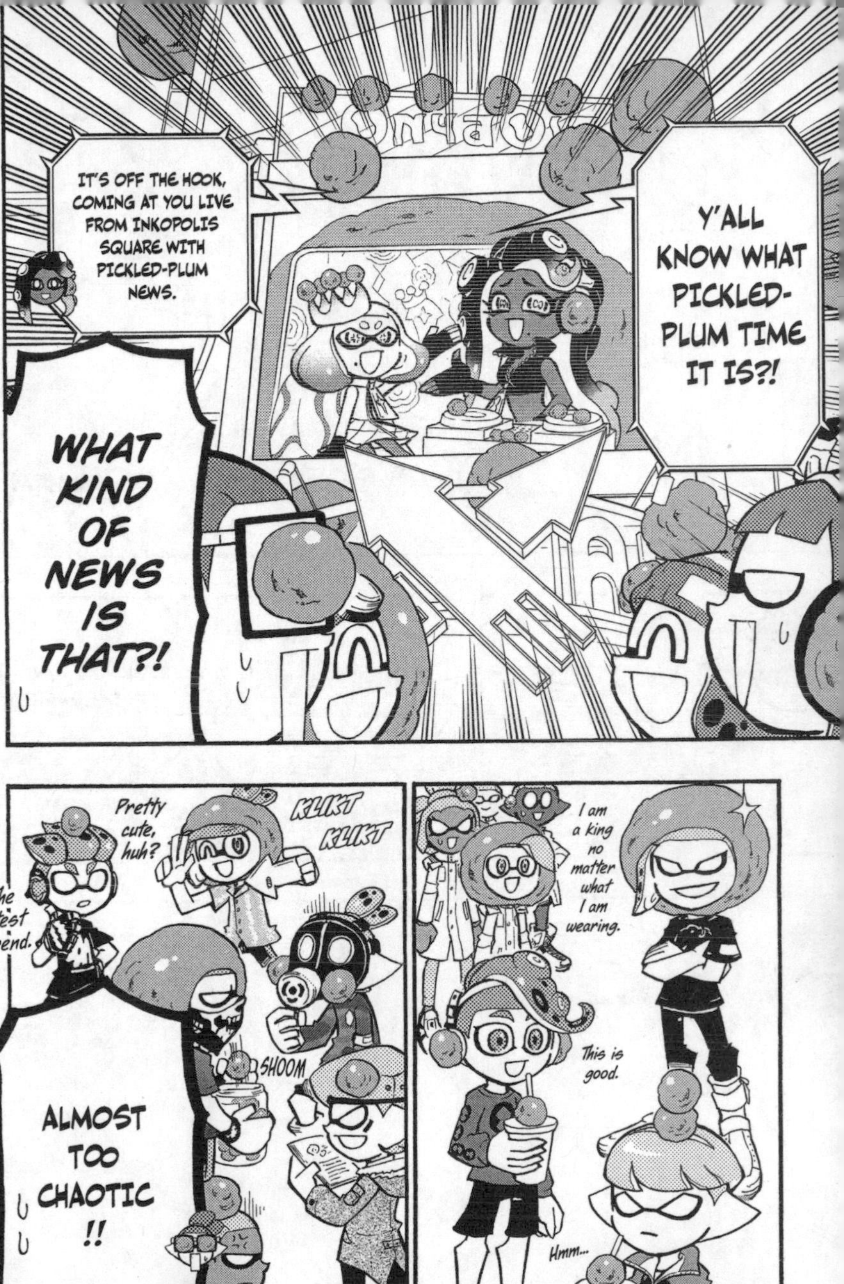
Y'ALL KNOW WHAT PICKLED-PLUM TIME IT IS?!
IT'S OFF THE HOOK, COMING AT YOU LIVE FROM INKOPOLIS SQUARE WITH PICKLED-PLUM NEWS.
WHAT KIND OF NEWS IS THAT?!
I am a king no matter what I am wearing.
This is good.
Hmm...
KLIKT
KLIKT
Pretty cute, huh?
The latest trend.
SHOOM
ALMOST TOO CHAOTIC!!

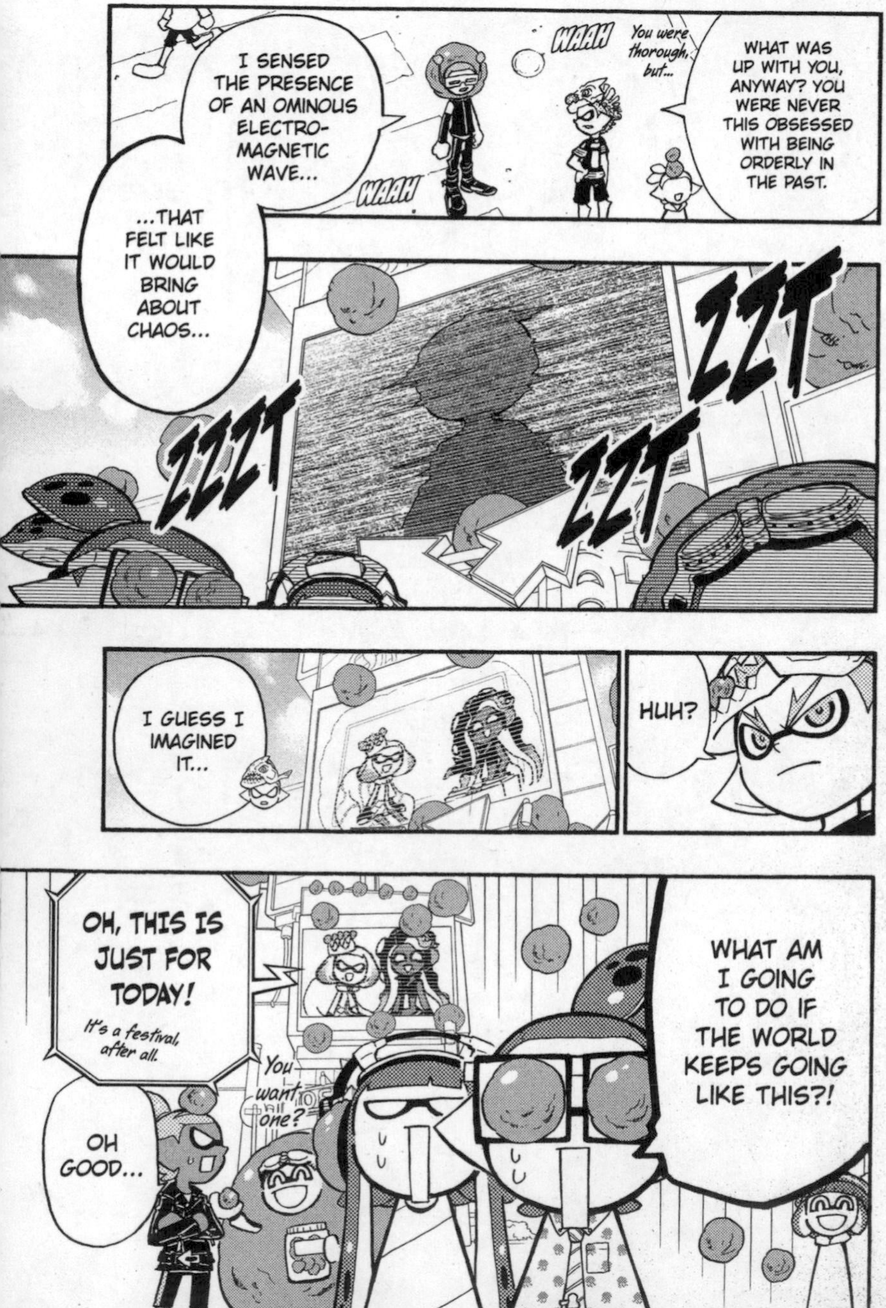
WHAT WAS UP WITH YOU, ANYWAY? YOU WERE NEVER THIS OBSESSED WITH BEING ORDERLY IN THE PAST.
You were thorough, but...
WAAH
I SENSED THE PRESENCE OF AN OMINOUS ELECTRO-MAGNETIC WAVE...
WAAH
...THAT FELT LIKE IT WOULD BRING ABOUT CHAOS...
ZZZT
ZZZT
ZZZT
HUH?
I GUESS I IMAGINED IT...
WHAT AM I GOING TO DO IF THE WORLD KEEPS GOING LIKE THIS?!
OH, THIS IS JUST FOR TODAY!
It's a festival, after all.
You want one?
OH GOOD...

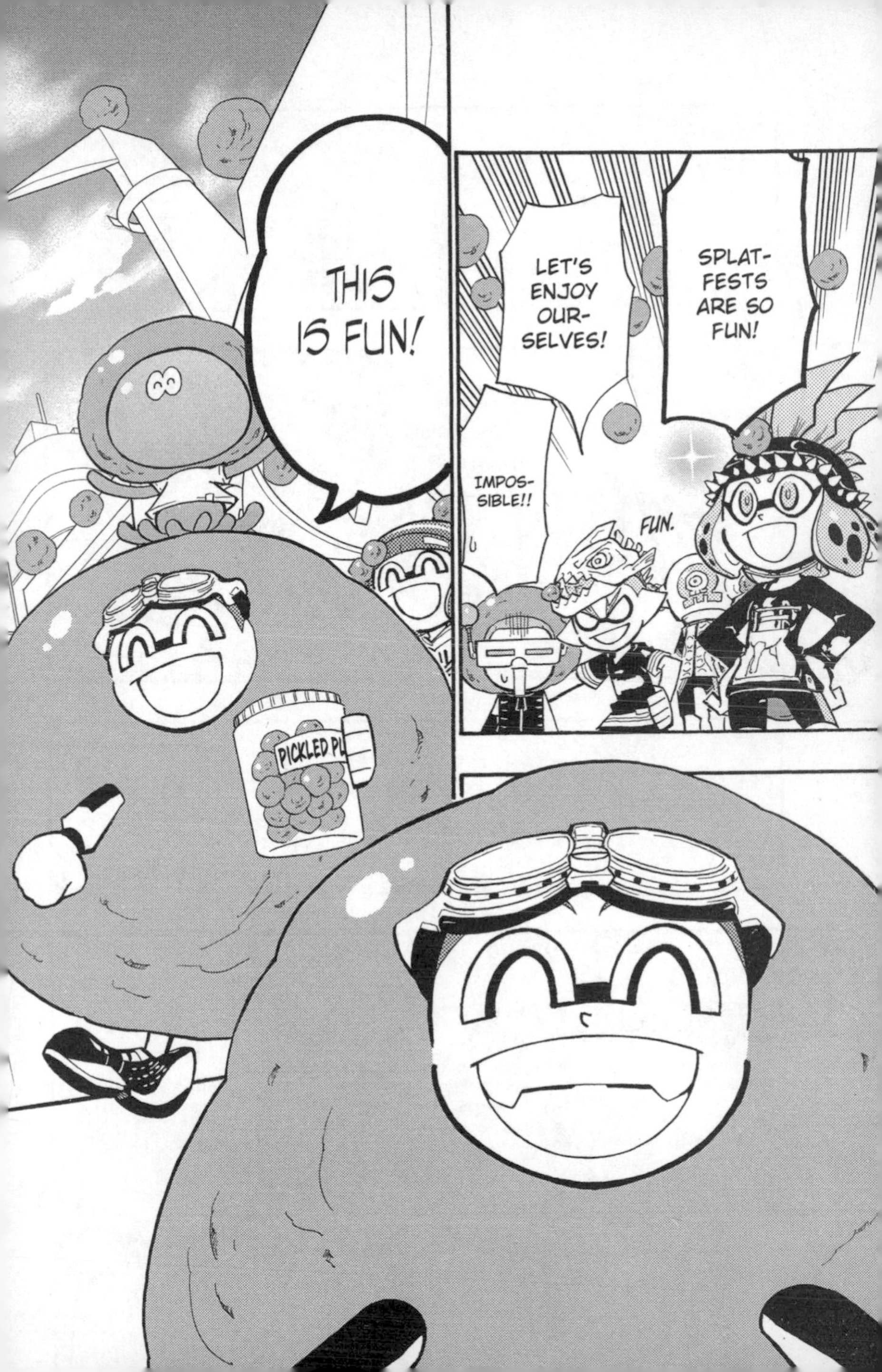
SPLAT-FESTS ARE SO FUN!
LET'S ENJOY OUR-SELVES!
FUN.
IMPOS-SIBLE!!
THIS IS FUN!
PICKLED PL

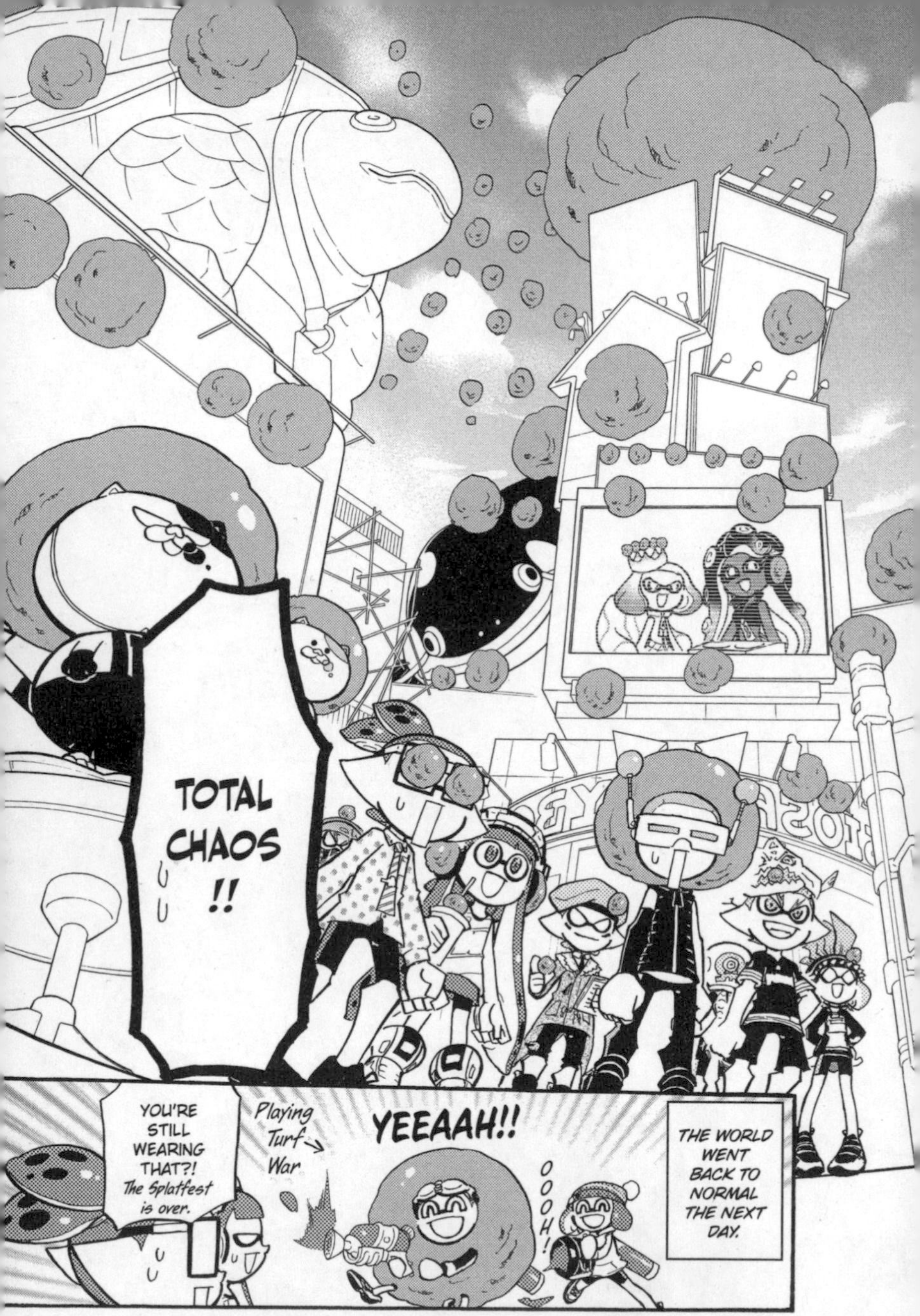
TOTAL CHAOS !!
THE WORLD WENT BACK TO NORMAL THE NEXT DAY.
OOOOH!
YEEAAH!!
Playing Turf War
YOU'RE STILL WEARING THAT?! The Splatfest is over.

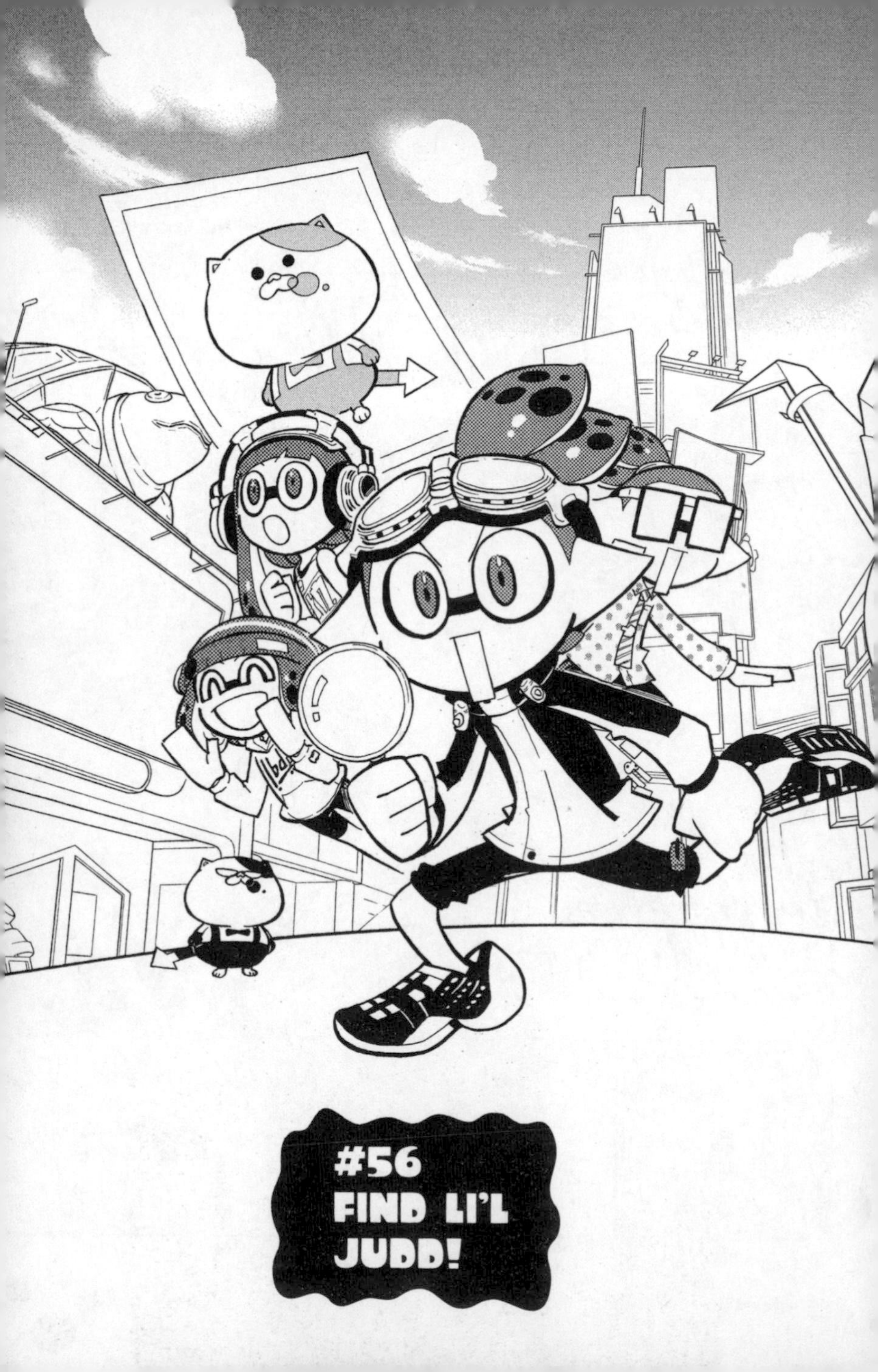
#56
FIND LI'L
JUDD!

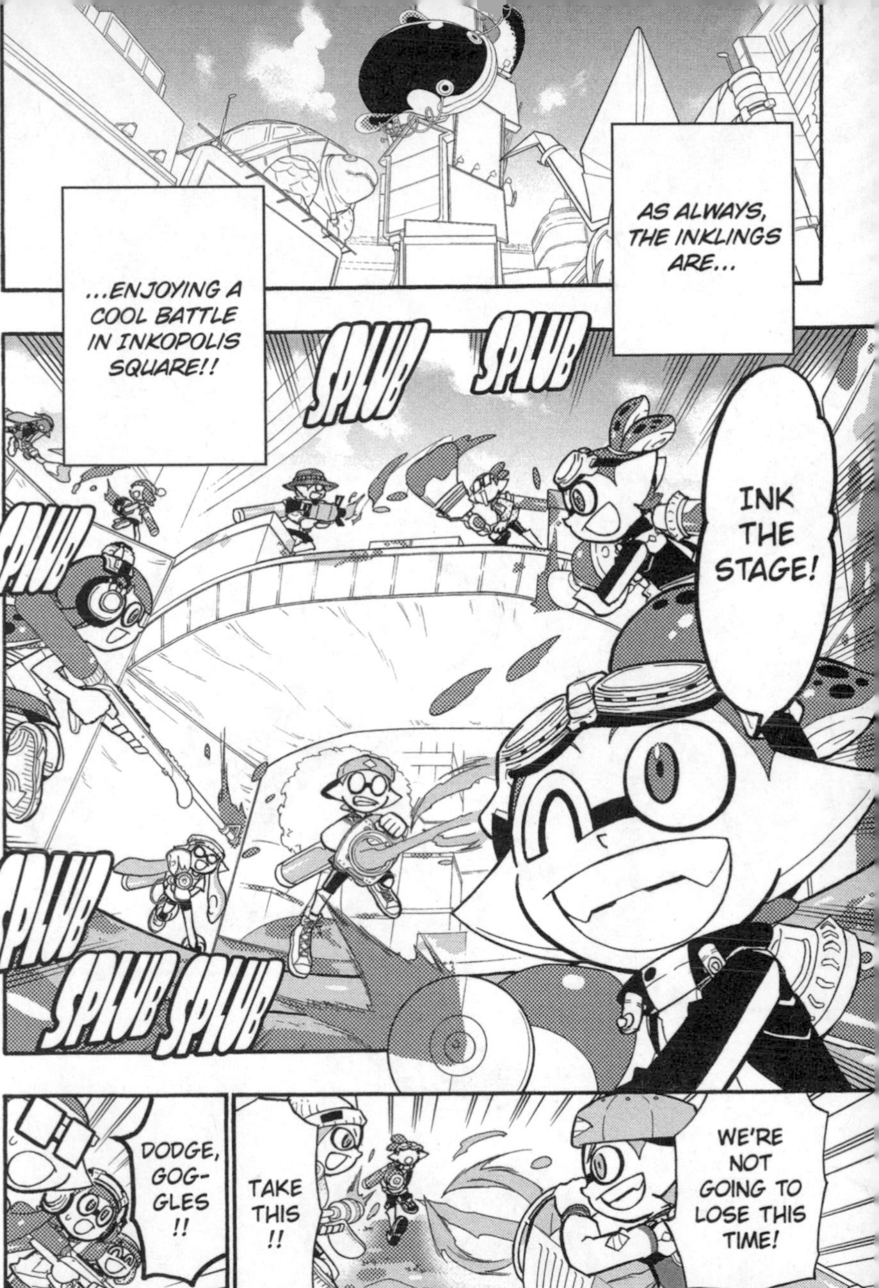
AS ALWAYS, THE INKLINGS ARE...
...ENJOYING A COOL BATTLE IN INKOPOLIS SQUARE!!
SPLUB SPLUB
INK THE STAGE!
SPLUB
SPLUB
SPLUB SPLUB
WE'RE NOT GOING TO LOSE THIS TIME!
TAKE THIS!!
DODGE, GOG-GLES!!

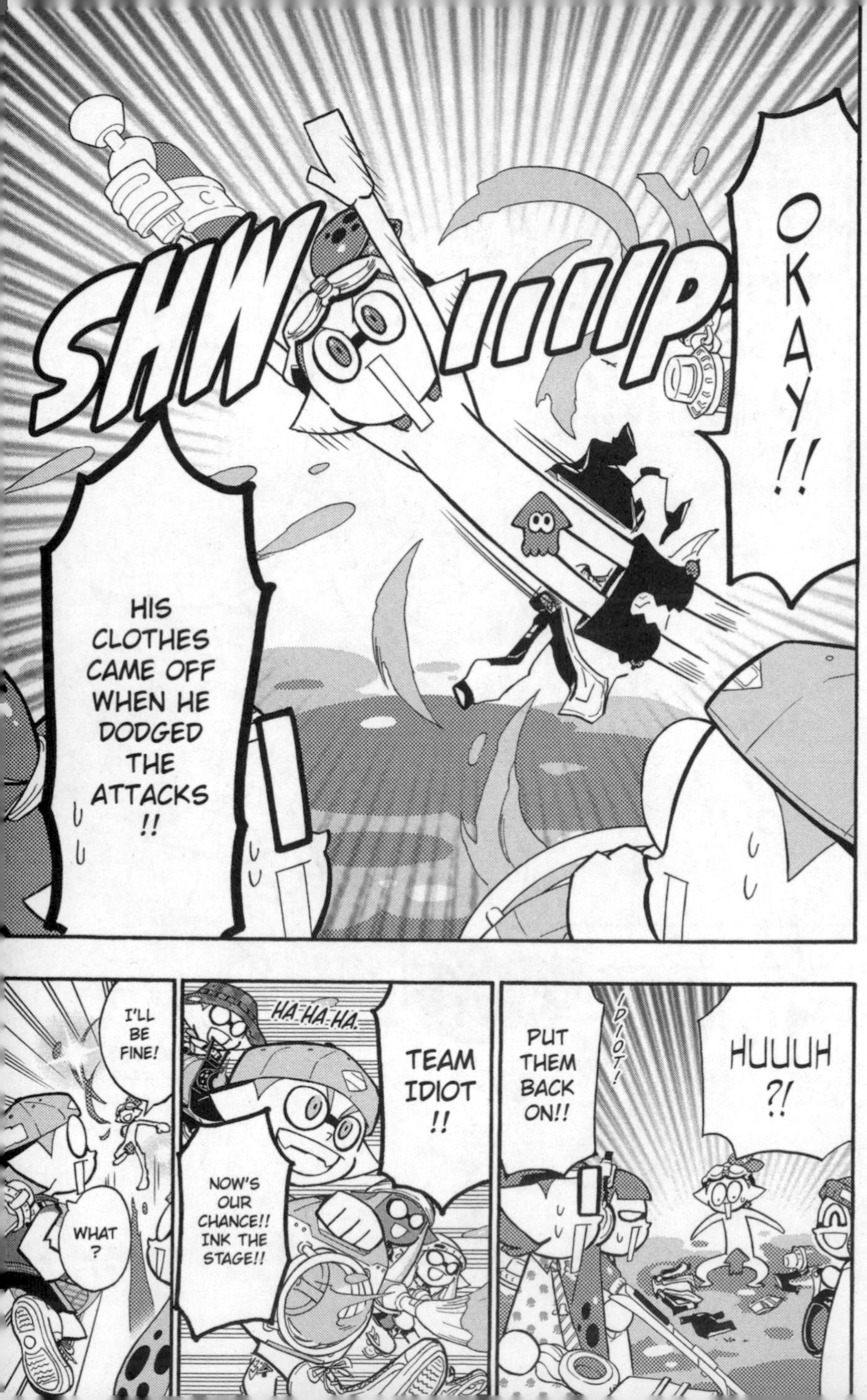
OKAY!!
SHWIIIIIP
HIS CLOTHES CAME OFF WHEN HE DODGED THE ATTACKS!!
HUUUH ?!
PUT THEM BACK ON!!
IDIOT!
TEAM IDIOT!!
HA-HA-HA.
NOW'S OUR CHANCE!! INK THE STAGE!!
I'LL BE FINE!
WHAT ?

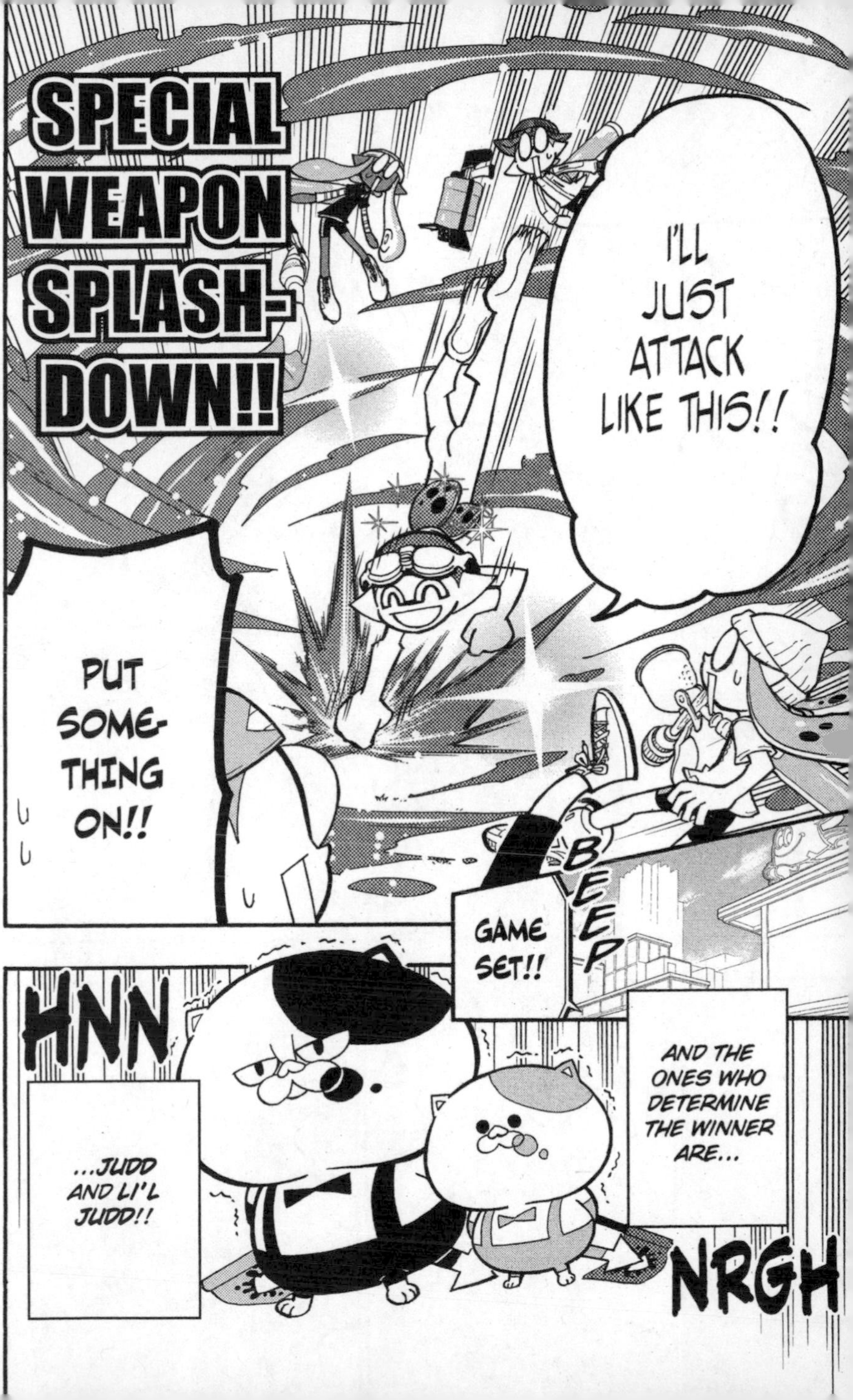
I'LL JUST ATTACK LIKE THIS!!
SPECIAL WEAPON SPLASH-DOWN!!
PUT SOME-THING ON!!
BEEP
GAME SET!!
AND THE ONES WHO DETERMINE THE WINNER ARE...
HNN
...JUDD AND LI'L JUDD!!
NRGH

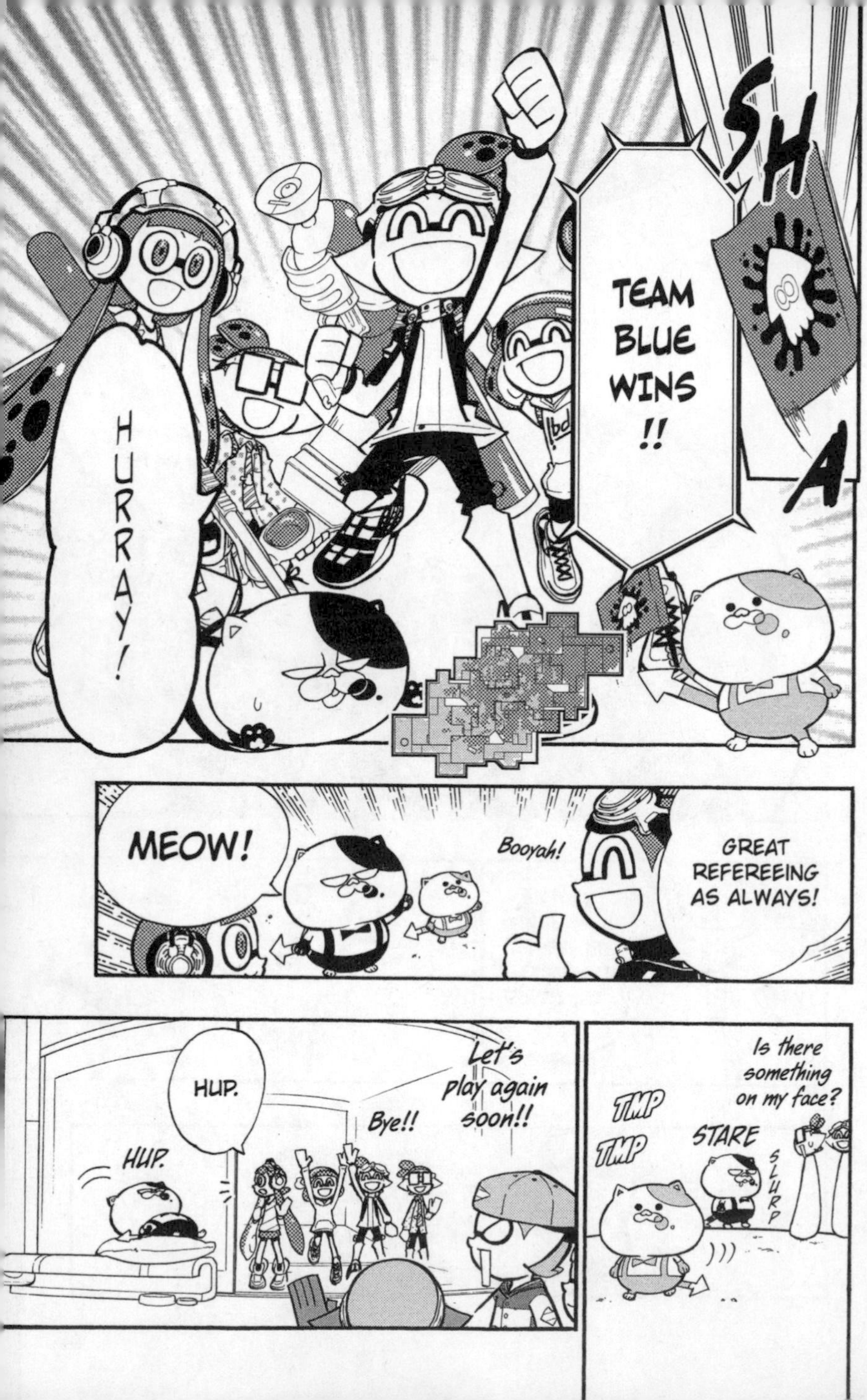
SHA
TEAM BLUE WINS !!
HURRAY!
GREAT REFEREEING AS ALWAYS!
Booyah!
MEOW!
Is there something on my face?
SLURP
STARE
TMP TMP
Let's play again soon!!
Bye!!
HUP.
HUP.

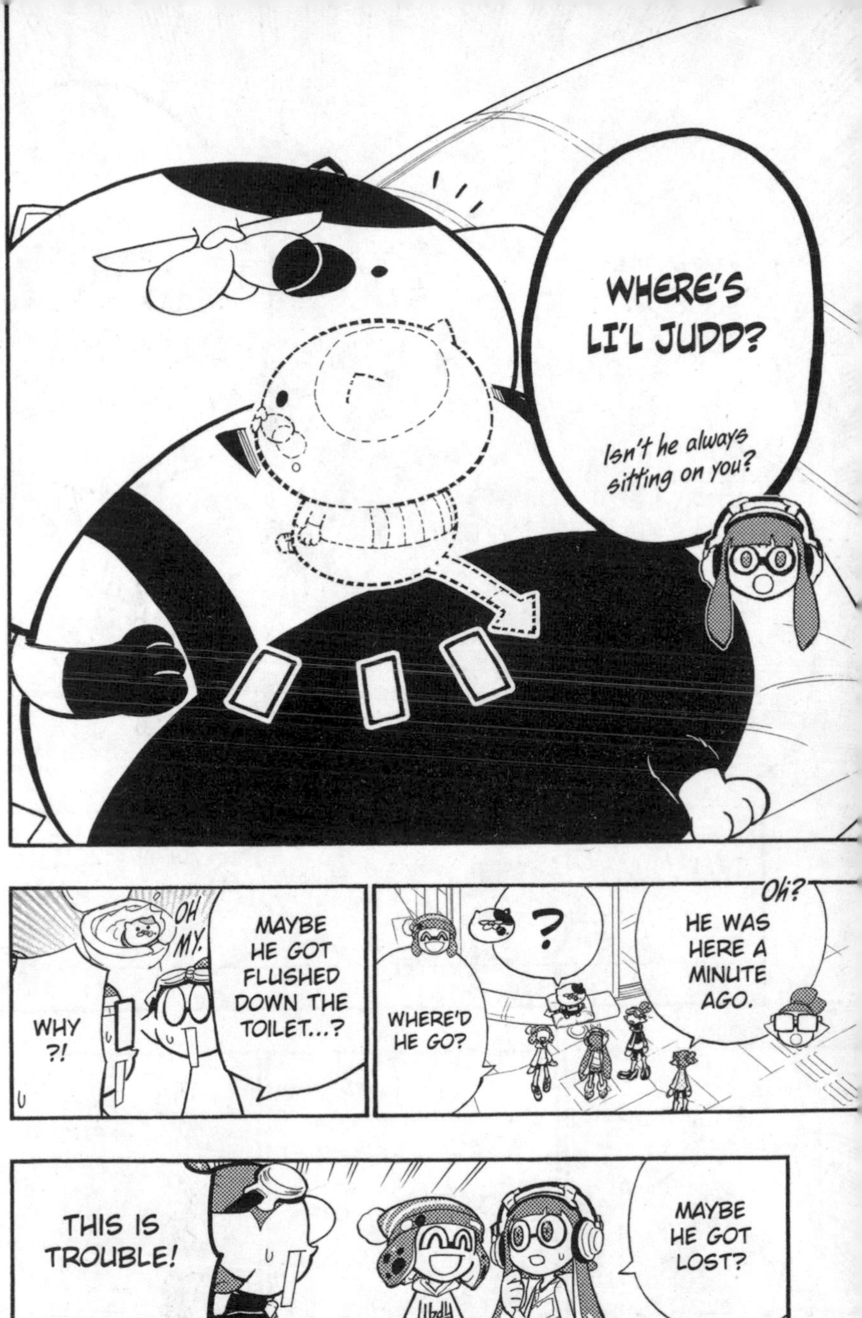
WHERE'S LI'L JUDD?
Isn't he always sitting on you?
Oh?
HE WAS HERE A MINUTE AGO.
?
WHERE'D HE GO?
MAYBE HE GOT FLUSHED DOWN THE TOILET...?
OH MY.
WHY ?!
MAYBE HE GOT LOST?
THIS IS TROUBLE!

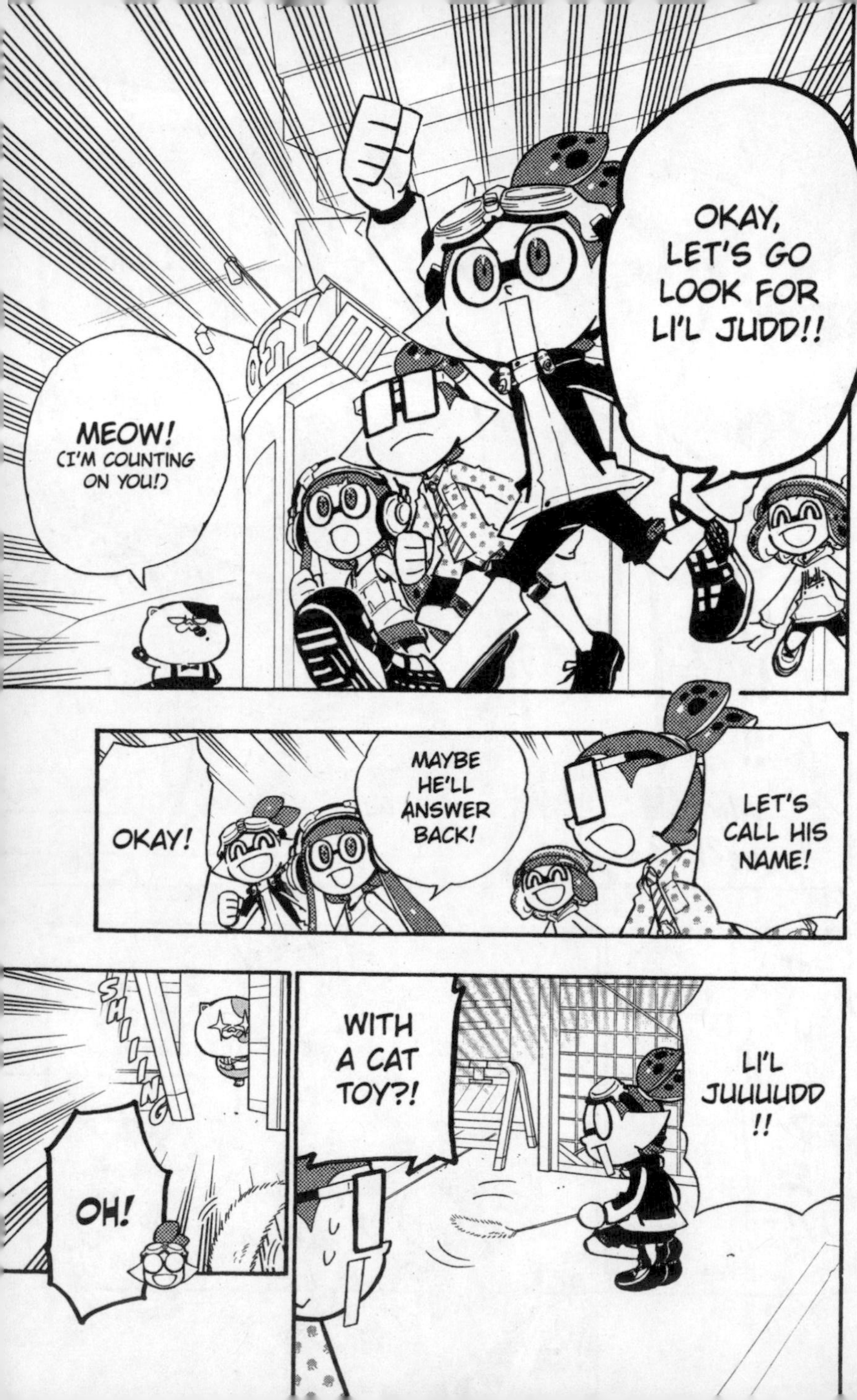
OKAY, LET'S GO LOOK FOR LI'L JUDD!!
MEOW! (I'M COUNTING ON YOU!)
LET'S CALL HIS NAME!
MAYBE HE'LL ANSWER BACK!
OKAY!
LI'L JUUUUDD !!
WITH A CAT TOY?!
SHIIIING
OH!

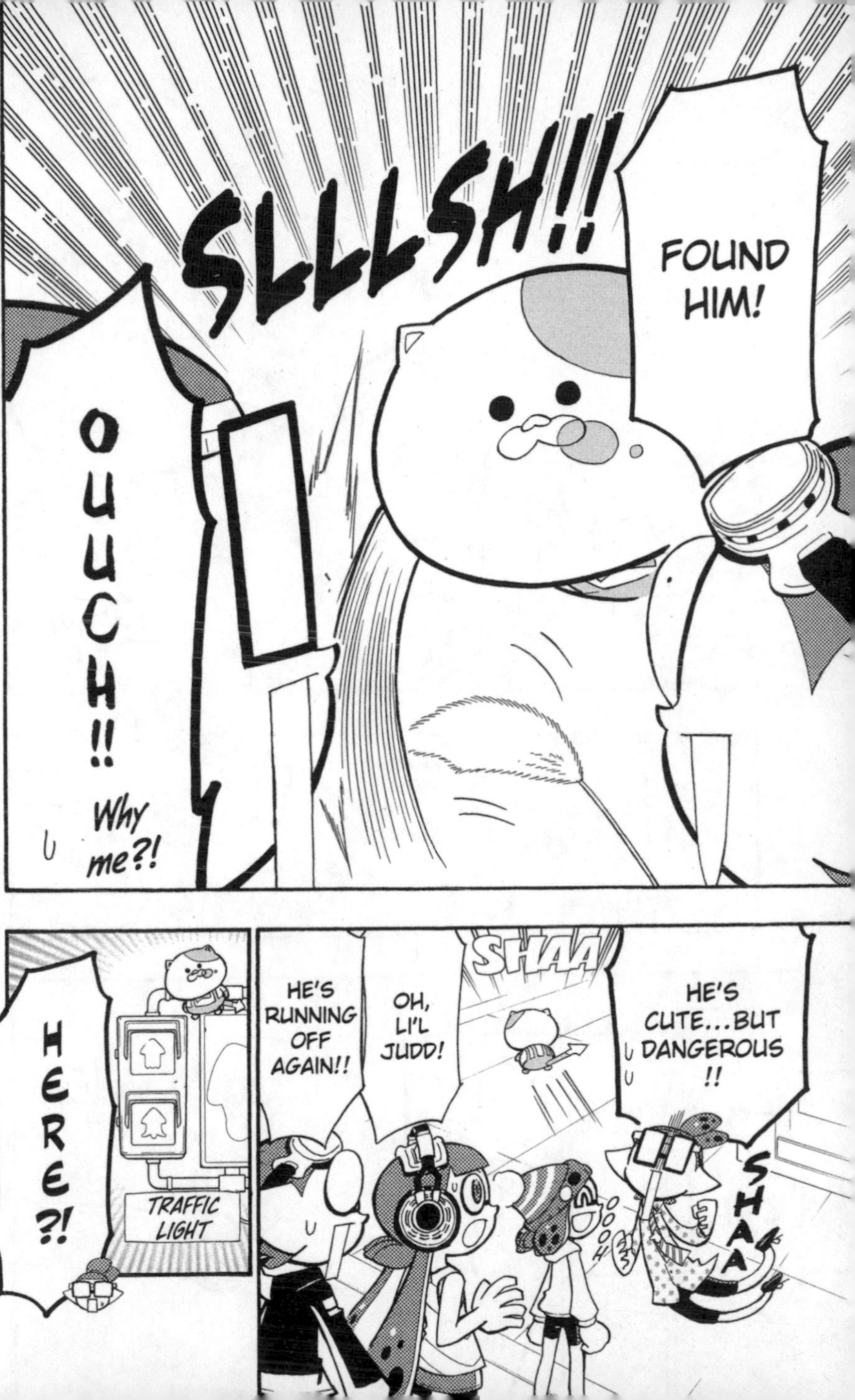
FOUND HIM!
SLLLSH!!
OUUCH!!
Why me?!
HE'S CUTE...BUT DANGEROUS!!
SHAA
OH, LI'L JUDD!
HE'S RUNNING OFF AGAIN!!
SHAA
HERE?!
TRAFFIC LIGHT

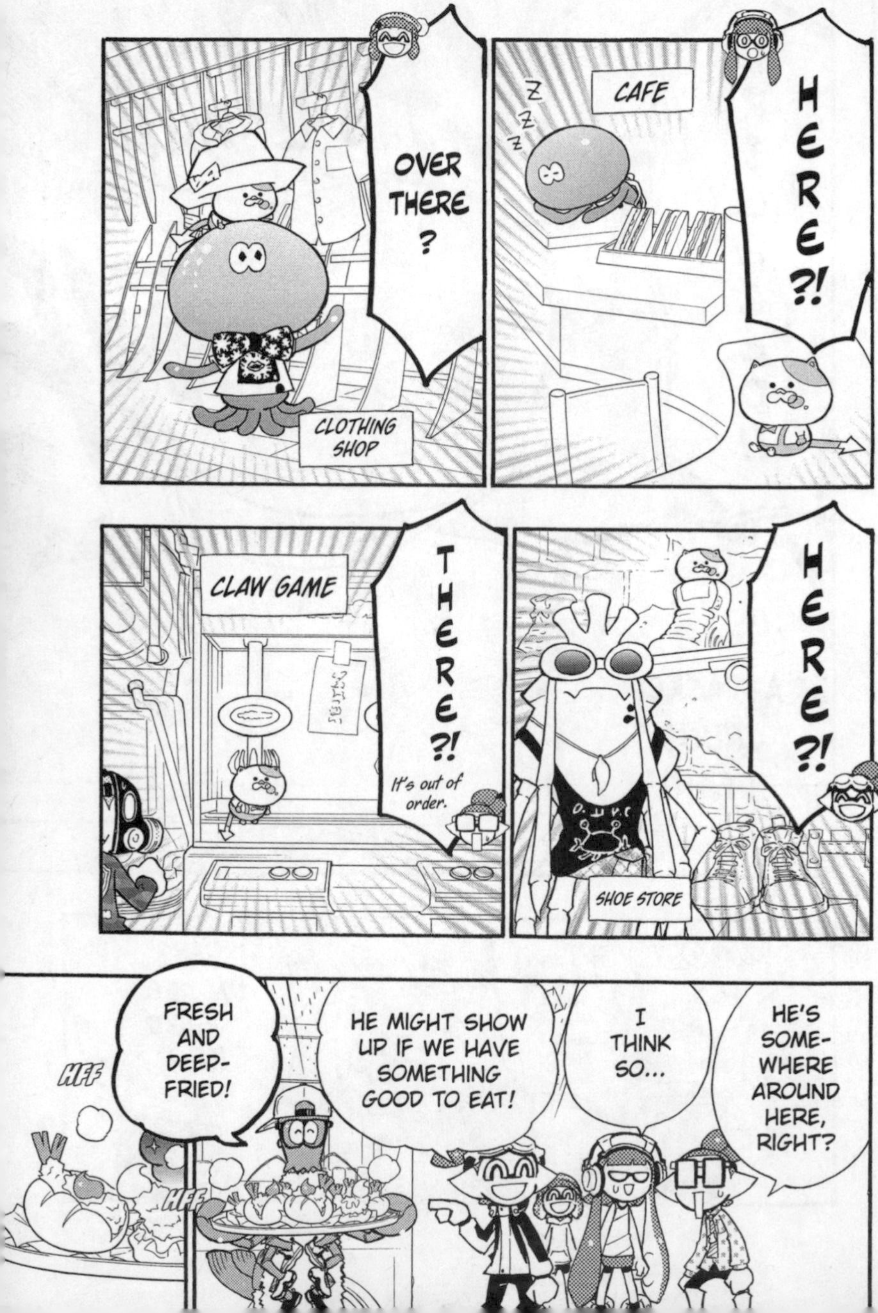
CAFE
HERE?!
OVER THERE?
CLOTHING SHOP
HERE?!
SHOE STORE
CLAW GAME
THERE?!
It's out of order.
HE'S SOME-WHERE AROUND HERE, RIGHT?
I THINK SO...
HE MIGHT SHOW UP IF WE HAVE SOMETHING GOOD TO EAT!
FRESH AND DEEP-FRIED!
HFF
HFF

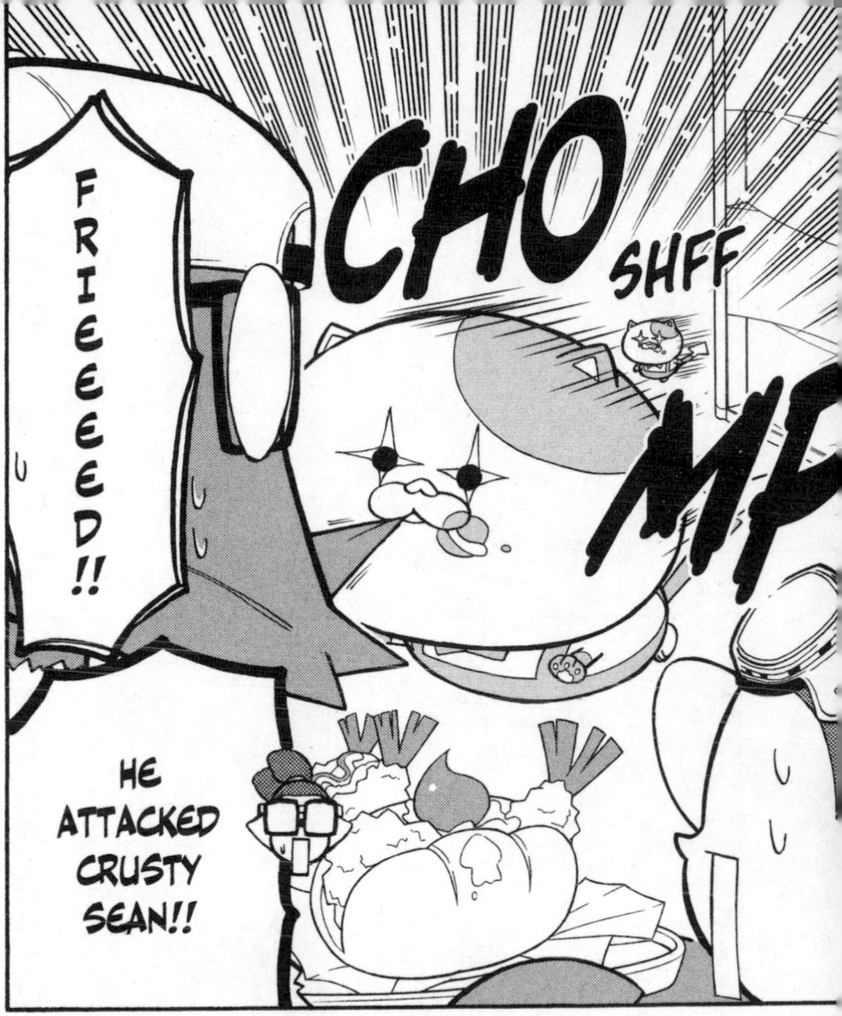
CHO
SHFF
MP
FRIEEEEED!!
HE ATTACKED CRUSTY SEAN!!

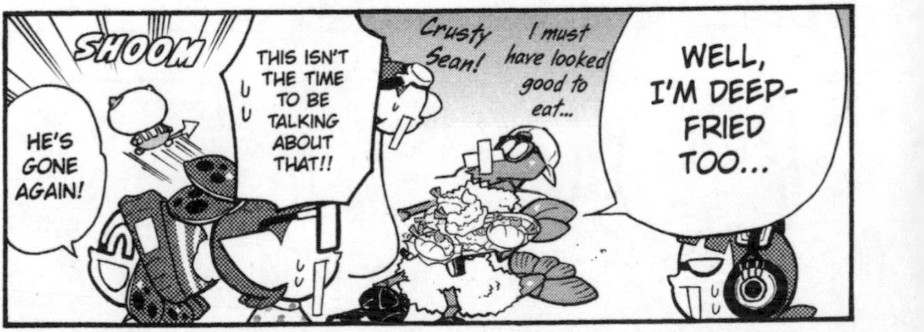
WELL, I'M DEEP-FRIED TOO...
I must have looked good to eat...
Crusty Sean!
THIS ISN'T THE TIME TO BE TALKING ABOUT THAT!!
SHOOM
HE'S GONE AGAIN!

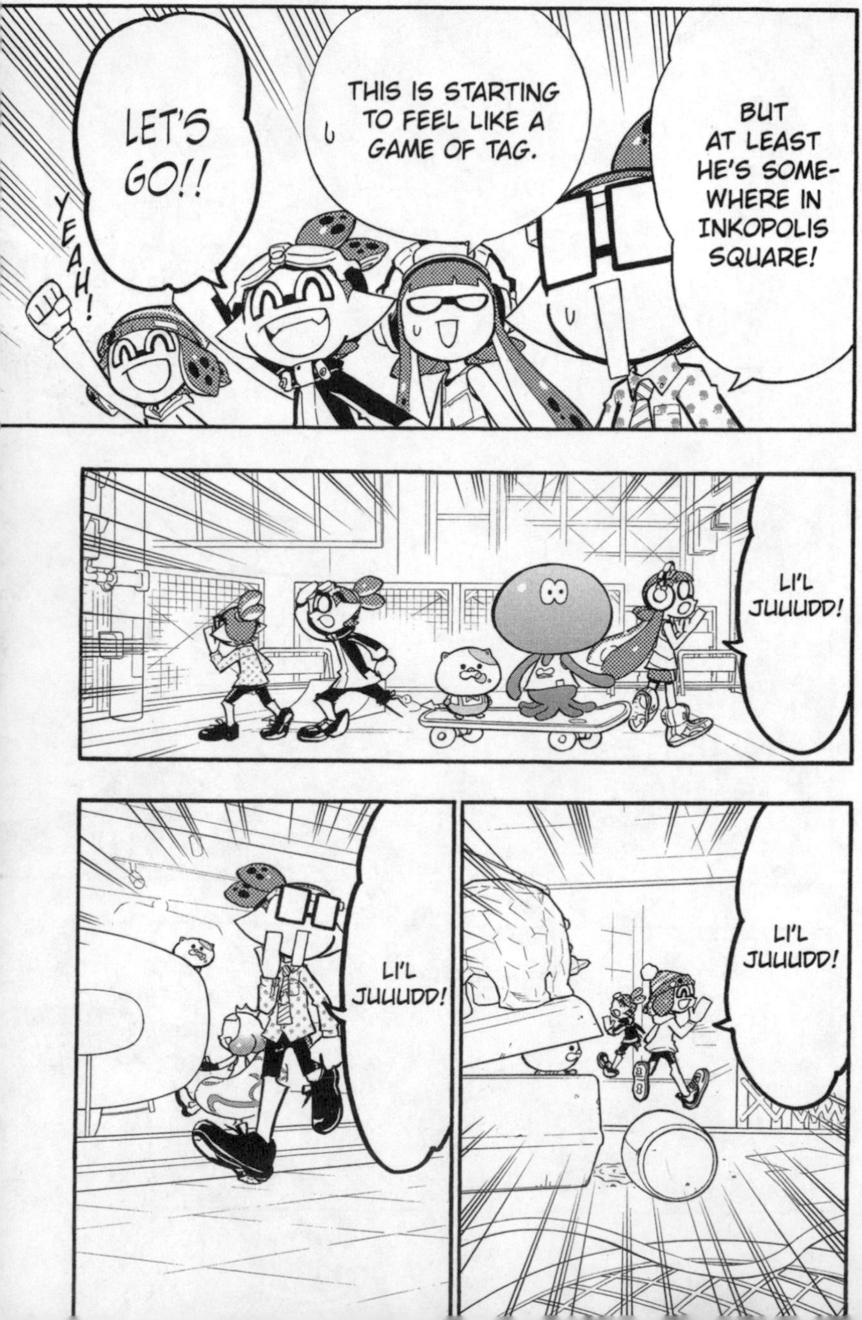
BUT AT LEAST HE'S SOME-WHERE IN INKOPOLIS SQUARE!
THIS IS STARTING TO FEEL LIKE A GAME OF TAG.
LET'S GO!!
YEAH!
LI'L JUUUDD!
LI'L JUUUDD!
LI'L JUUUDD!

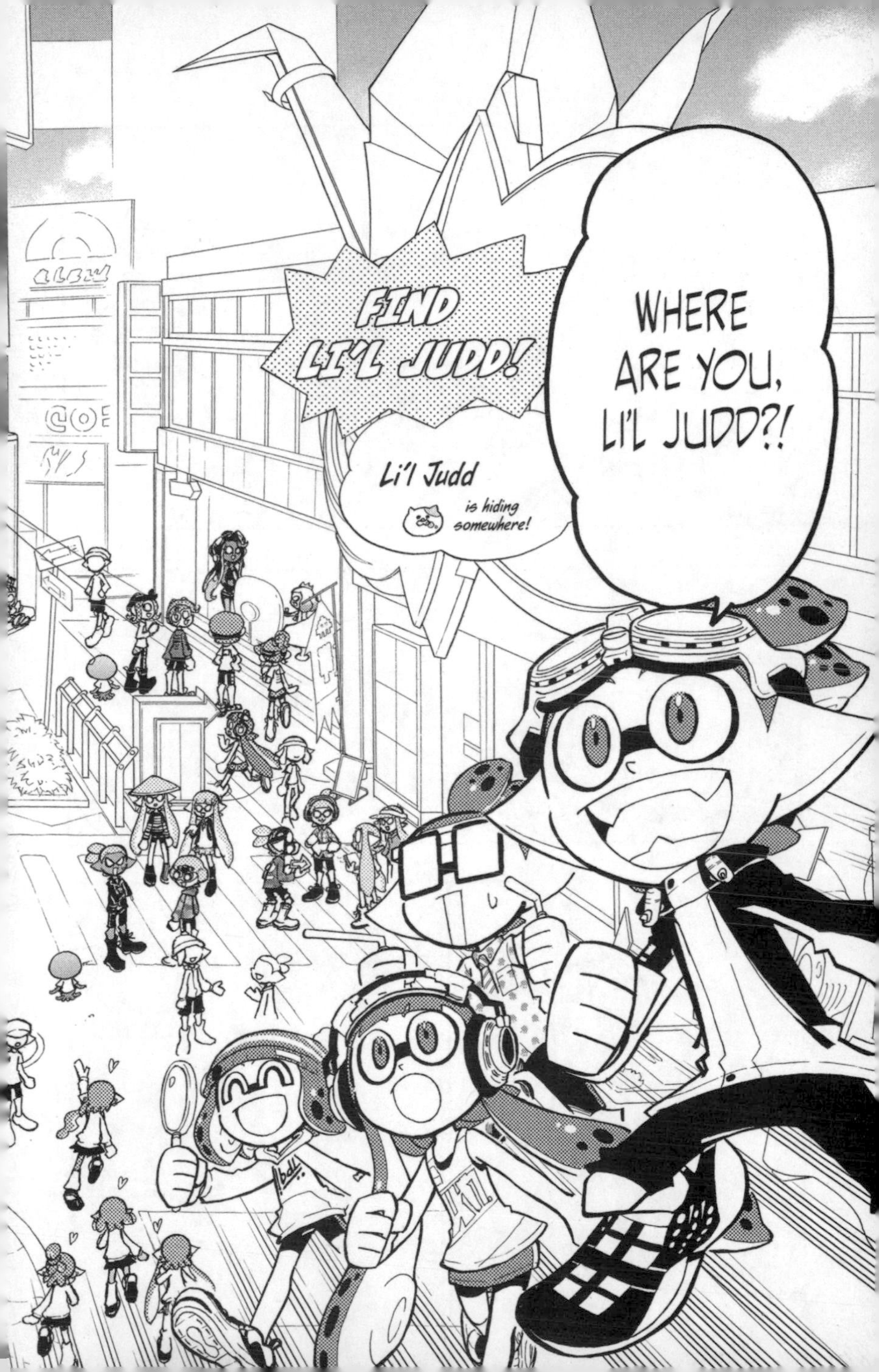
WHERE ARE YOU, LI'L JUDD?!
FIND LI'L JUDD!
Li'l Judd is hiding somewhere!

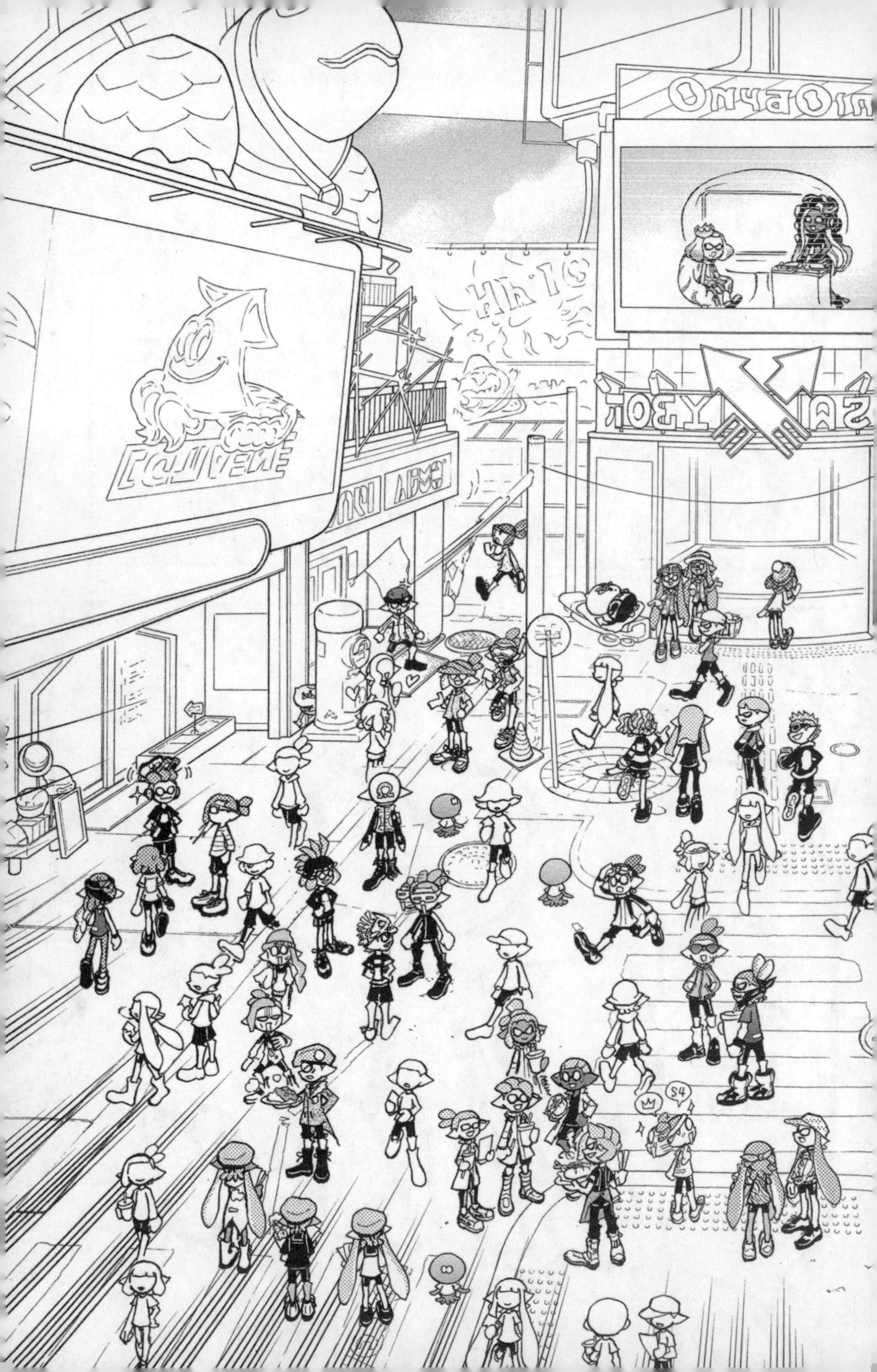

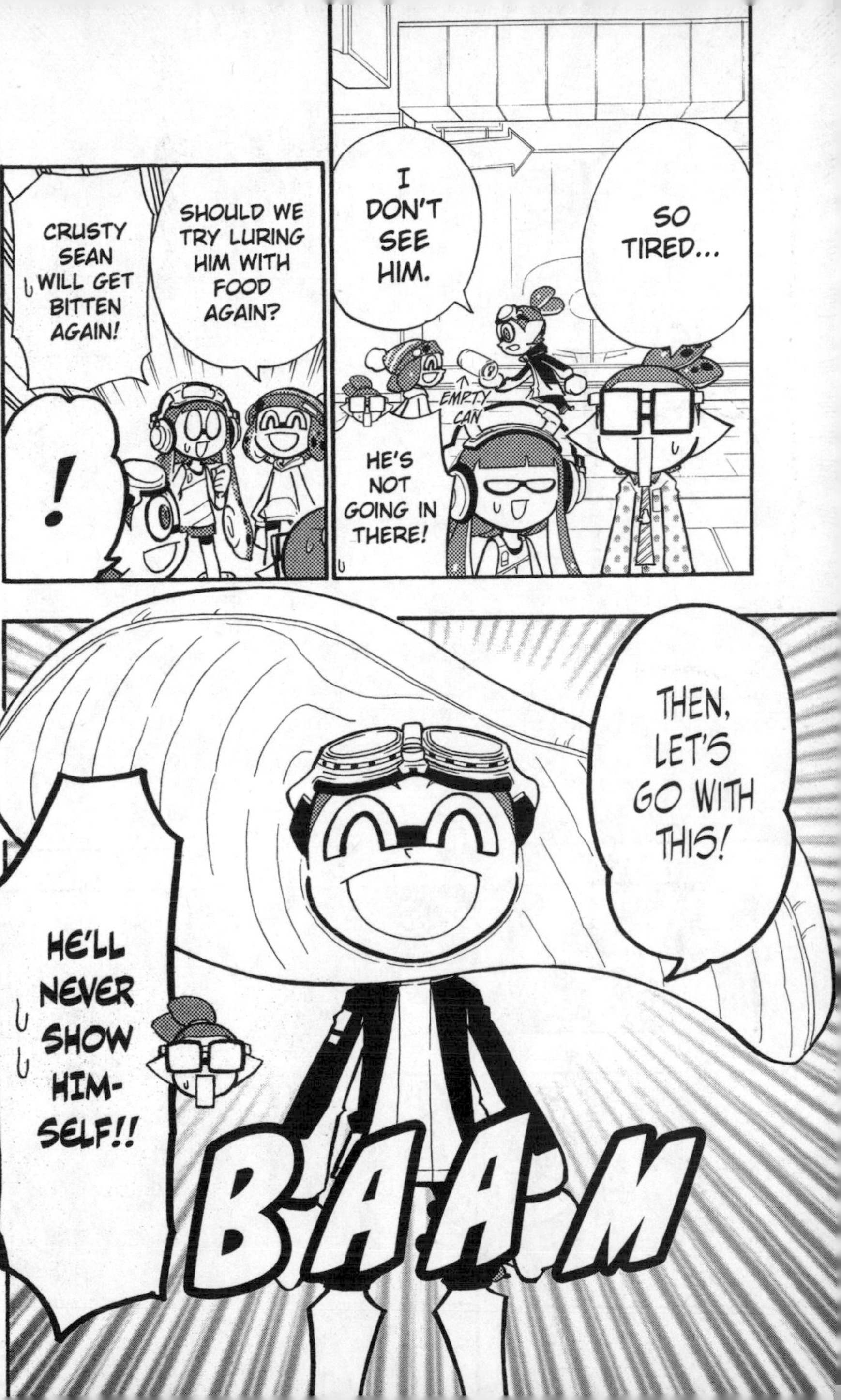
SO TIRED...
I DON'T SEE HIM.
EMPTY CAN
HE'S NOT GOING IN THERE!
SHOULD WE TRY LURING HIM WITH FOOD AGAIN?
CRUSTY SEAN WILL GET BITTEN AGAIN!
!
THEN, LET'S GO WITH THIS!
HE'LL NEVER SHOW HIMSELF!!
BAAM

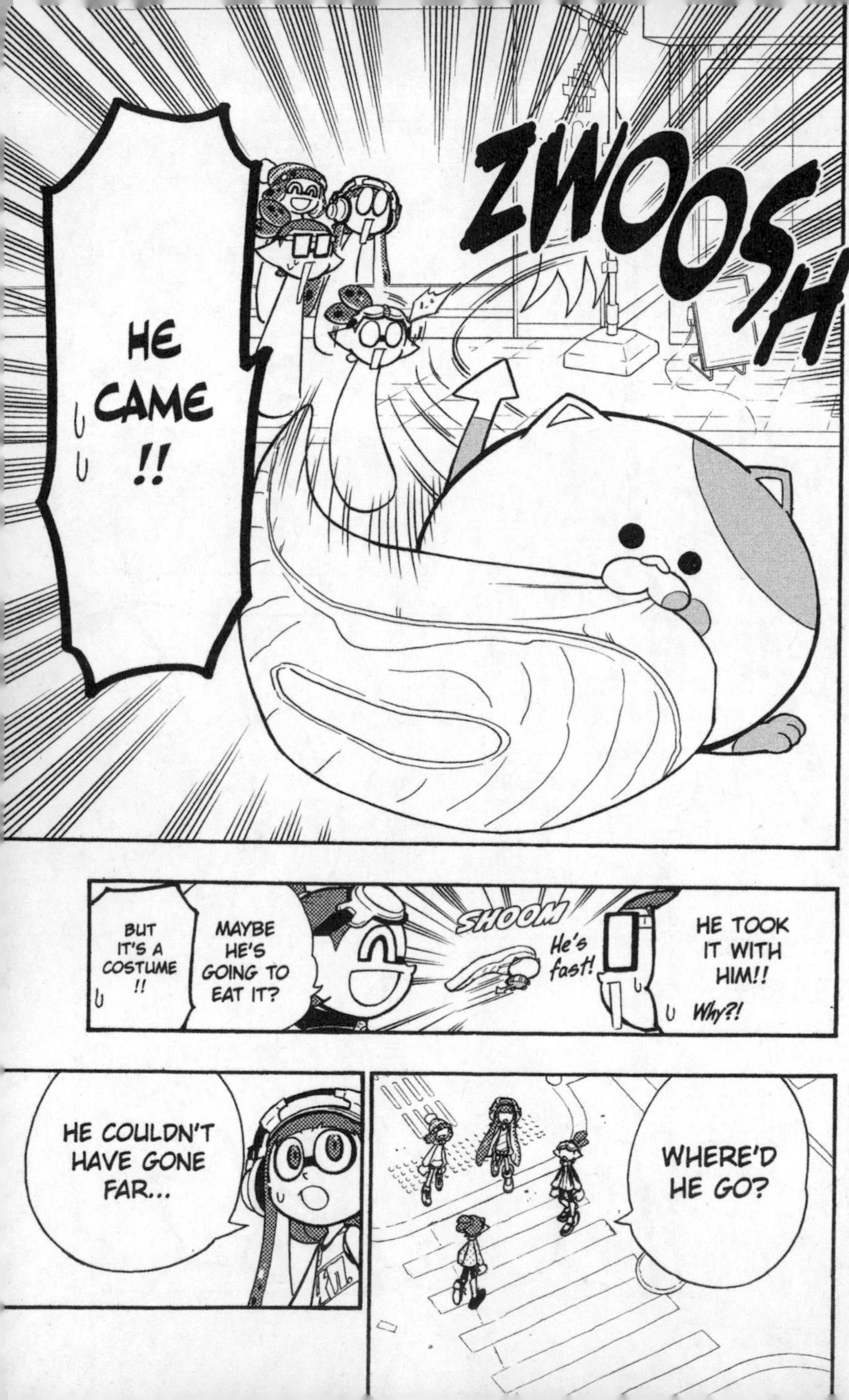
ZWOOSH
HE CAME !!
HE TOOK IT WITH HIM!!
Why?!
He's fast!
SHOOM
MAYBE HE'S GOING TO EAT IT?
BUT IT'S A COSTUME !!
WHERE'D HE GO?
HE COULDN'T HAVE GONE FAR...

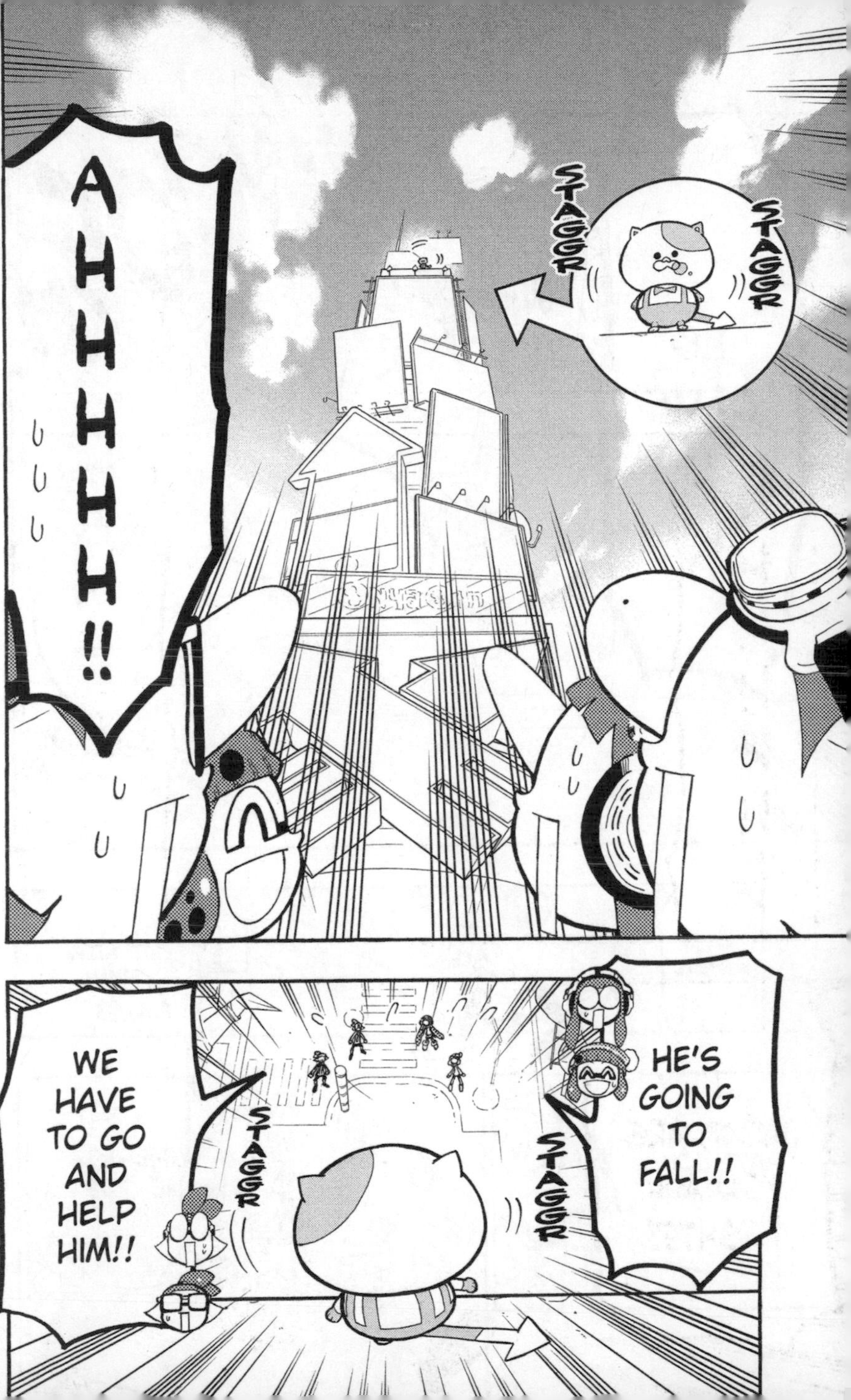
STAGGR
STAGGR
AHHHHHH!!
HE'S GOING TO FALL!!
STAGGR
STAGGR
WE HAVE TO GO AND HELP HIM!!

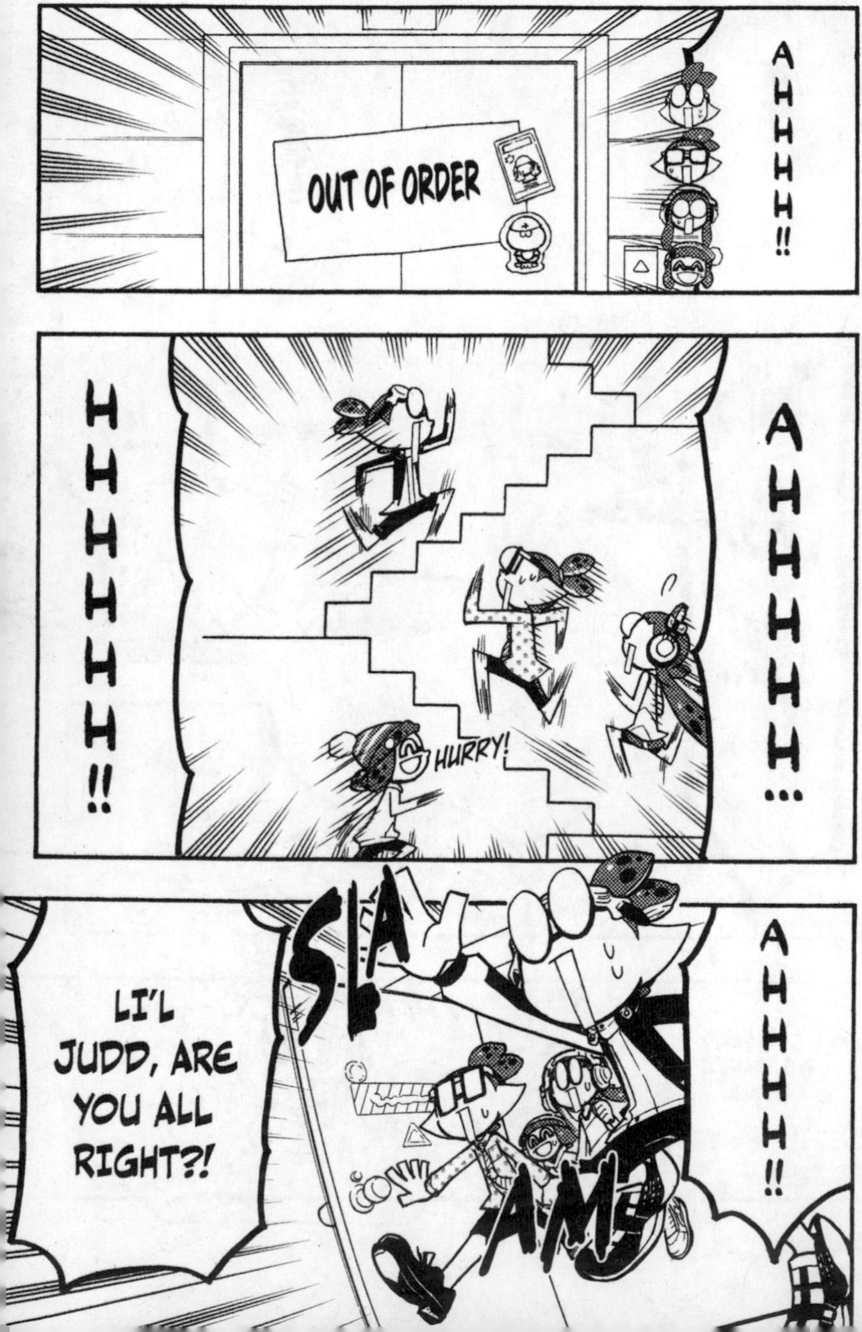
AHHHH!!
OUT OF ORDER
AHHHHH...
HURRY!
HHHHHH!!
AHHHH!!
SLAM
LI'L JUDD, ARE YOU ALL RIGHT?!

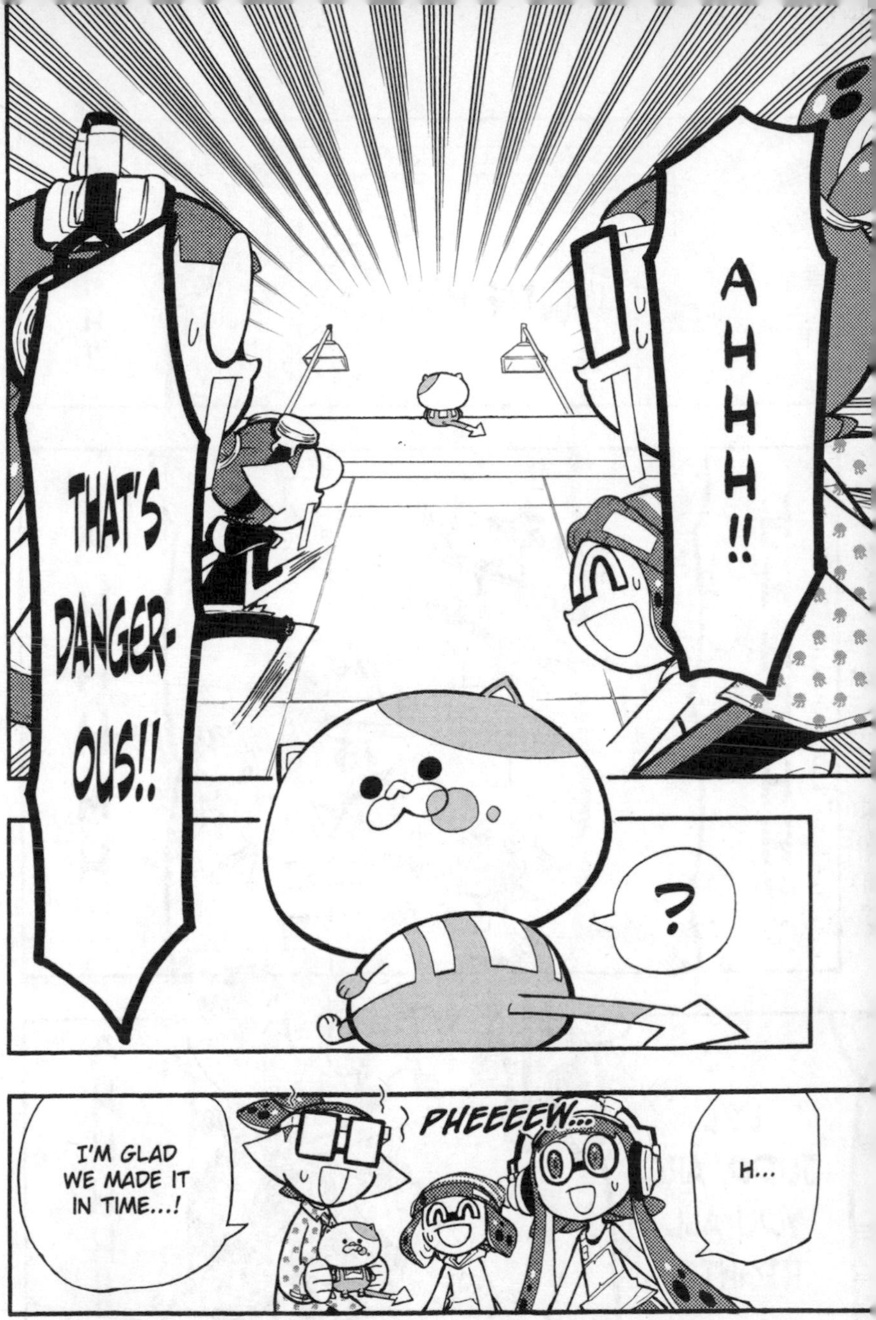
AHHH!!
THAT'S DANGER-OUS!!
?
H...
PHEEEEW...
I'M GLAD WE MADE IT IN TIME...!

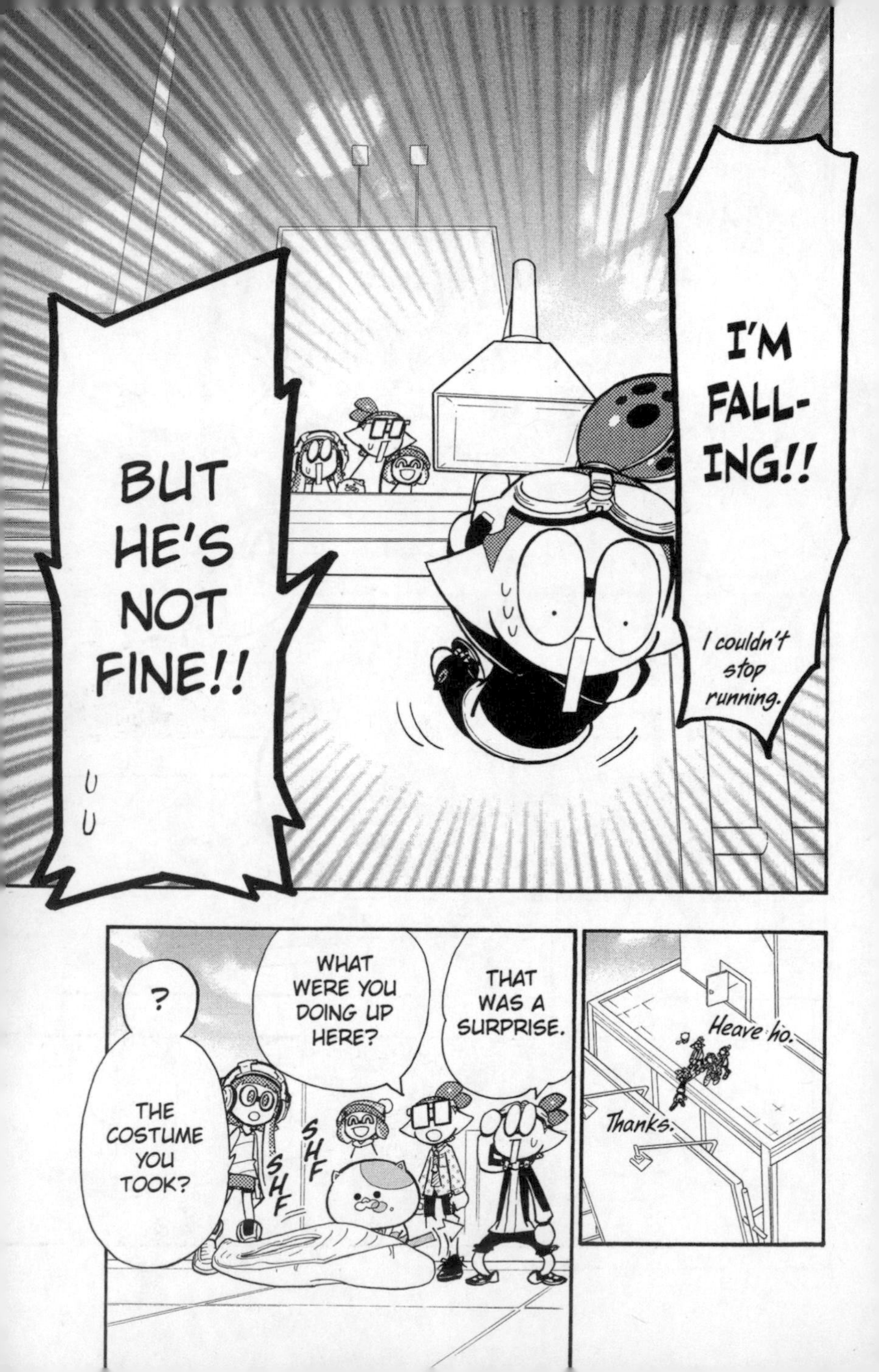
I'M FALLING!!
I couldn't stop running.
BUT HE'S NOT FINE!!
Heave ho.
Thanks.
THAT WAS A SURPRISE.
WHAT WERE YOU DOING UP HERE?
?
THE COSTUME YOU TOOK?
SHF
SHF

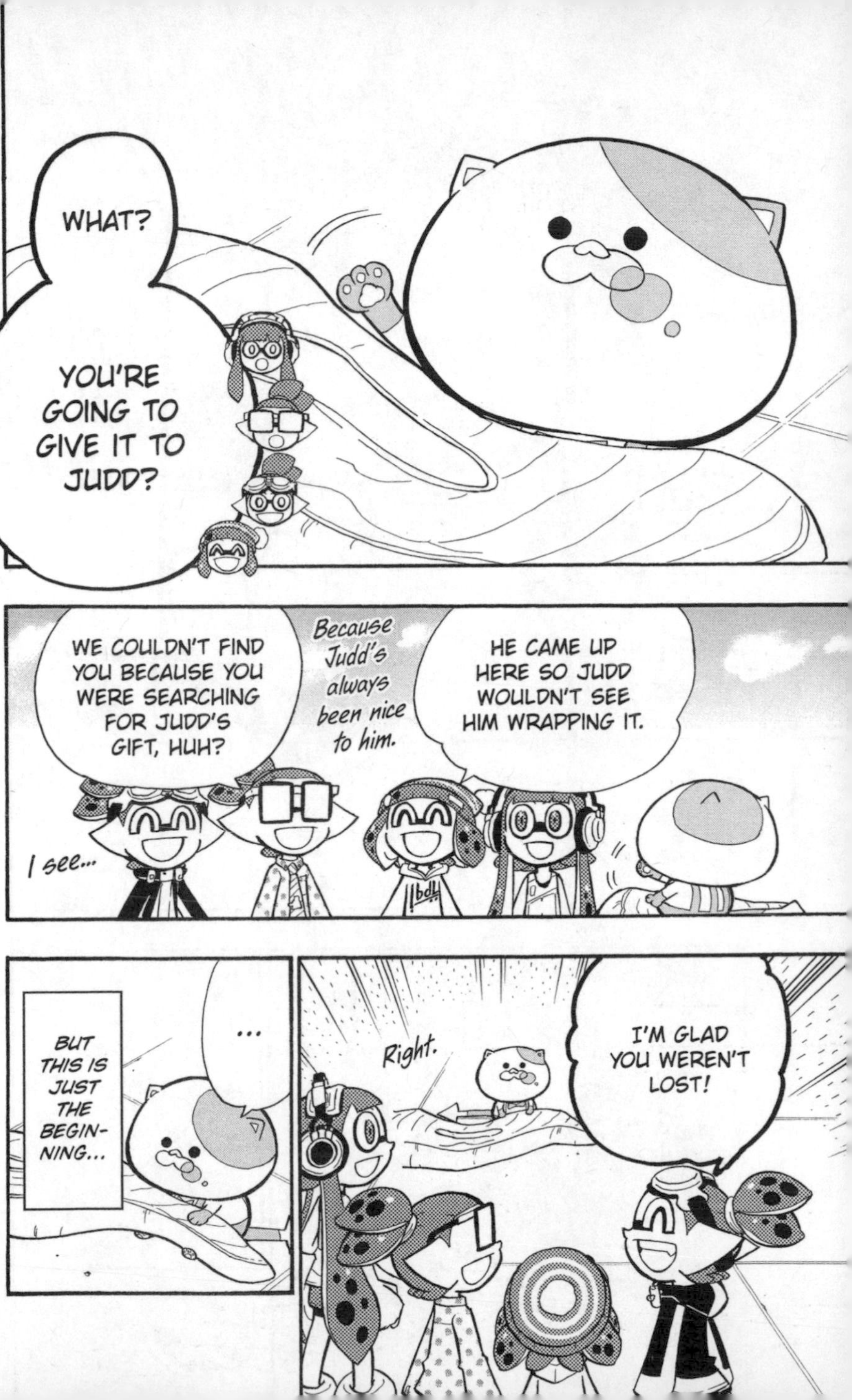
WHAT?
YOU'RE GOING TO GIVE IT TO JUDD?
HE CAME UP HERE SO JUDD WOULDN'T SEE HIM WRAPPING IT.
Because Judd's always been nice to him.
WE COULDN'T FIND YOU BECAUSE YOU WERE SEARCHING FOR JUDD'S GIFT, HUH?
I see...
I'M GLAD YOU WEREN'T LOST!
Right.
...
BUT THIS IS JUST THE BEGIN-NING...

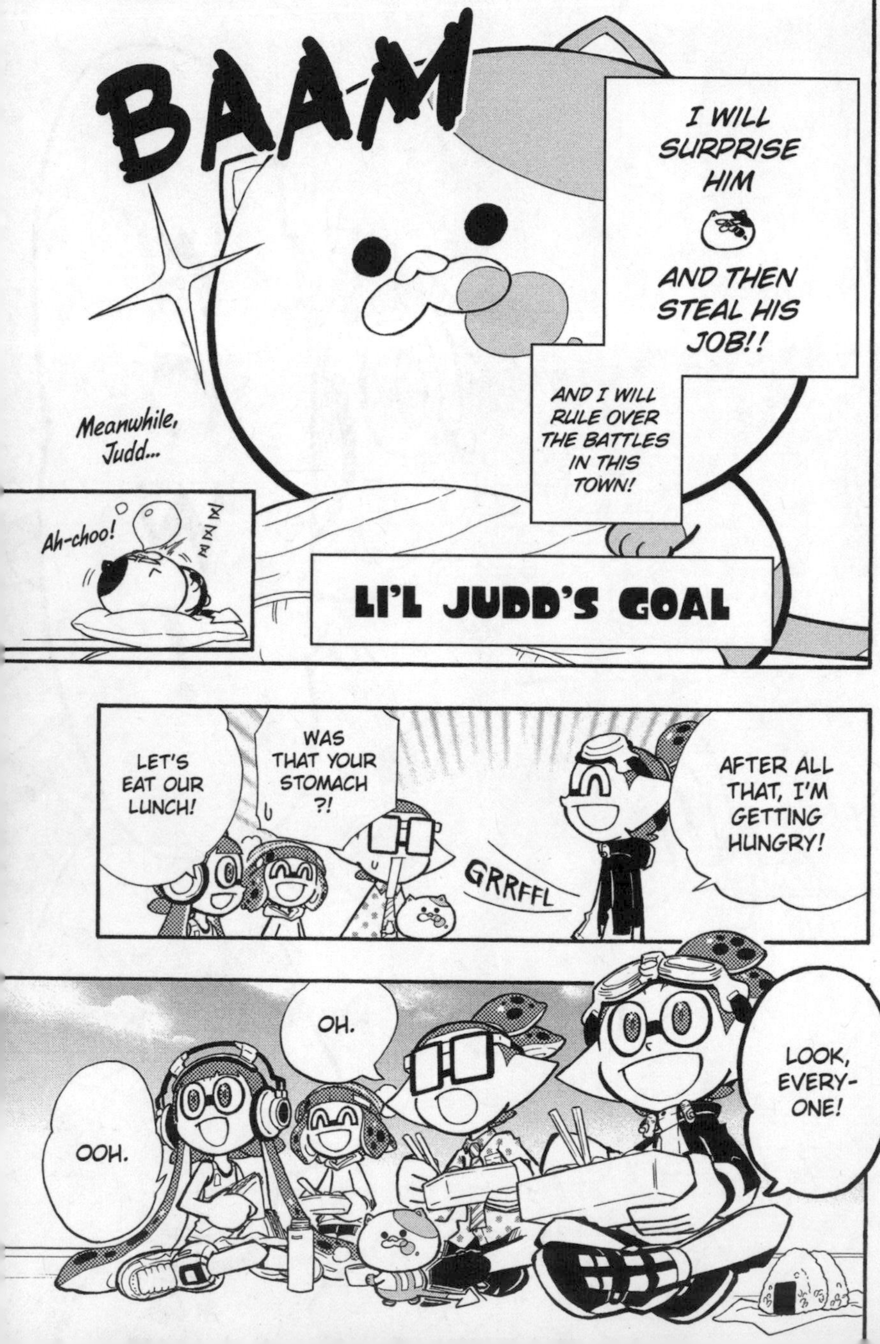
I WILL SURPRISE HIM
AND THEN STEAL HIS JOB!!
AND I WILL RULE OVER THE BATTLES IN THIS TOWN!
BAAM
Meanwhile, Judd...
LI'L JUDD'S GOAL
Ah-choo!
AFTER ALL THAT, I'M GETTING HUNGRY!
GRRFFL
WAS THAT YOUR STOMACH ?!
LET'S EAT OUR LUNCH!
LOOK, EVERY-ONE!
OH.
OOH.

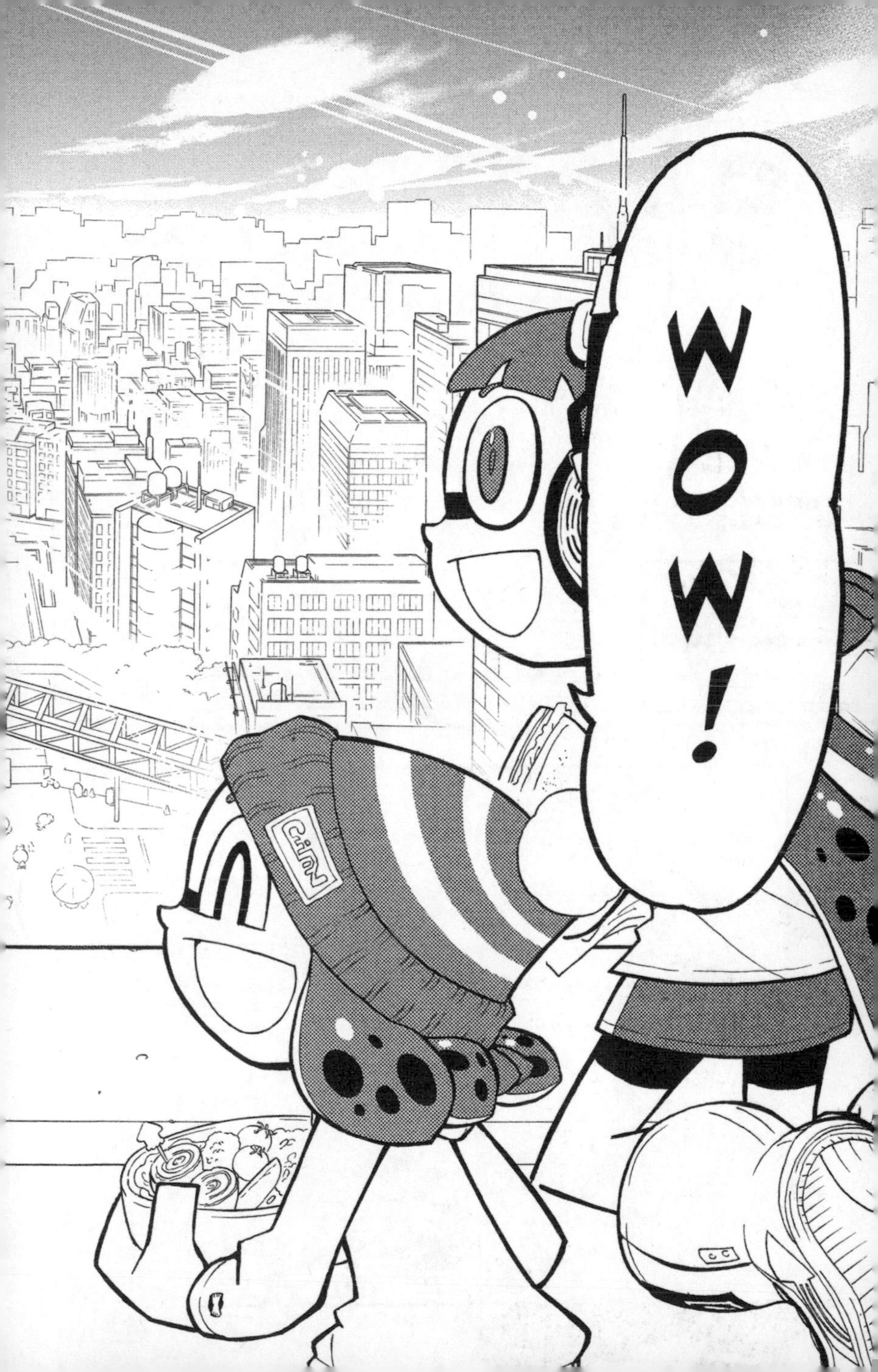
WOW!

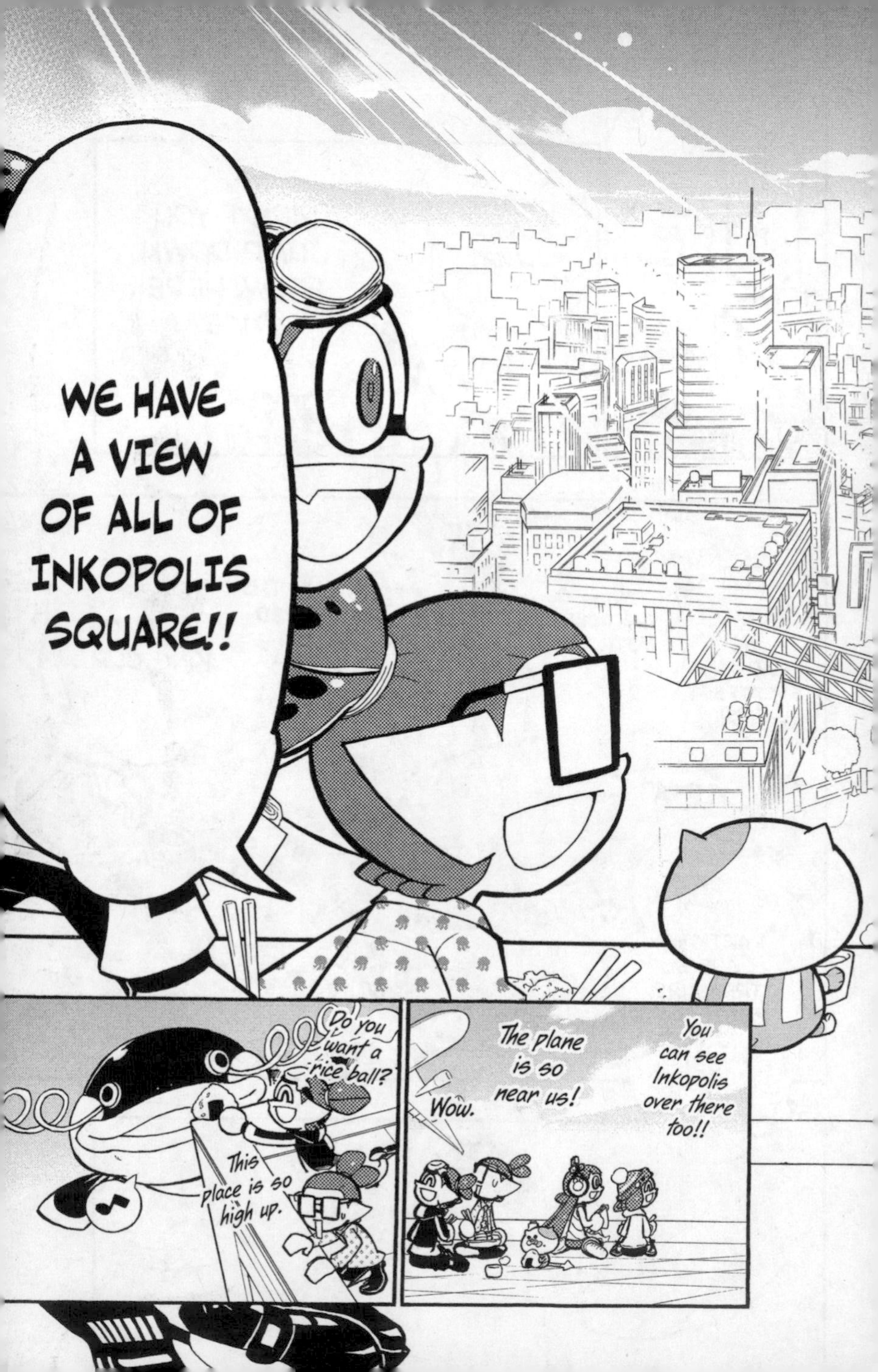
WE HAVE A VIEW OF ALL OF INKOPOLIS SQUARE!!
You can see Inkopolis over there too!!
The plane is so near us!
Wow.
Do you want a rice ball?
This place is so high up.

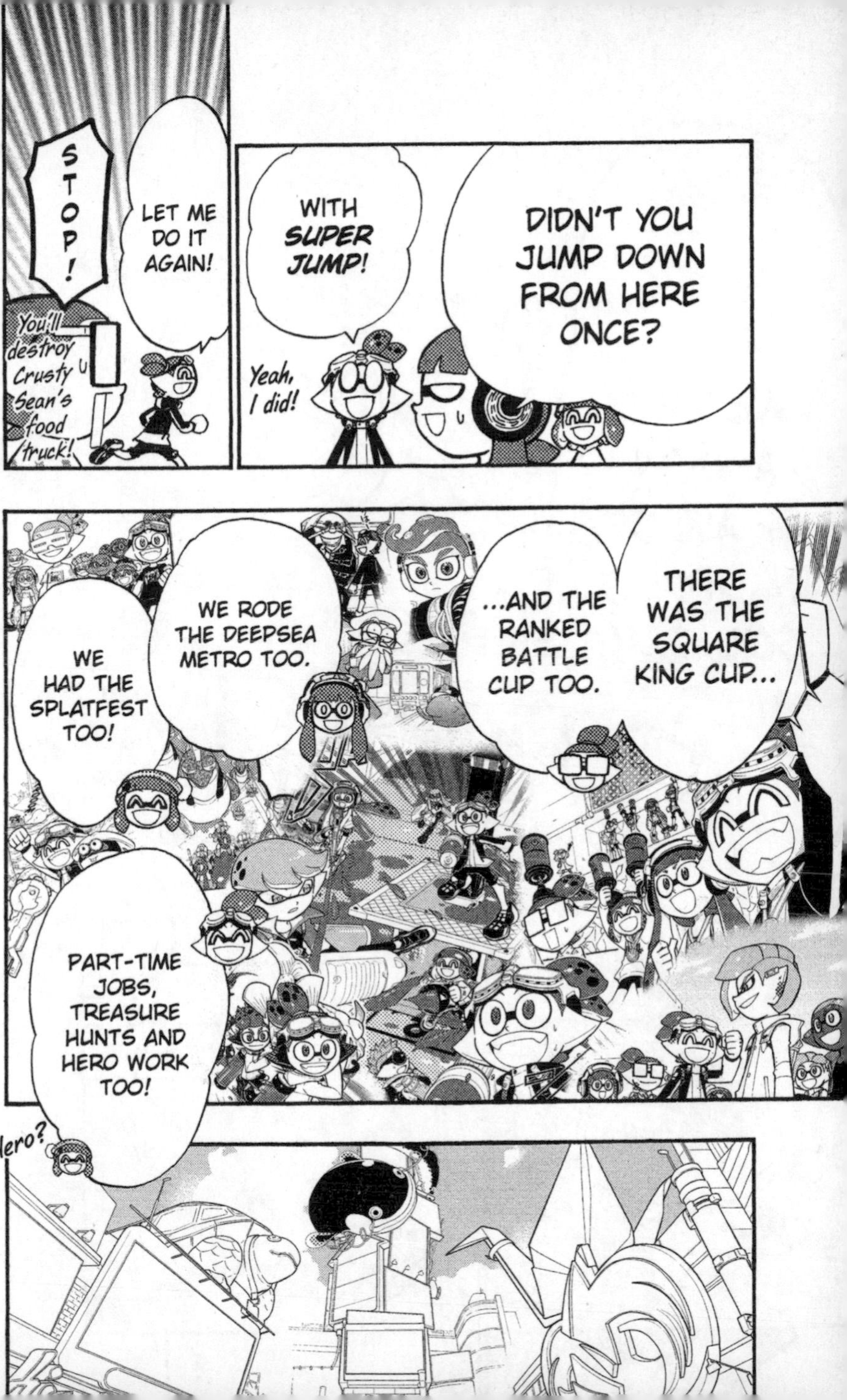
DIDN'T YOU JUMP DOWN FROM HERE ONCE?
WITH SUPER JUMP!
Yeah, I did!
LET ME DO IT AGAIN!
STOP!
You'll destroy Crusty Sean's food truck!
THERE WAS THE SQUARE KING CUP...
...AND THE RANKED BATTLE CUP TOO.
WE RODE THE DEEPSEA METRO TOO.
WE HAD THE SPLATFEST TOO!
PART-TIME JOBS, TREASURE HUNTS AND HERO WORK TOO!
Hero?

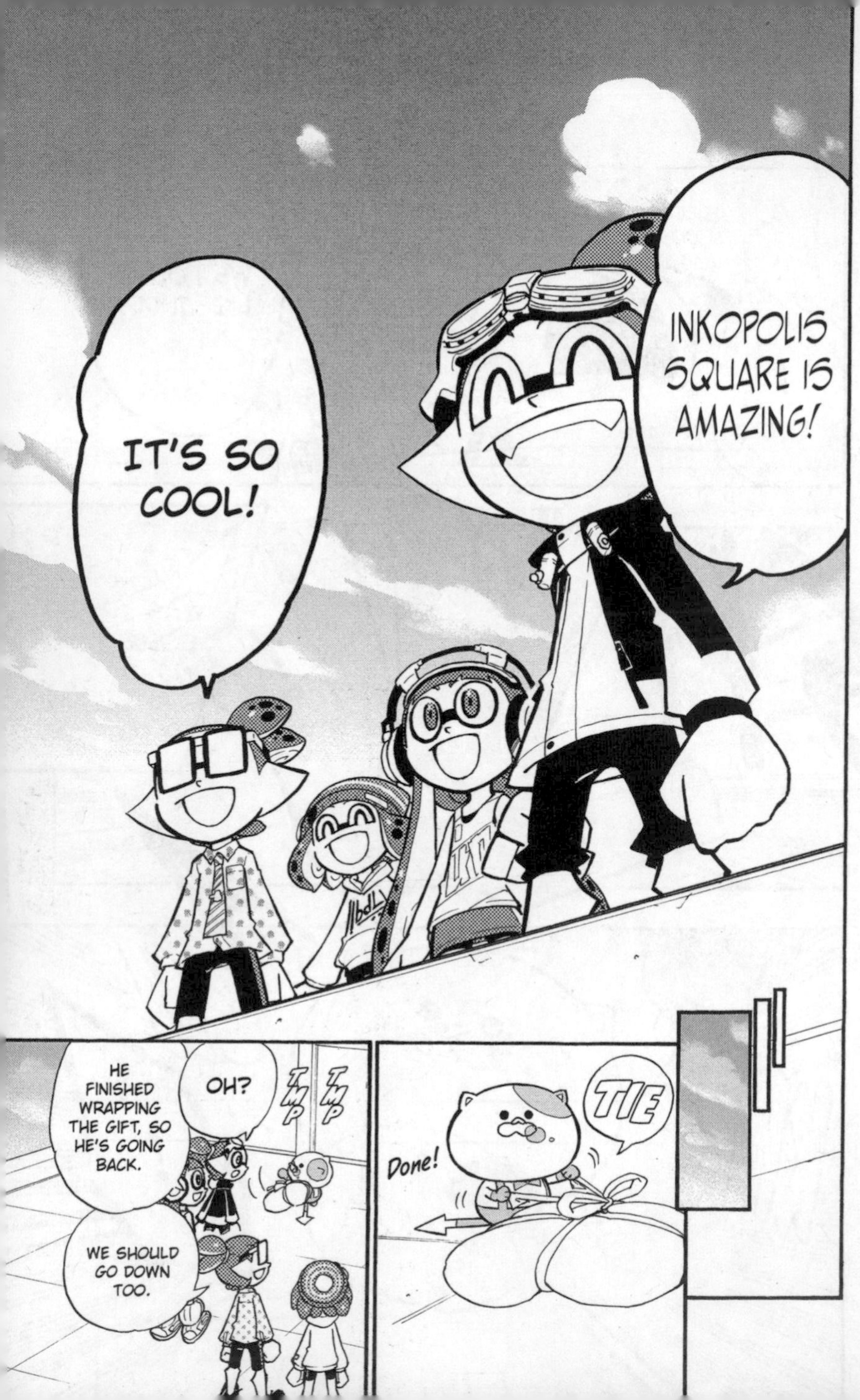
INKOPOLIS SQUARE IS AMAZING!
IT'S SO COOL!
TIE
Done!
OH?
TMP TMP
HE FINISHED WRAPPING THE GIFT, SO HE'S GOING BACK.
WE SHOULD GO DOWN TOO.

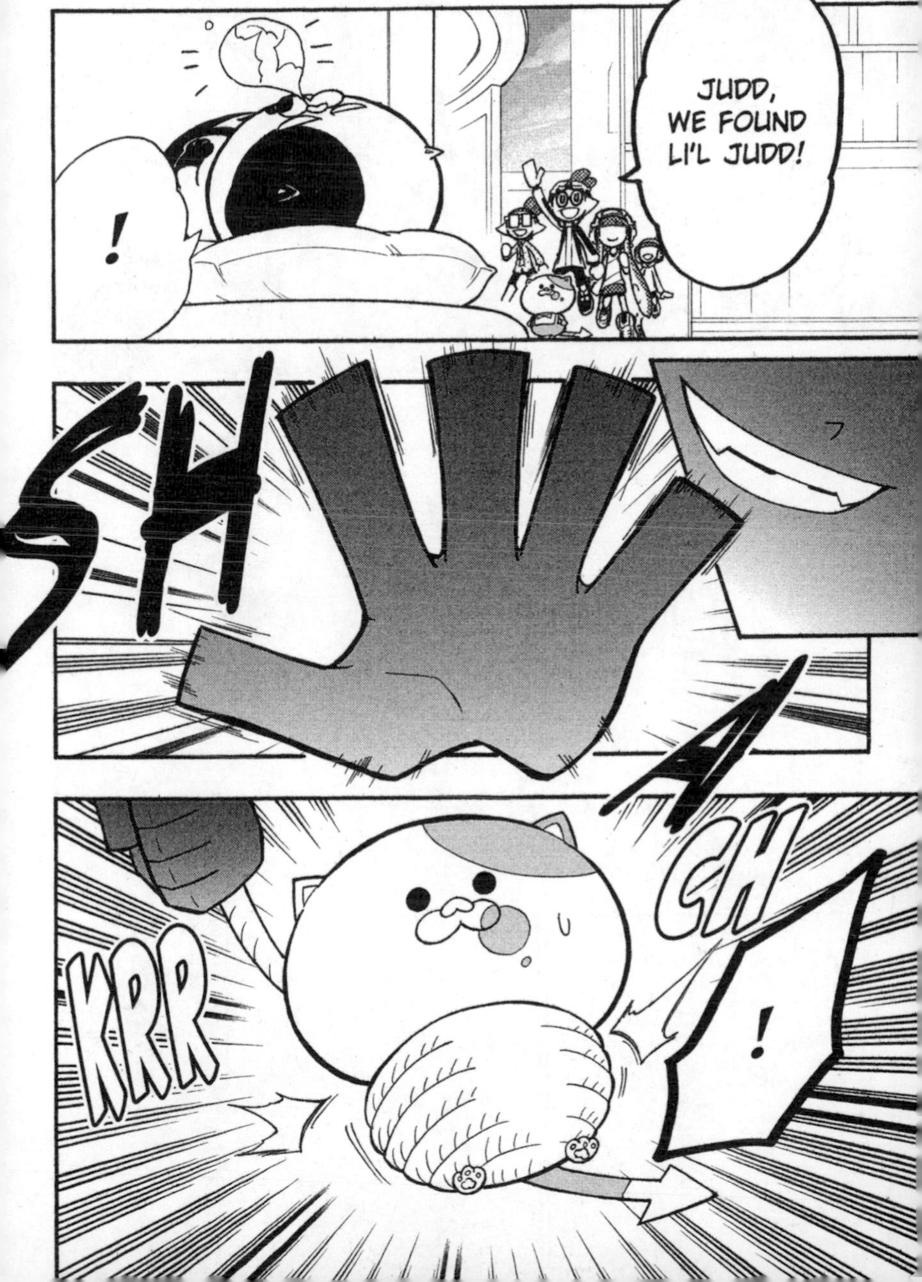
JUDD, WE FOUND LI'L JUDD!
!
SH
A
CH
!
KRR

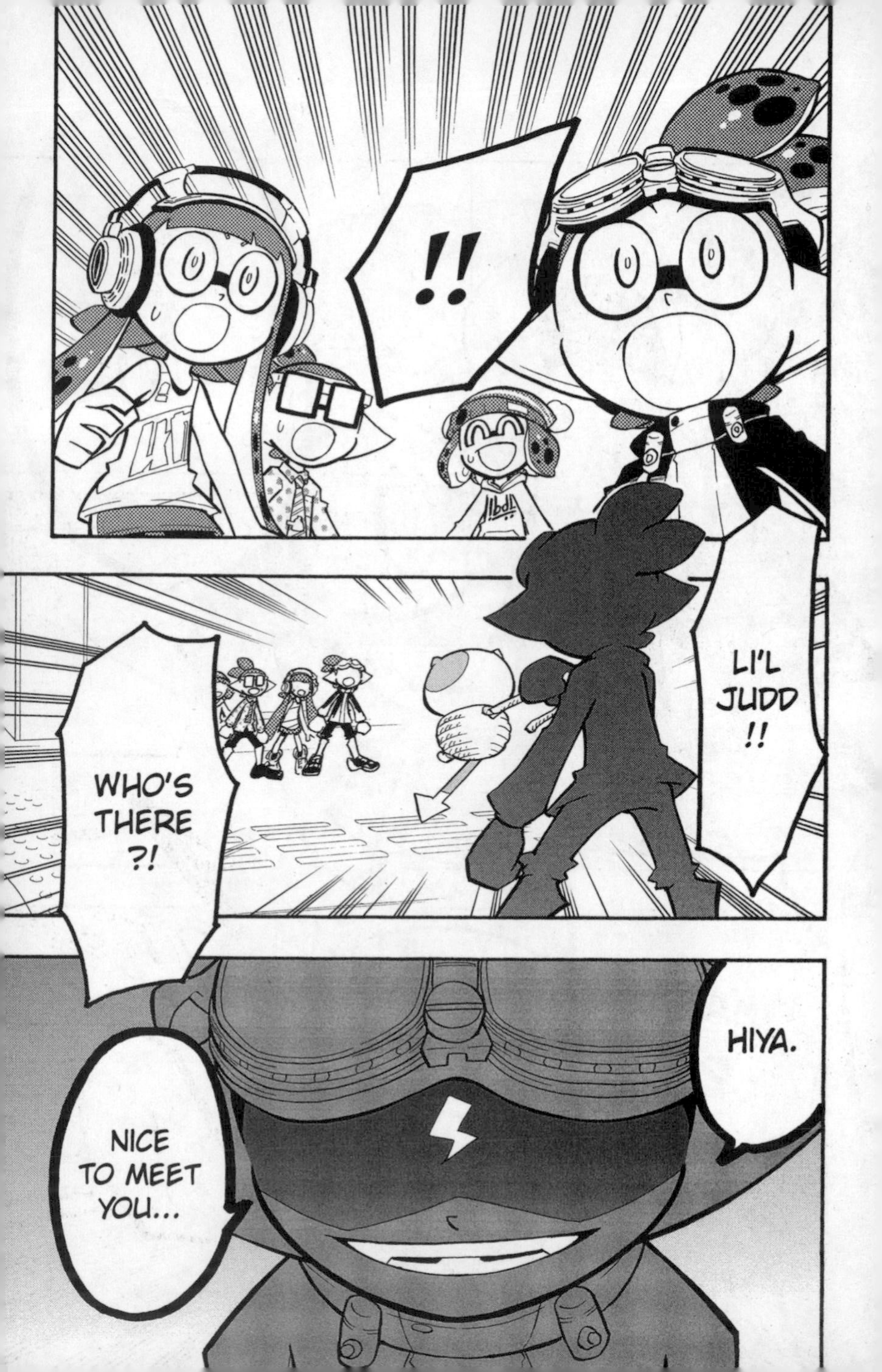
!!
LI'L JUDD!!
WHO'S THERE?!
HIYA.
NICE TO MEET YOU...

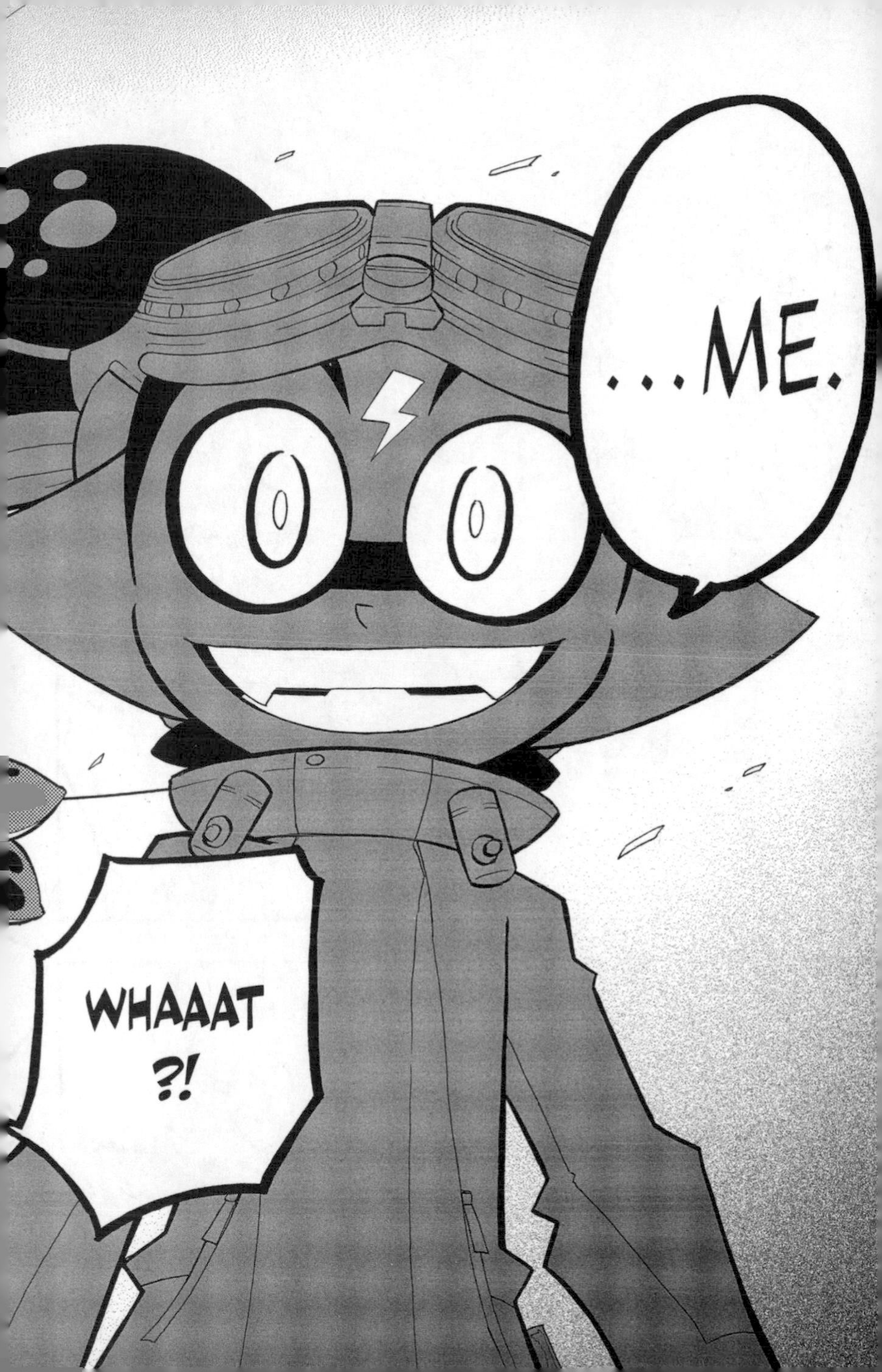
...ME.
WHAAAT ?!

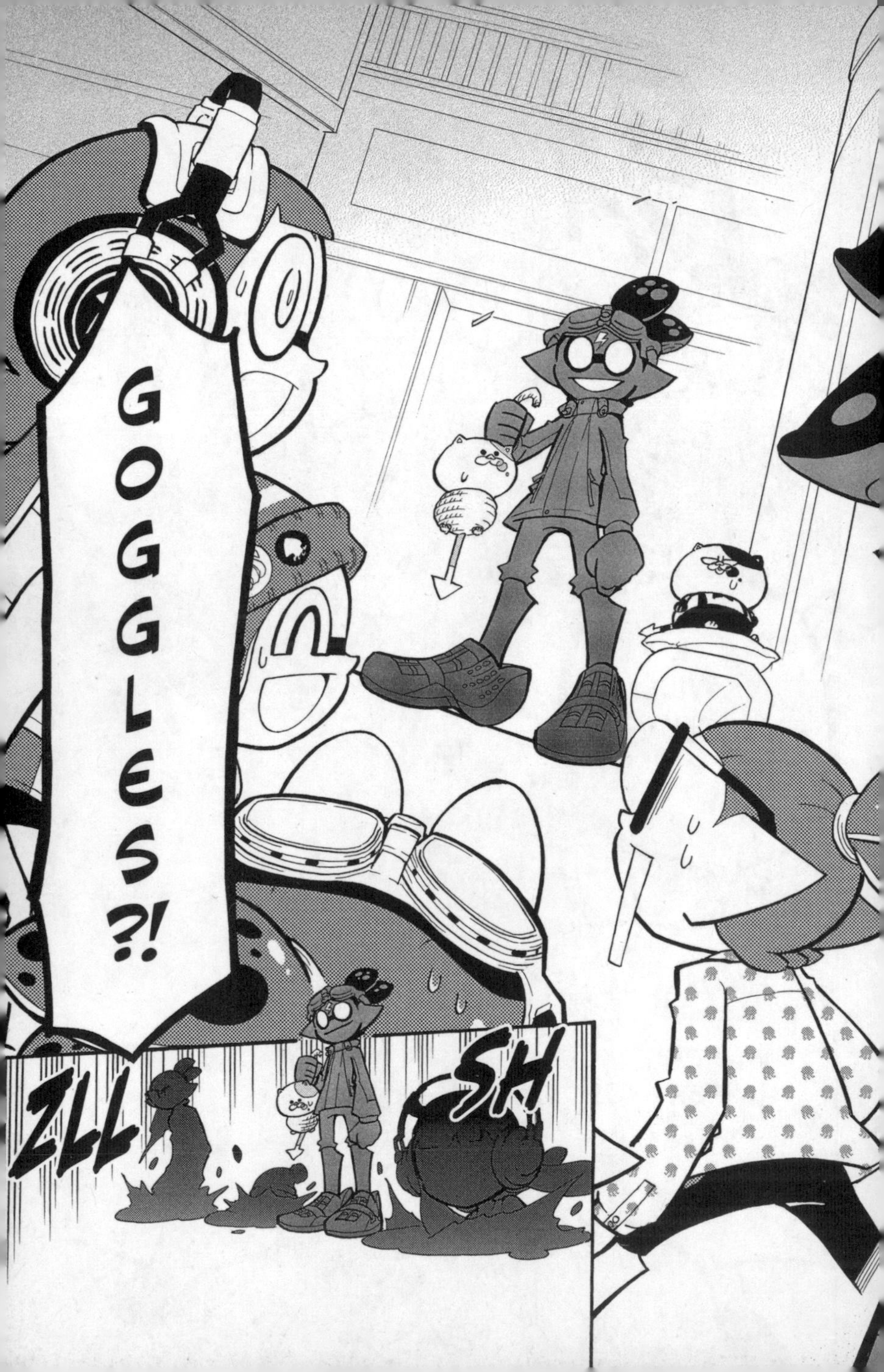
GOGGLES?!
SH
ZLL

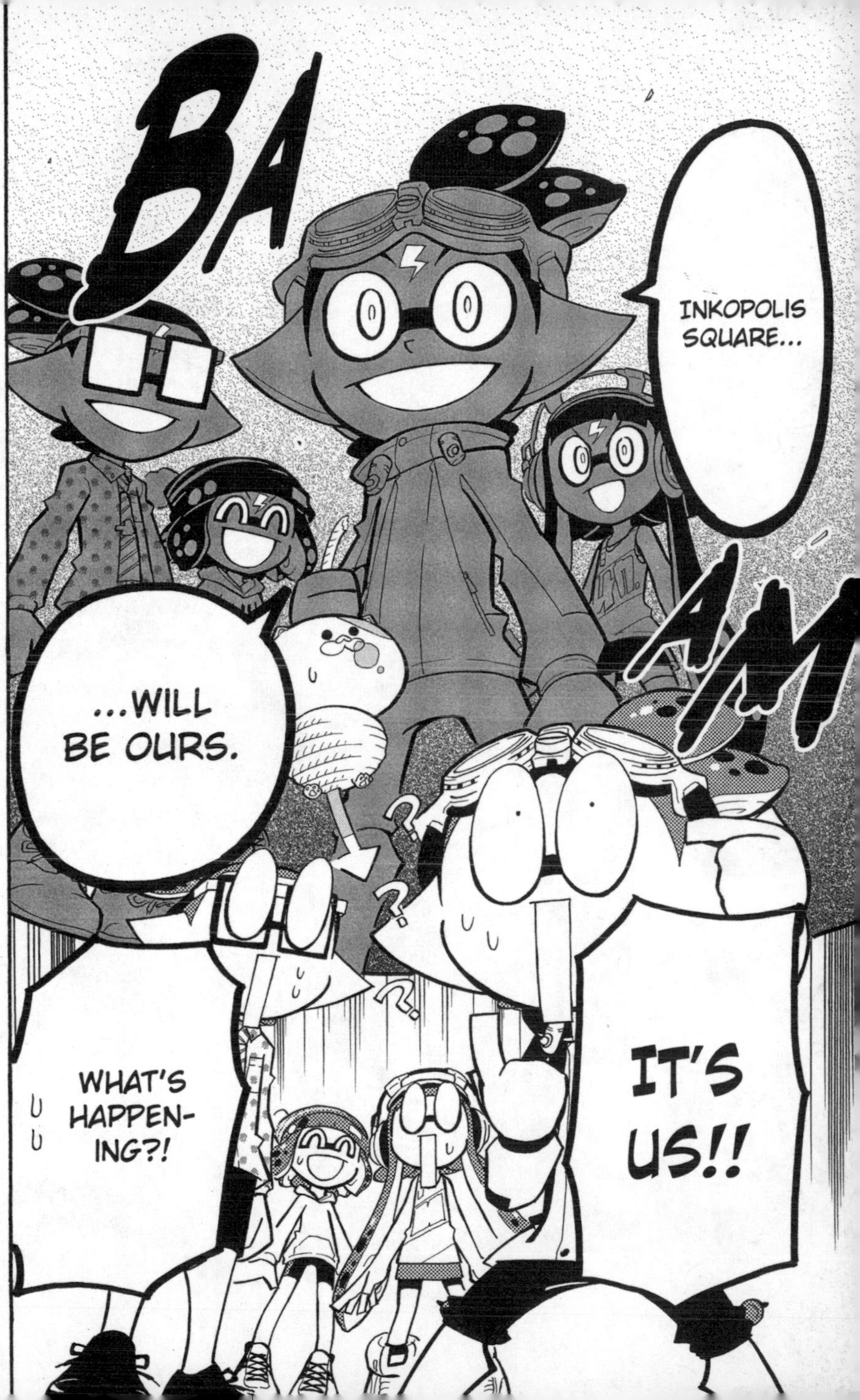
INKOPOLIS SQUARE...
BA
AM
...WILL BE OURS.
IT'S US!!
WHAT'S HAPPEN-ING?!

Where are you?

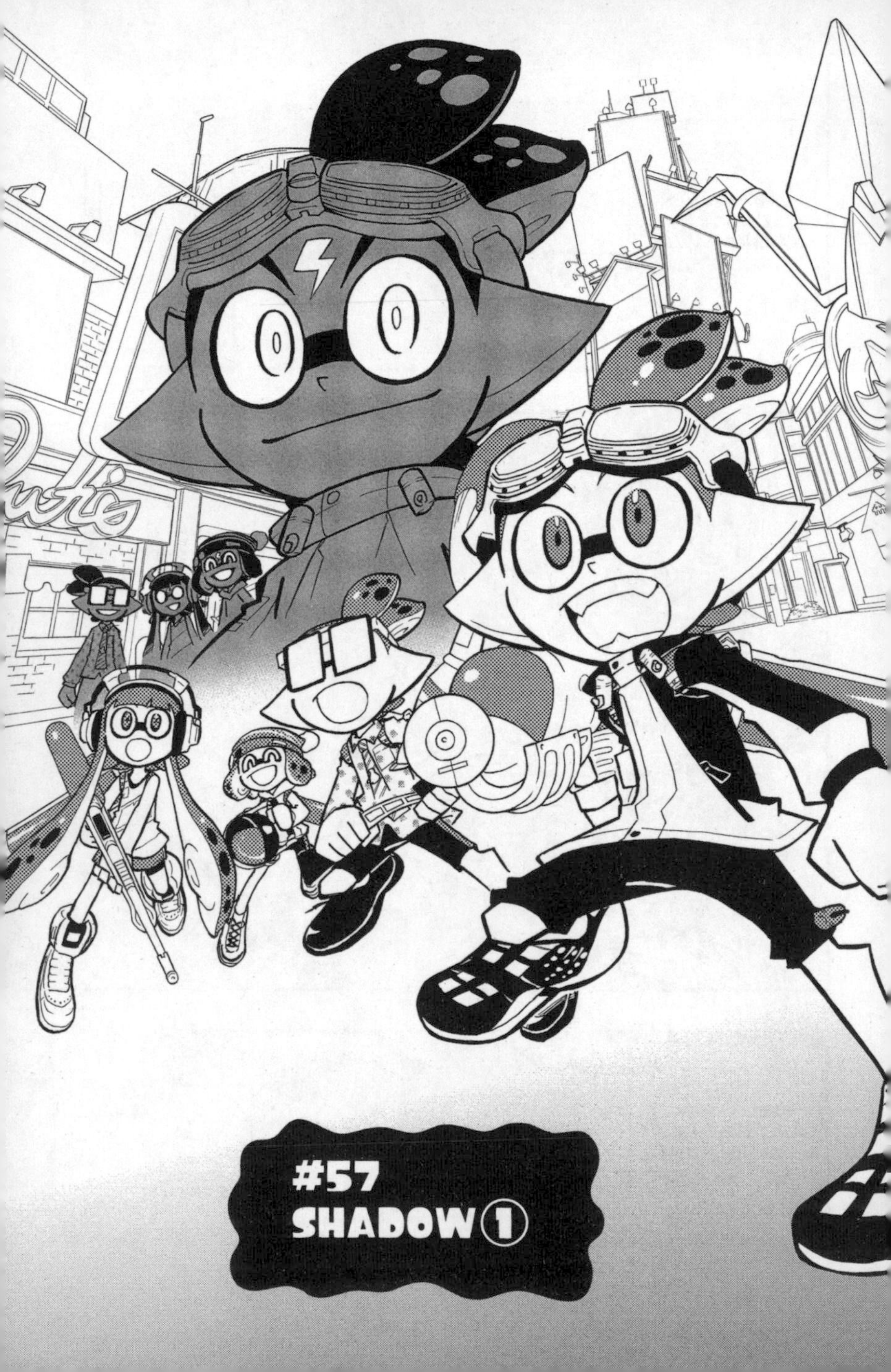
#57
SHADOW ①

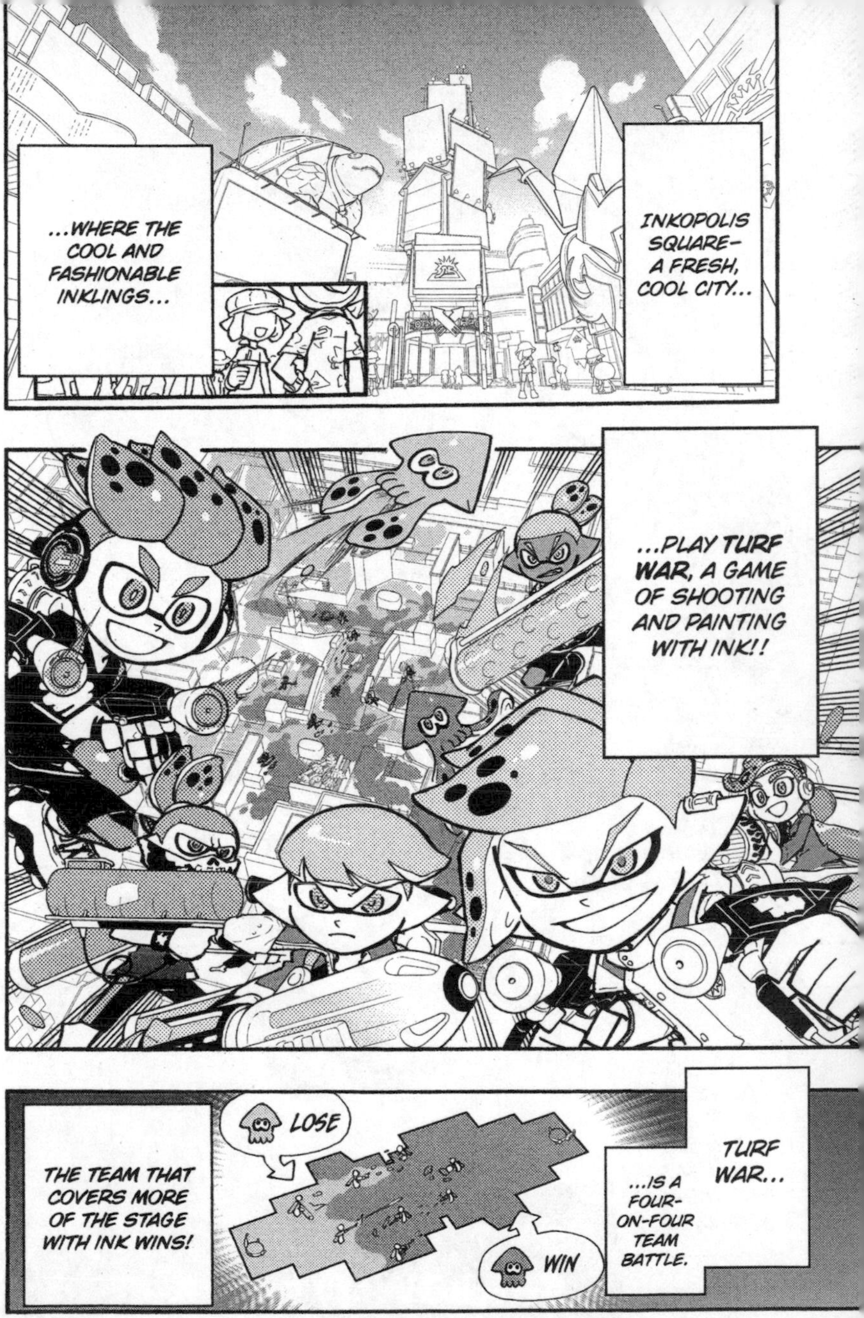
INKOPOLIS SQUARE– A FRESH, COOL CITY...
...WHERE THE COOL AND FASHIONABLE INKLINGS...
...PLAY TURF WAR, A GAME OF SHOOTING AND PAINTING WITH INK!!
TURF WAR...
...IS A FOUR-ON-FOUR TEAM BATTLE.
LOSE
WIN
THE TEAM THAT COVERS MORE OF THE STAGE WITH INK WINS!

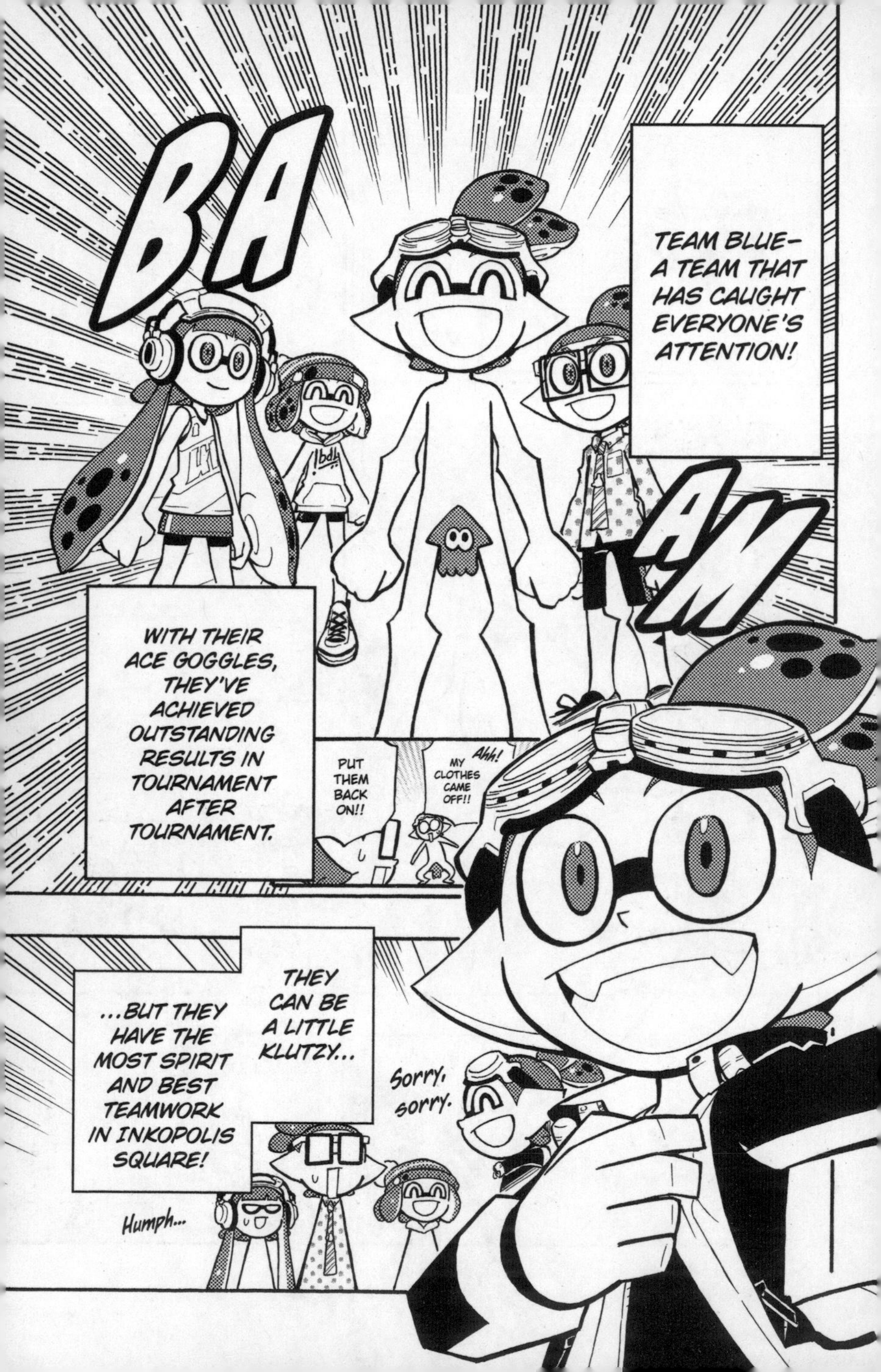

TEAM BLUE—A TEAM THAT HAS CAUGHT EVERYONE'S ATTENTION!
BA AM
WITH THEIR ACE GOGGLES, THEY'VE ACHIEVED OUTSTANDING RESULTS IN TOURNAMENT AFTER TOURNAMENT.
Ahh! MY CLOTHES CAME OFF!!
PUT THEM BACK ON!!
THEY CAN BE A LITTLE KLUTZY...
...BUT THEY HAVE THE MOST SPIRIT AND BEST TEAMWORK IN INKOPOLIS SQUARE!
Sorry, sorry.
Humph...

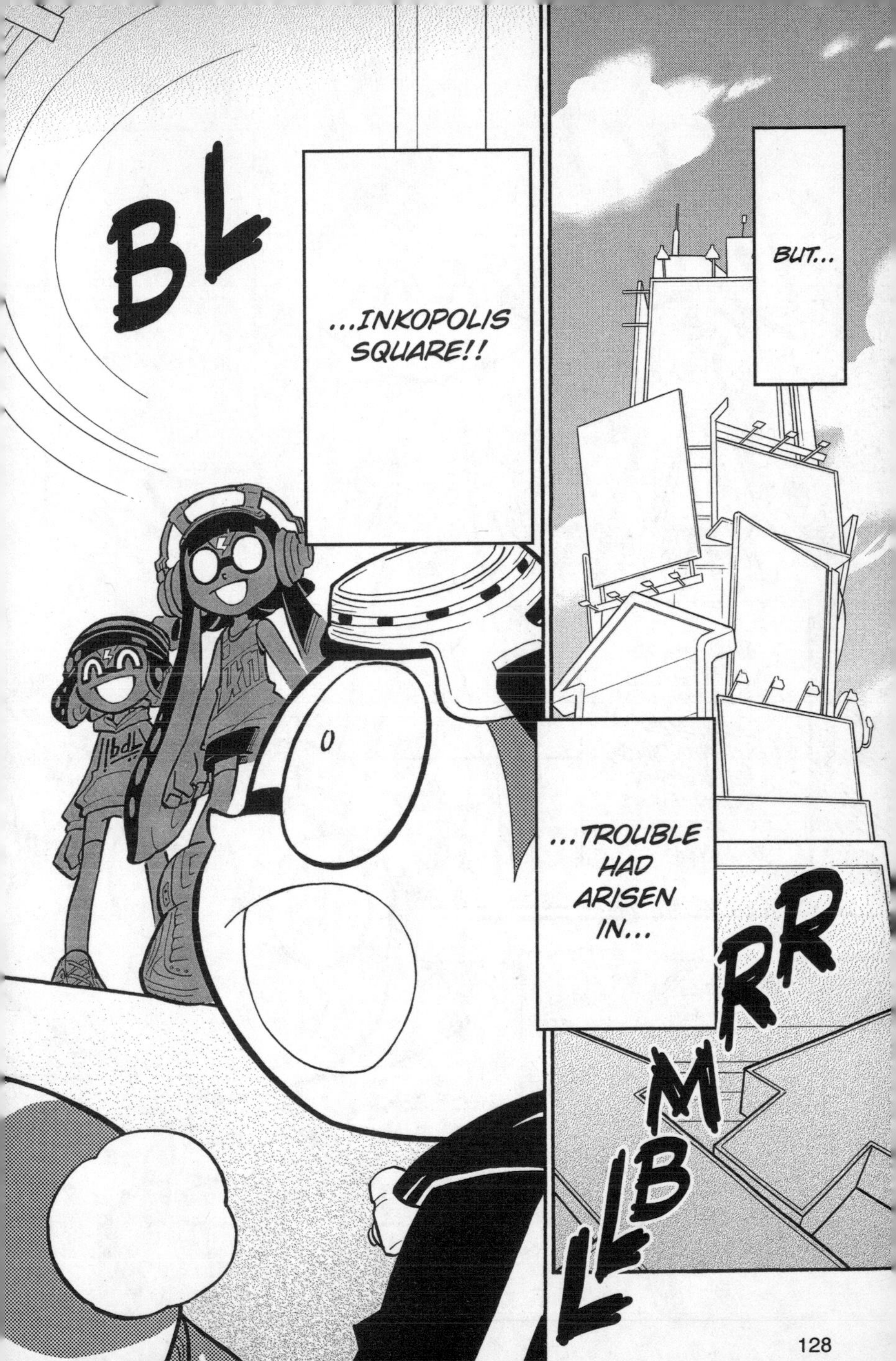
BUT...
...TROUBLE HAD ARISEN IN...
RRMBLL
BL
...INKOPOLIS SQUARE!!

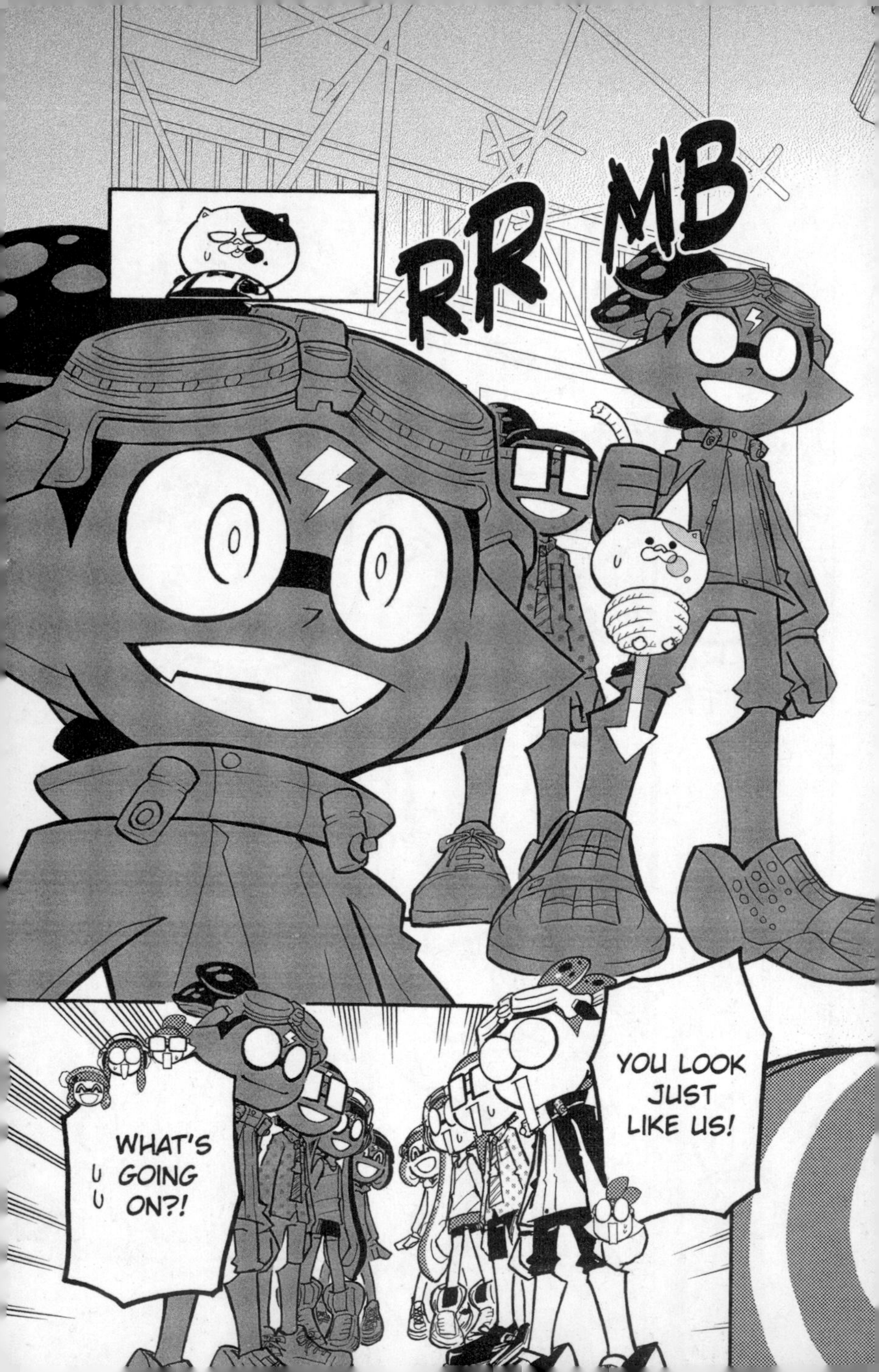
RRMB
YOU LOOK JUST LIKE US!
WHAT'S GOING ON?!

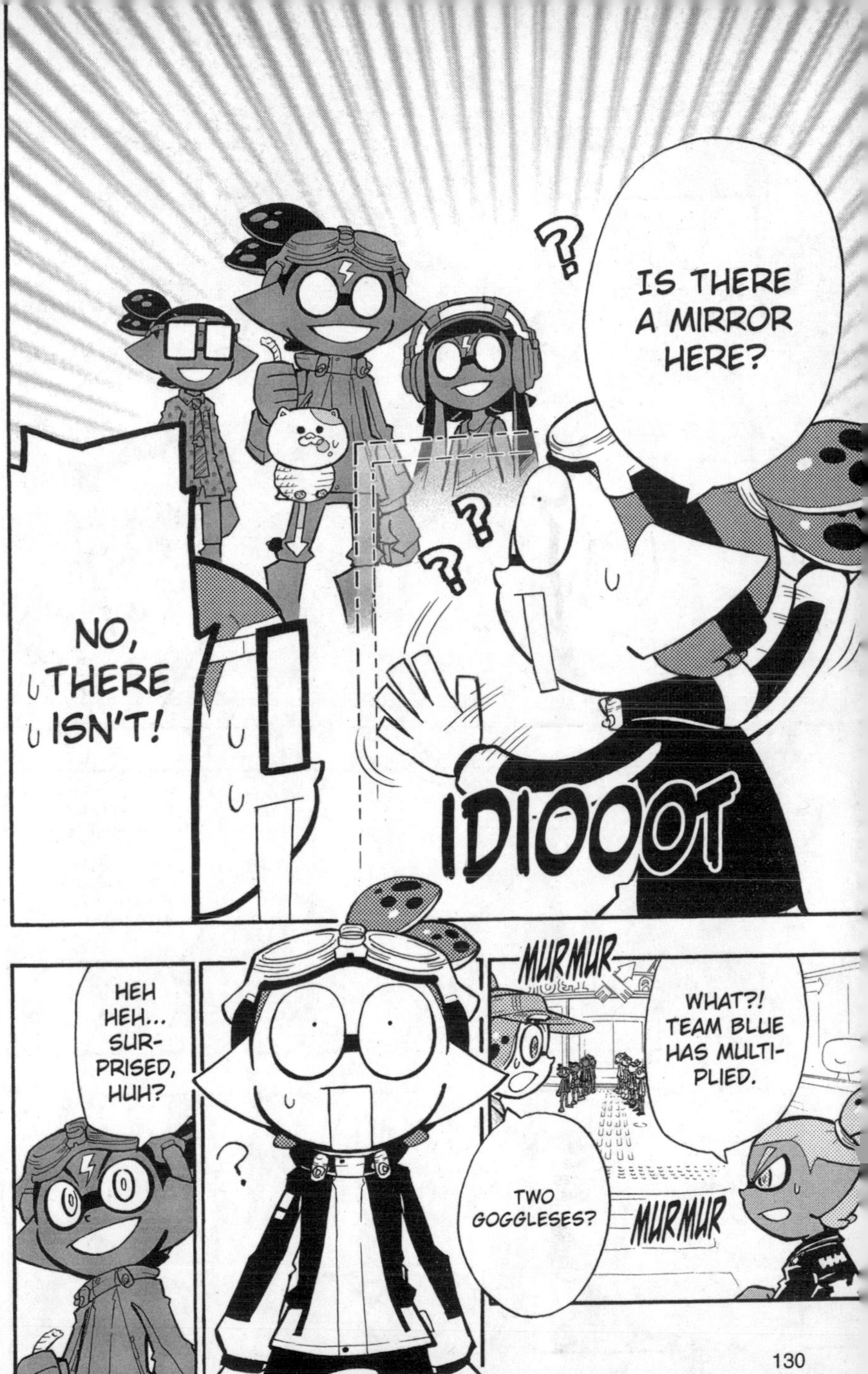
IS THERE A MIRROR HERE?
IDIOOOT
NO, THERE ISN'T!
MURMUR
WHAT?! TEAM BLUE HAS MULTI-PLIED.
TWO GOGGLESES?
MURMUR
HEH HEH... SUR-PRISED, HUH?

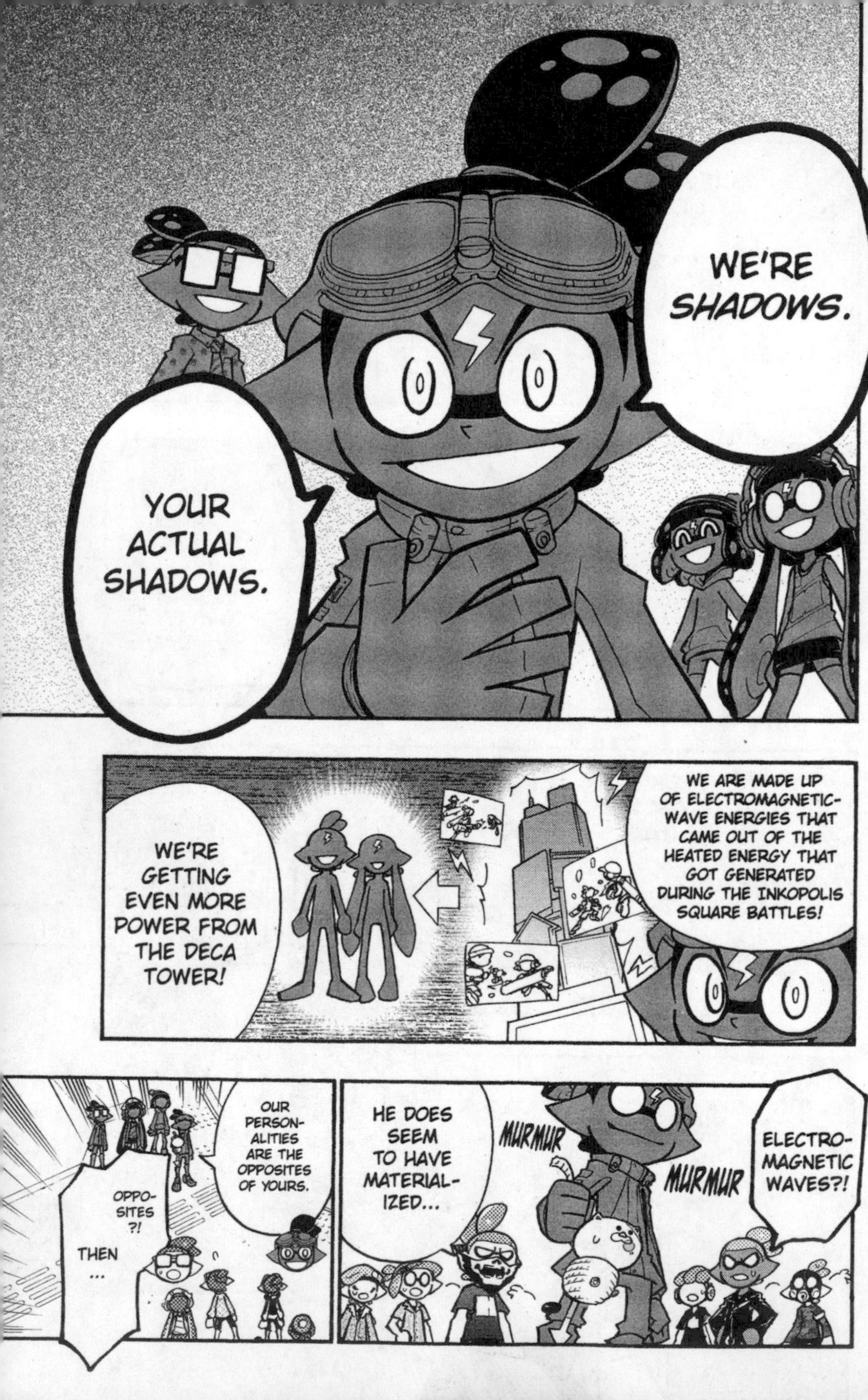
WE'RE SHADOWS.
YOUR ACTUAL SHADOWS.
WE ARE MADE UP OF ELECTROMAGNETIC-WAVE ENERGIES THAT CAME OUT OF THE HEATED ENERGY THAT GOT GENERATED DURING THE INKOPOLIS SQUARE BATTLES!
WE'RE GETTING EVEN MORE POWER FROM THE DECA TOWER!
ELECTRO-MAGNETIC WAVES?!
MURMUR
MURMUR
HE DOES SEEM TO HAVE MATERIAL-IZED...
OUR PERSON-ALITIES ARE THE OPPOSITES OF YOURS.
OPPO-SITES ?!
THEN ...

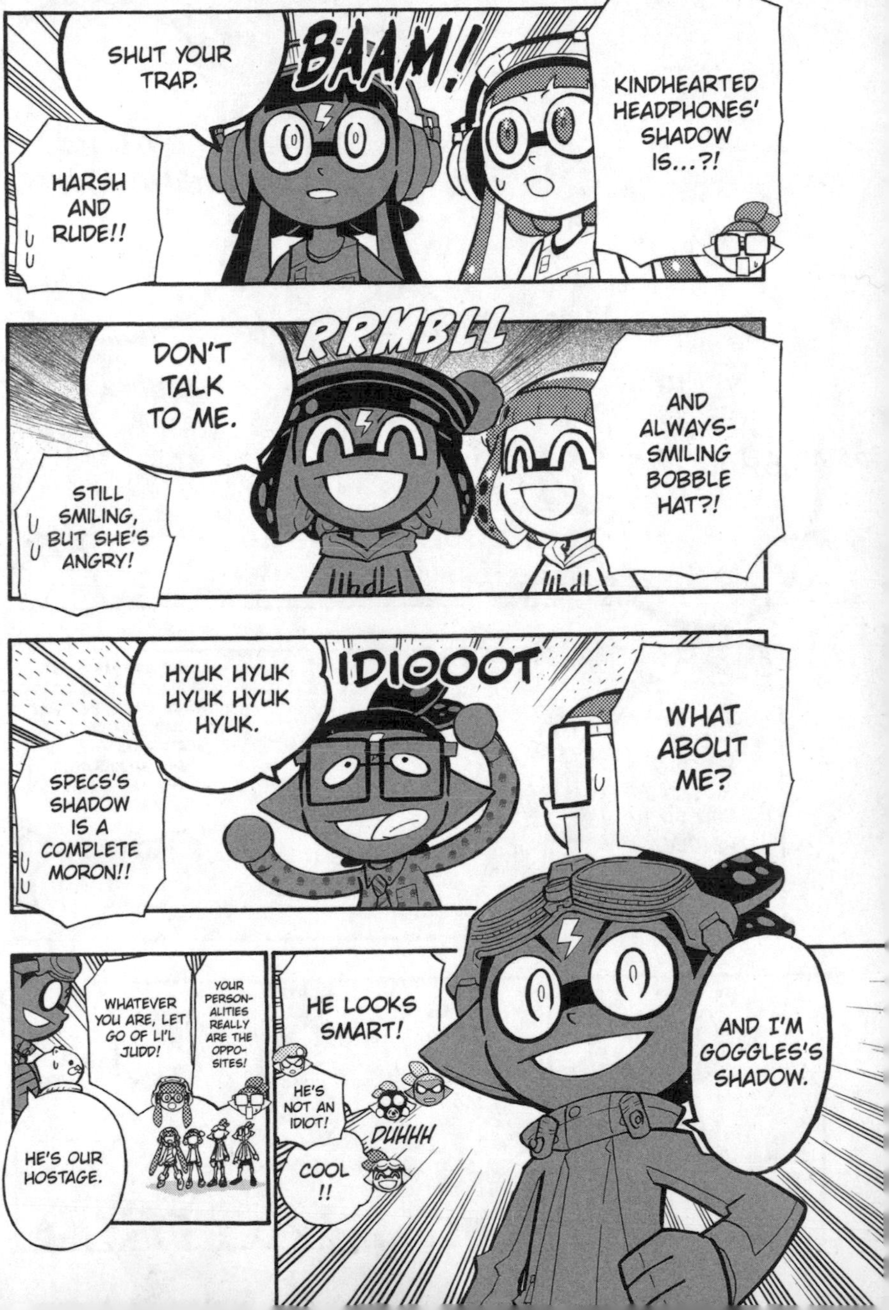
KINDHEARTED HEADPHONES' SHADOW IS...?!
BAAM!
SHUT YOUR TRAP.
HARSH AND RUDE!!
AND ALWAYS-SMILING BOBBLE HAT?!
RRMBLL
DON'T TALK TO ME.
STILL SMILING, BUT SHE'S ANGRY!
WHAT ABOUT ME?
IDIOOOT
HYUK HYUK HYUK HYUK HYUK.
SPECS'S SHADOW IS A COMPLETE MORON!!
AND I'M GOGGLES'S SHADOW.
HE LOOKS SMART!
HE'S NOT AN IDIOT!
DUHHH
COOL!!
YOUR PERSONALITIES REALLY ARE THE OPPOSITES!
WHATEVER YOU ARE, LET GO OF LI'L JUDD!
HE'S OUR HOSTAGE.

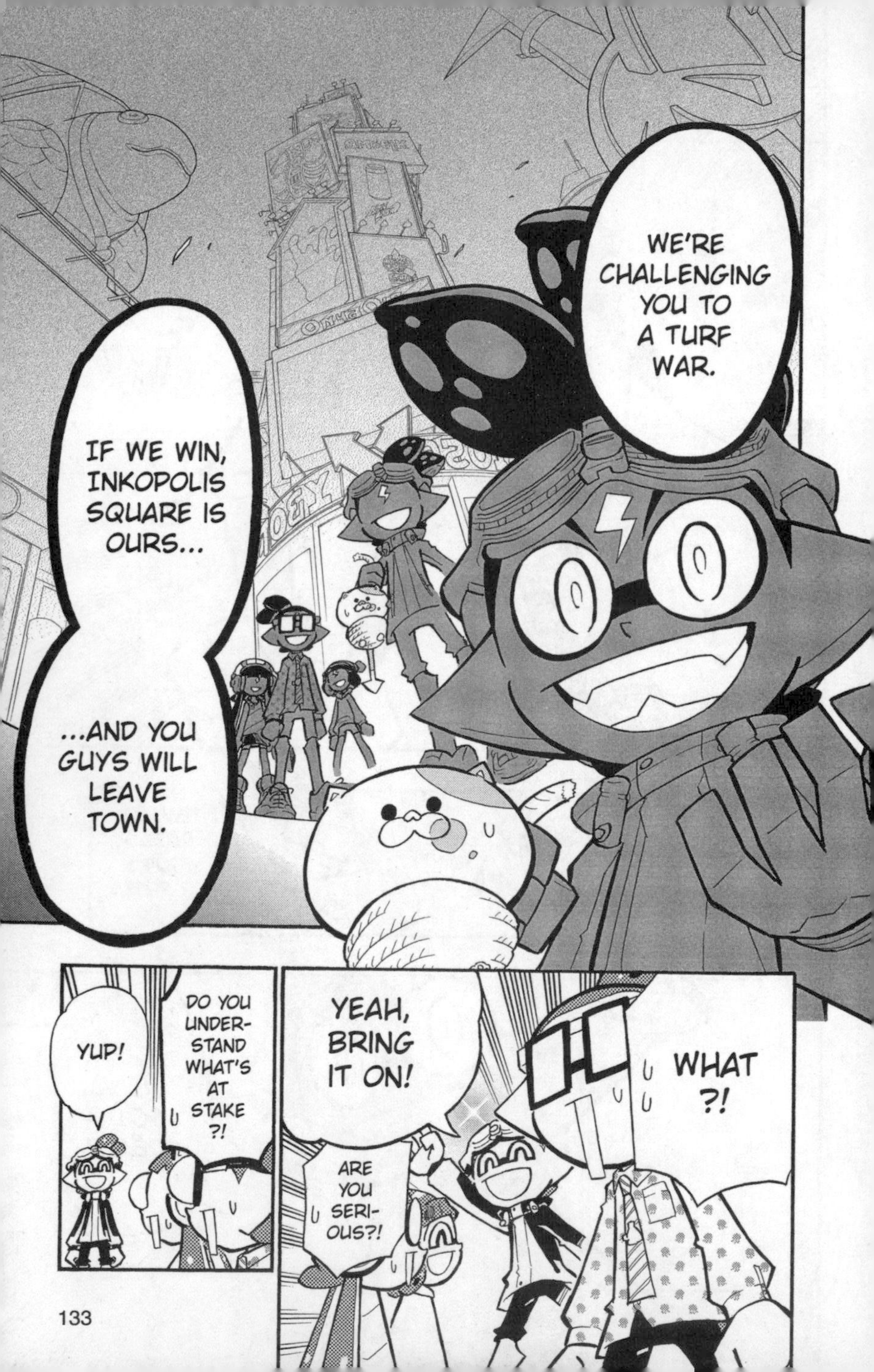
WE'RE CHALLENGING YOU TO A TURF WAR.
IF WE WIN, INKOPOLIS SQUARE IS OURS...
...AND YOU GUYS WILL LEAVE TOWN.
WHAT ?!
YEAH, BRING IT ON!
ARE YOU SERI-OUS?!
DO YOU UNDER-STAND WHAT'S AT STAKE ?!
YUP!

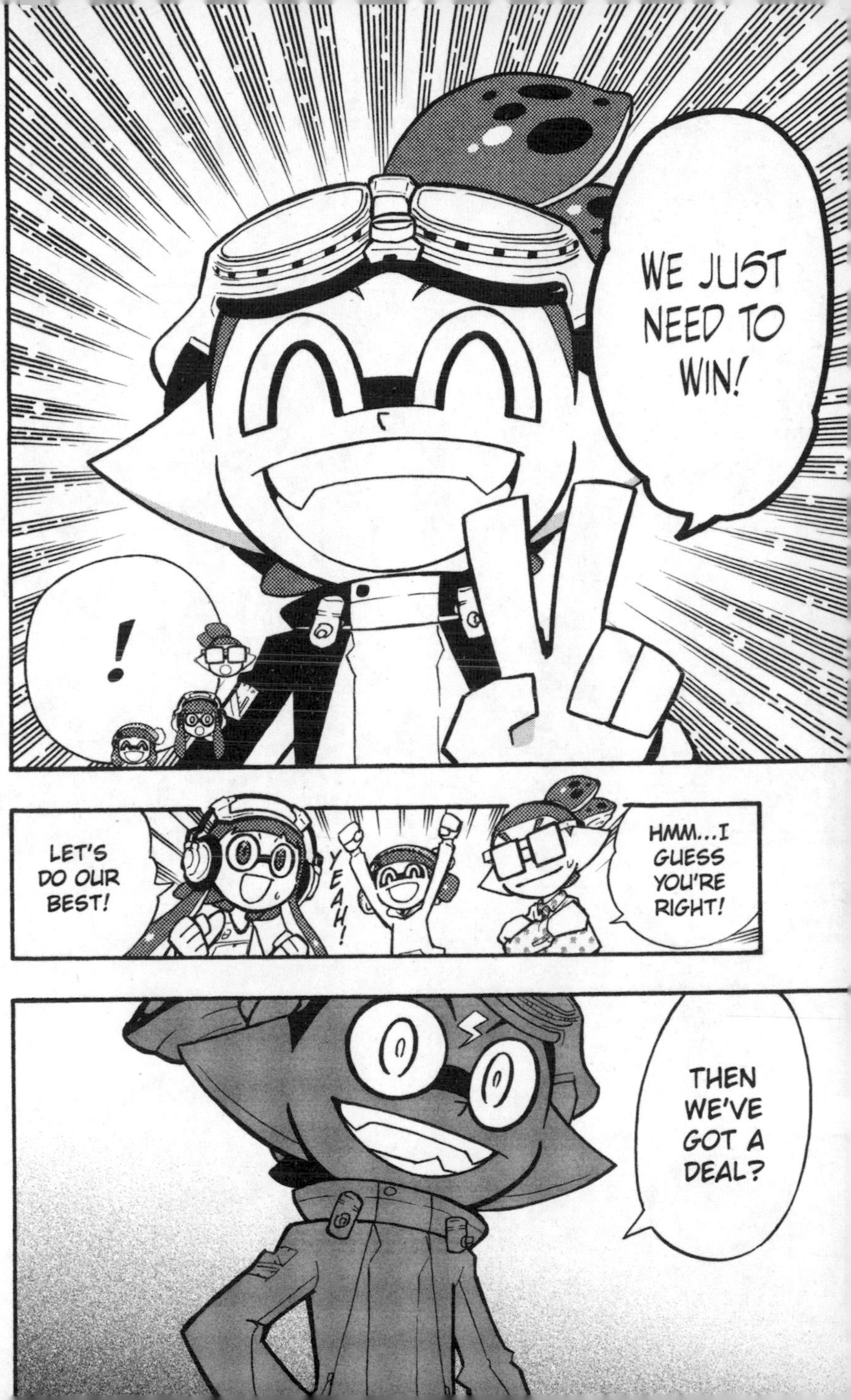
WE JUST NEED TO WIN!
!
HMM...I GUESS YOU'RE RIGHT!
YEAH!
LET'S DO OUR BEST!
THEN WE'VE GOT A DEAL?

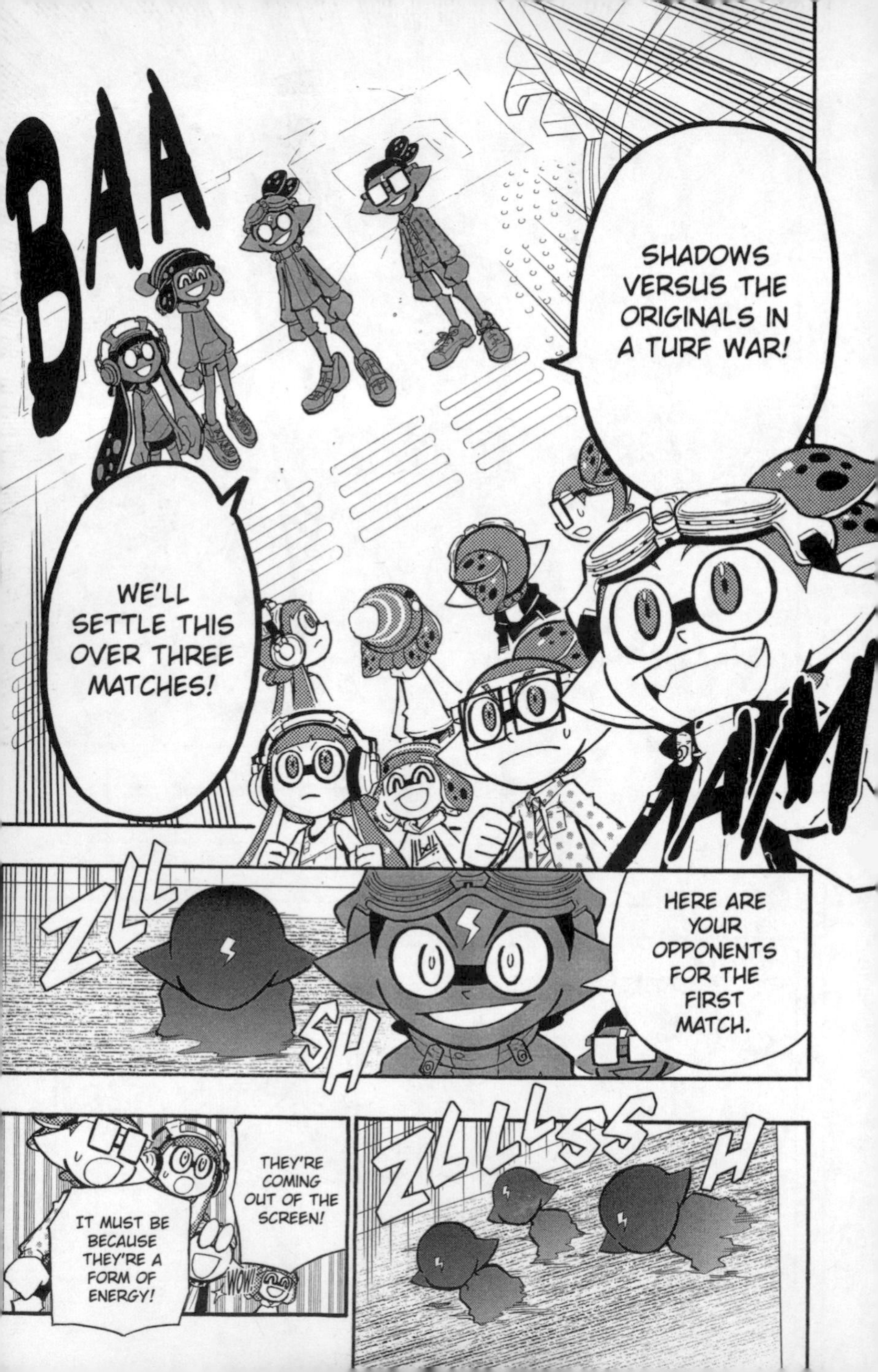
SHADOWS VERSUS THE ORIGINALS IN A TURF WAR!
BAA
AAM
WE'LL SETTLE THIS OVER THREE MATCHES!
HERE ARE YOUR OPPONENTS FOR THE FIRST MATCH.
SH
ZLL
ZLLLSSH
THEY'RE COMING OUT OF THE SCREEN!
IT MUST BE BECAUSE THEY'RE A FORM OF ENERGY!
WOW!

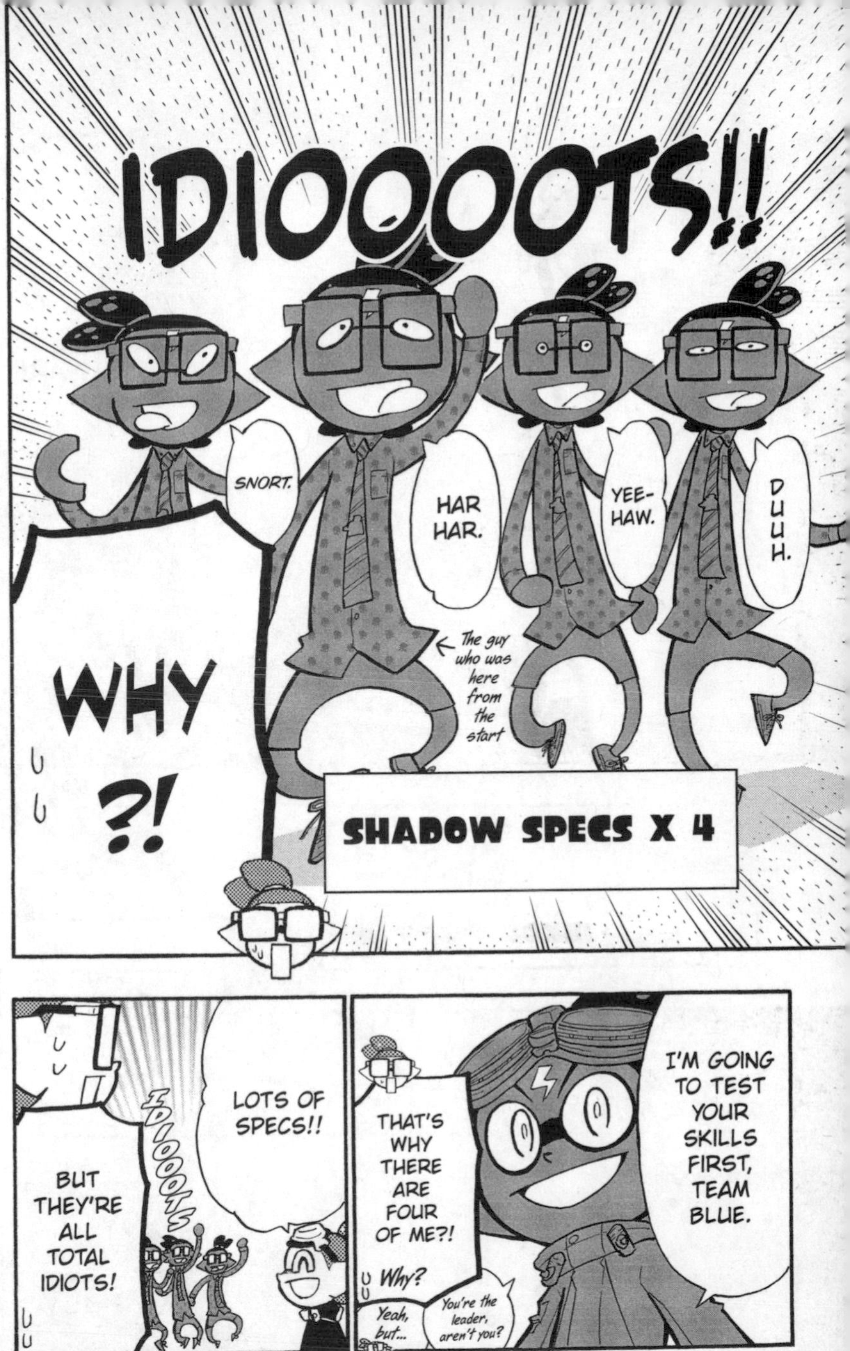
IDIOOOOTS!!
DUUH.
YEE-HAW.
HAR HAR.
SNORT.
The guy who was here from the start
WHY?!
SHADOW SPECS X 4
I'M GOING TO TEST YOUR SKILLS FIRST, TEAM BLUE.
THAT'S WHY THERE ARE FOUR OF ME?!
Why?
You're the leader, aren't you?
Yeah, but...
LOTS OF SPECS!!
IDIOOOOTS
BUT THEY'RE ALL TOTAL IDIOTS!

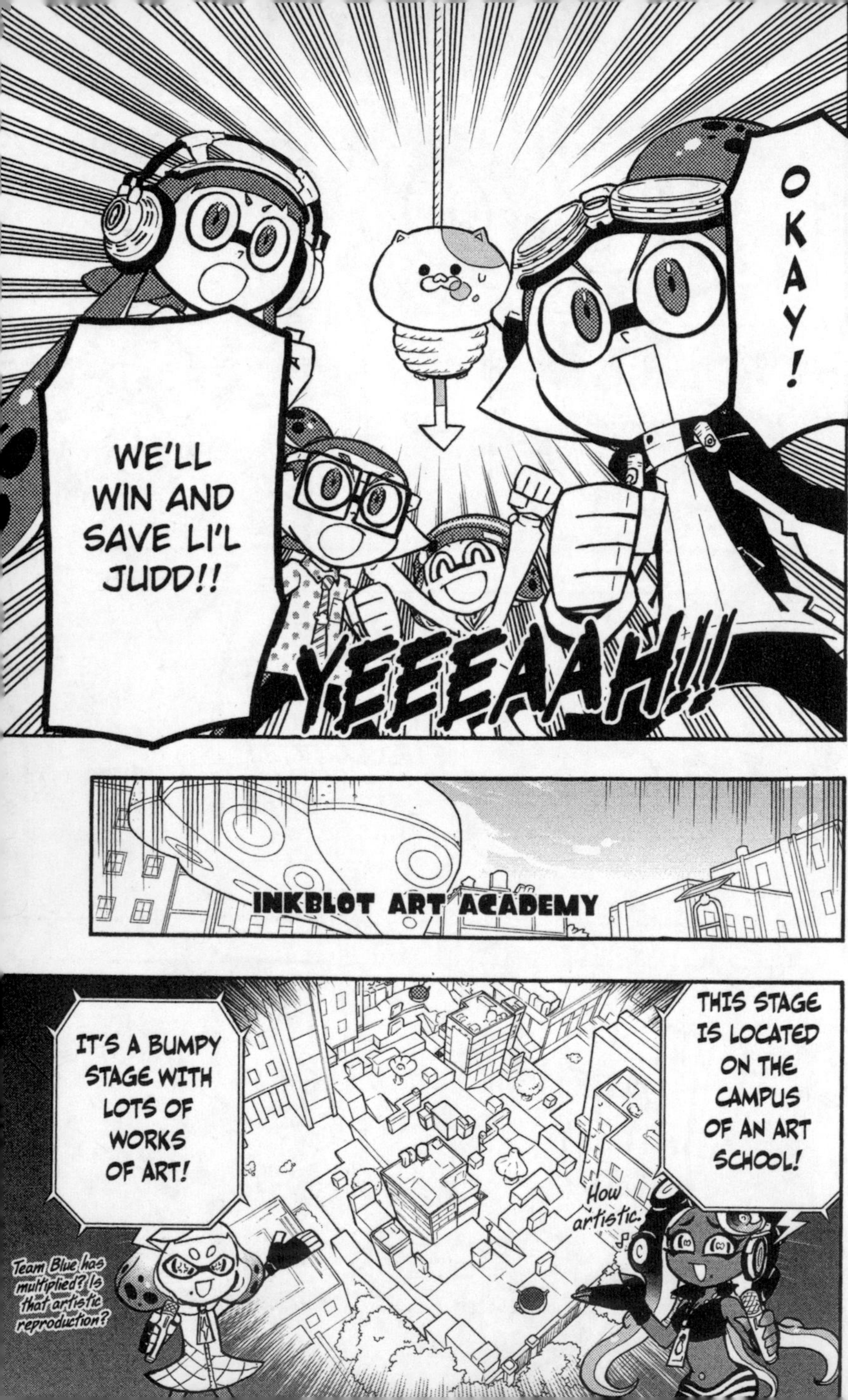
OKAY!
WE'LL WIN AND SAVE LI'L JUDD!!
YEEEAAH!!
INKBLOT ART ACADEMY
THIS STAGE IS LOCATED ON THE CAMPUS OF AN ART SCHOOL!
How artistic.
IT'S A BUMPY STAGE WITH LOTS OF WORKS OF ART!
Team Blue has multiplied? Is that artistic reproduction?

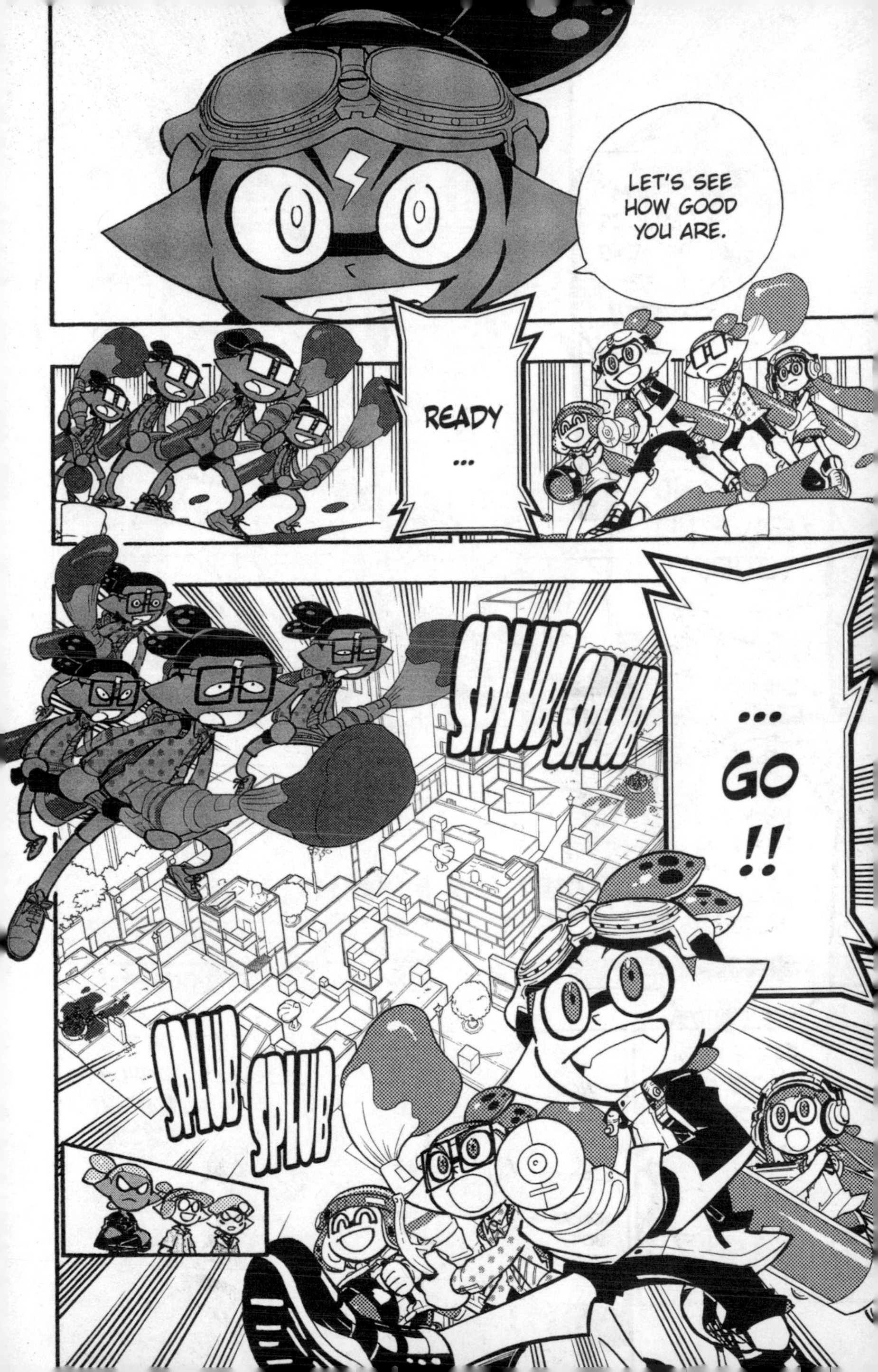
LET'S SEE HOW GOOD YOU ARE.
READY ...
... GO !!
SPLUB SPLUB
SPLUB SPLUB

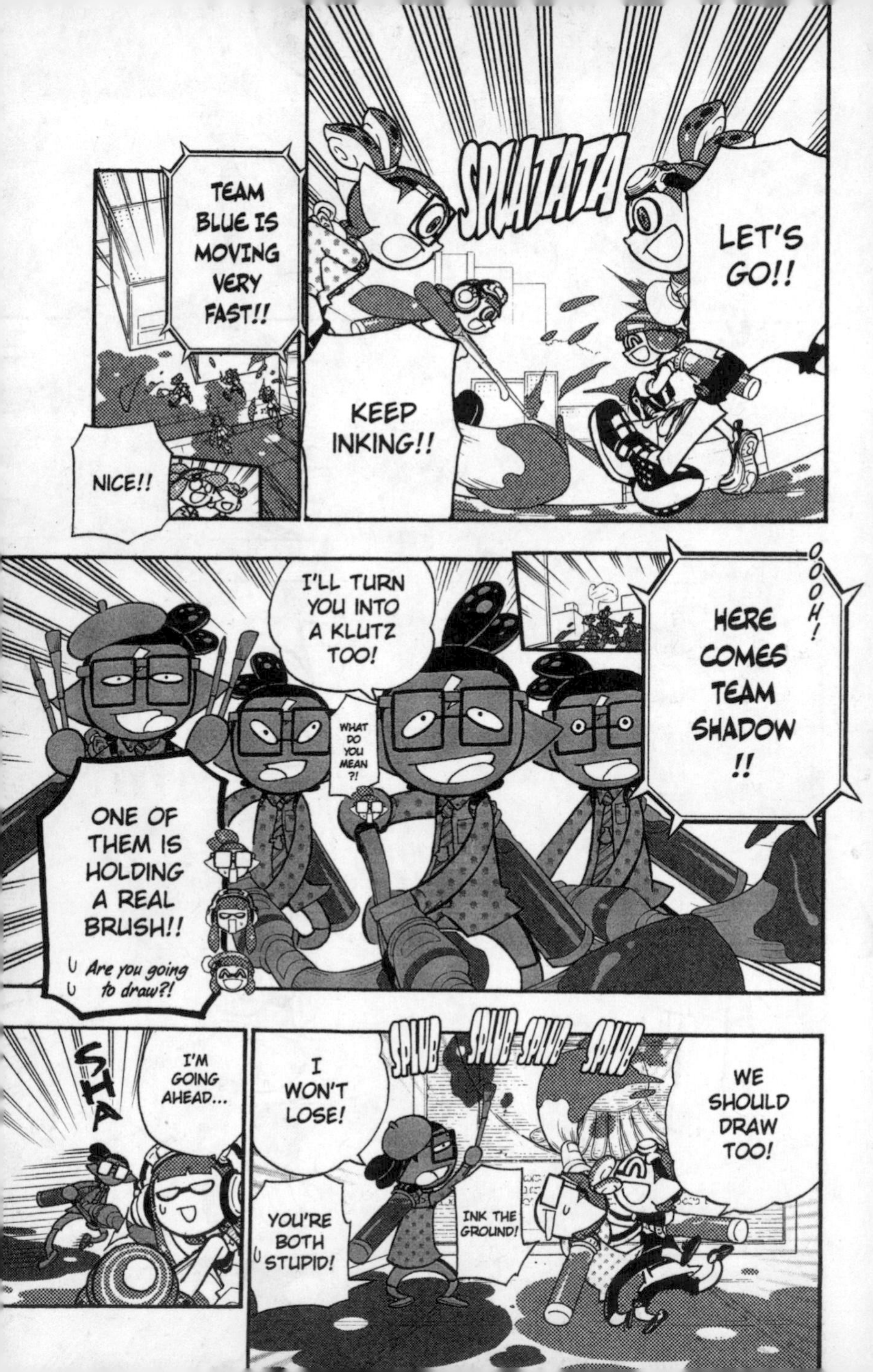
LET'S GO!!
SPLATATA
KEEP INKING!!
TEAM BLUE IS MOVING VERY FAST!!
NICE!!
OOOOH!
HERE COMES TEAM SHADOW!!
I'LL TURN YOU INTO A KLUTZ TOO!
WHAT DO YOU MEAN?!
ONE OF THEM IS HOLDING A REAL BRUSH!!
Are you going to draw?!
SPLUB
SPLUB
SPLUB
SPLUB
WE SHOULD DRAW TOO!
I WON'T LOSE!
INK THE GROUND!
YOU'RE BOTH STUPID!
SHA
I'M GOING AHEAD...

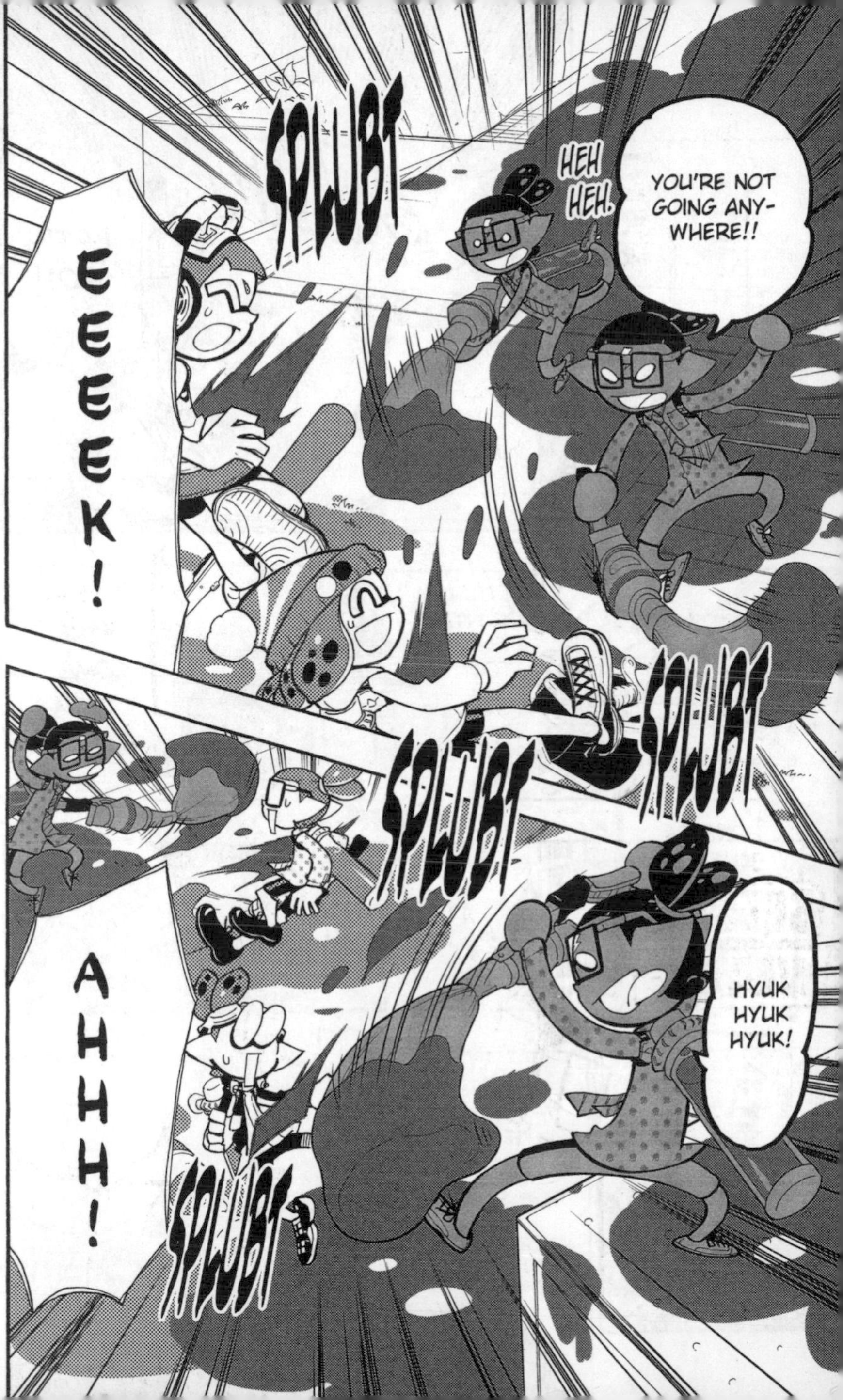
YOU'RE NOT GOING ANY-WHERE!!
HEH HEH.
SPLUBT
EEEEEK!
SPLUBT
SPLUBT
HYUK HYUK HYUK!
SPLUBT
AHHH!

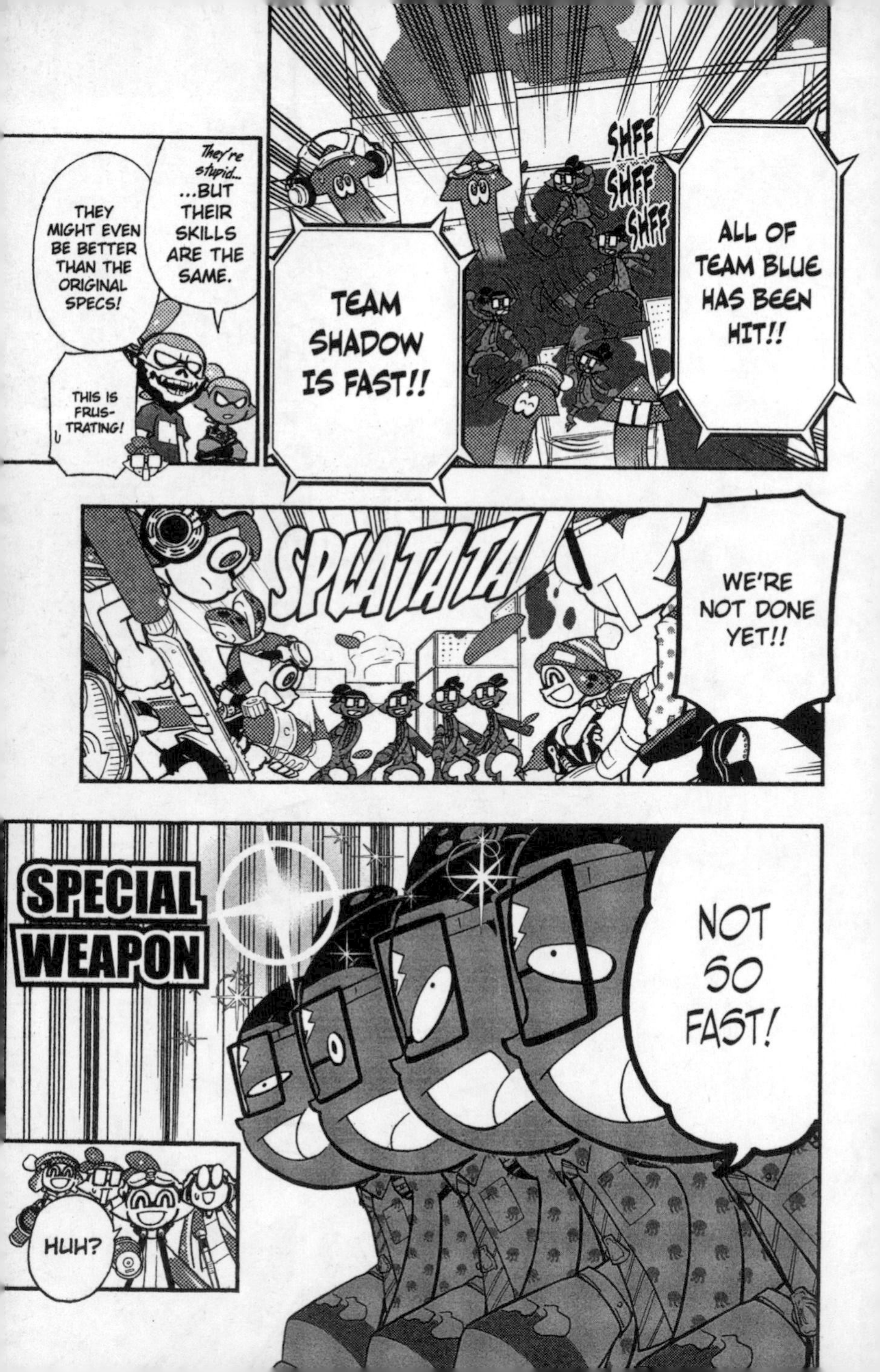
SHFF SHFF SHFF
ALL OF TEAM BLUE HAS BEEN HIT!!
TEAM SHADOW IS FAST!!
They're stupid...
...BUT THEIR SKILLS ARE THE SAME.
THEY MIGHT EVEN BE BETTER THAN THE ORIGINAL SPECS!
THIS IS FRUS-TRATING!
WE'RE NOT DONE YET!!
SPLATATA
NOT SO FAST!
SPECIAL WEAPON
HUH?

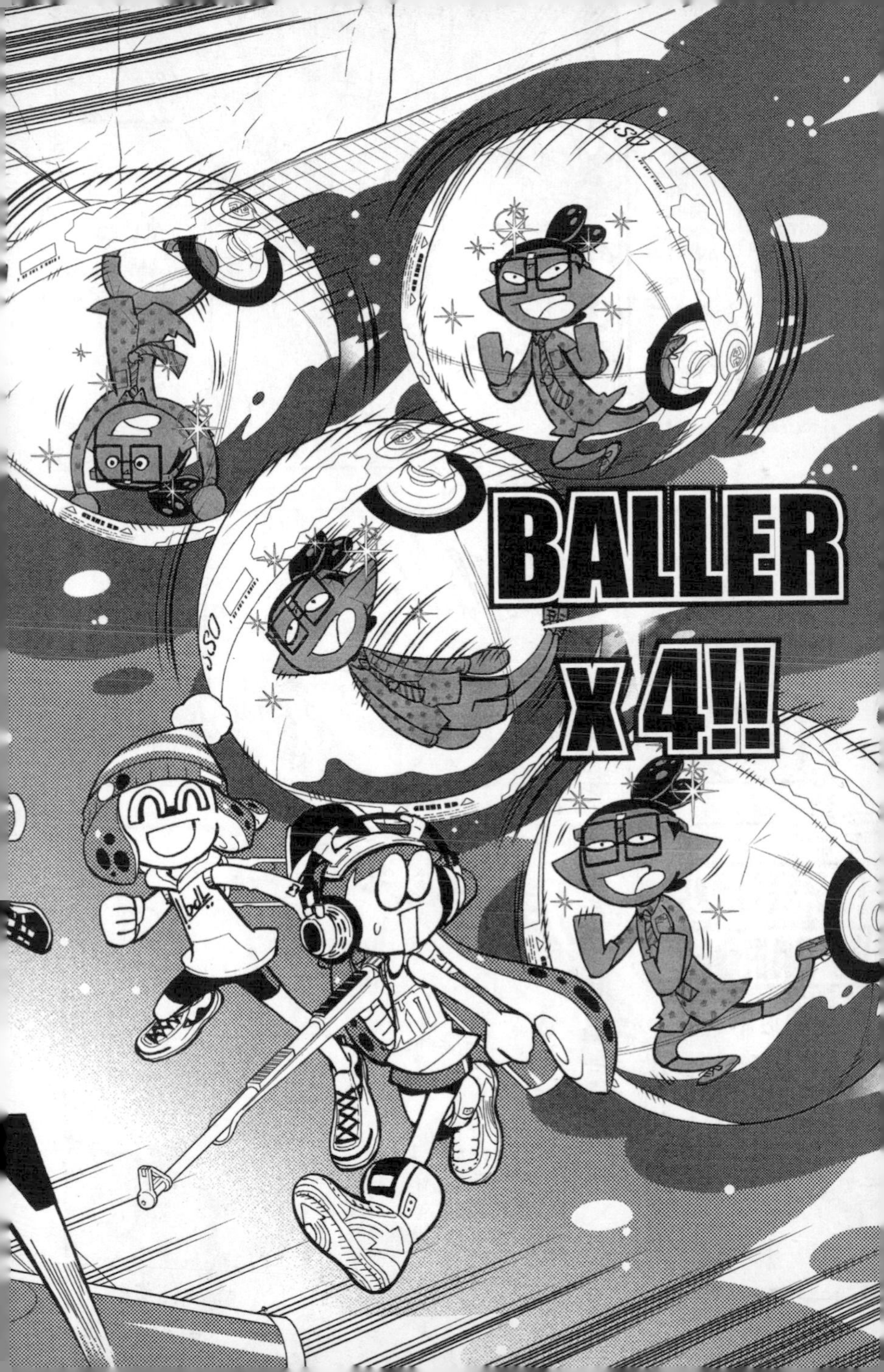
BALLER x 4!!

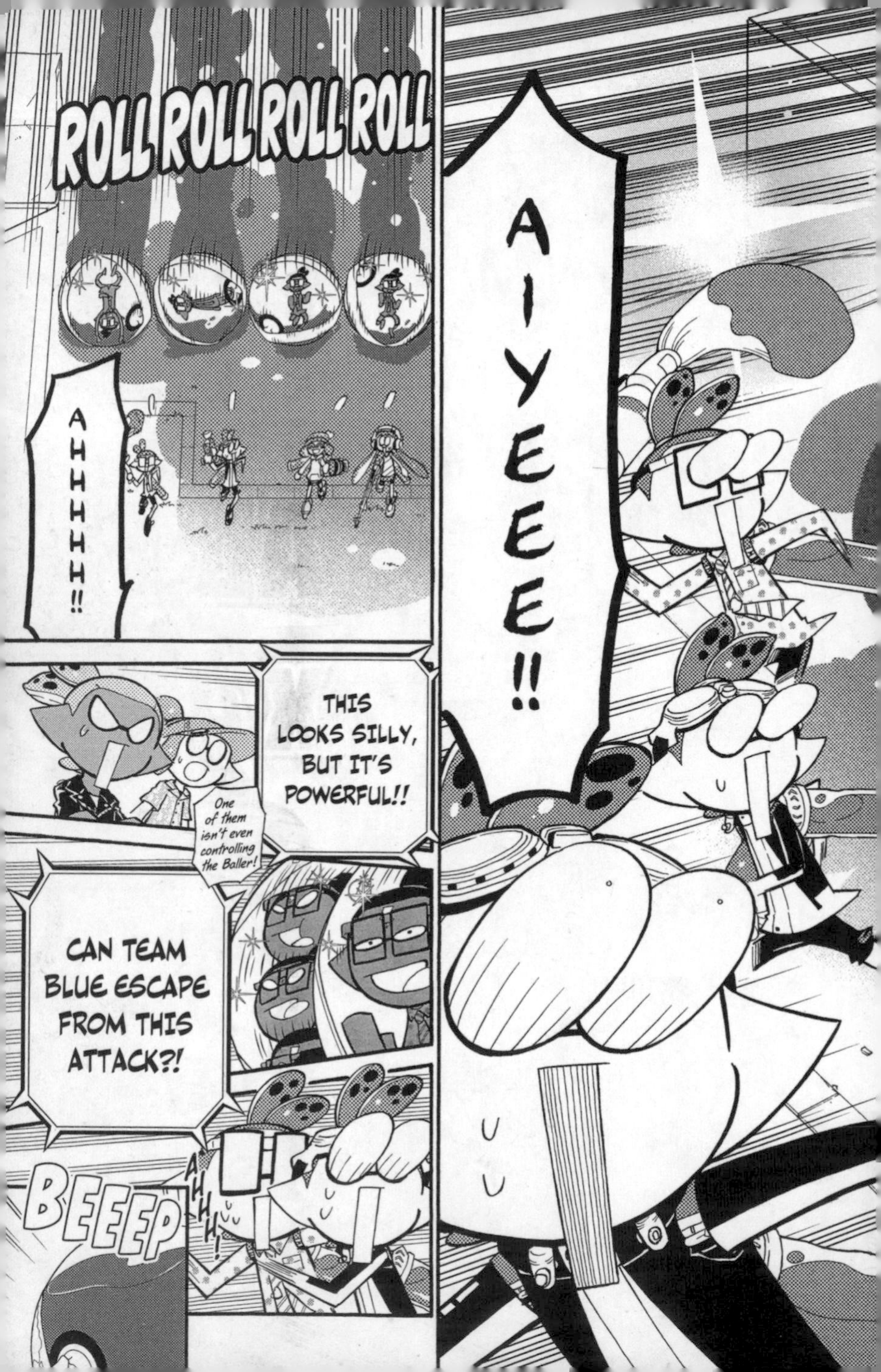
AIYEEE!!
ROLL ROLL ROLL ROLL
AHHHHHH!!
THIS LOOKS SILLY, BUT IT'S POWERFUL!!
One of them isn't even controlling the Baller!
CAN TEAM BLUE ESCAPE FROM THIS ATTACK?!
BEEEEP
AHHH!

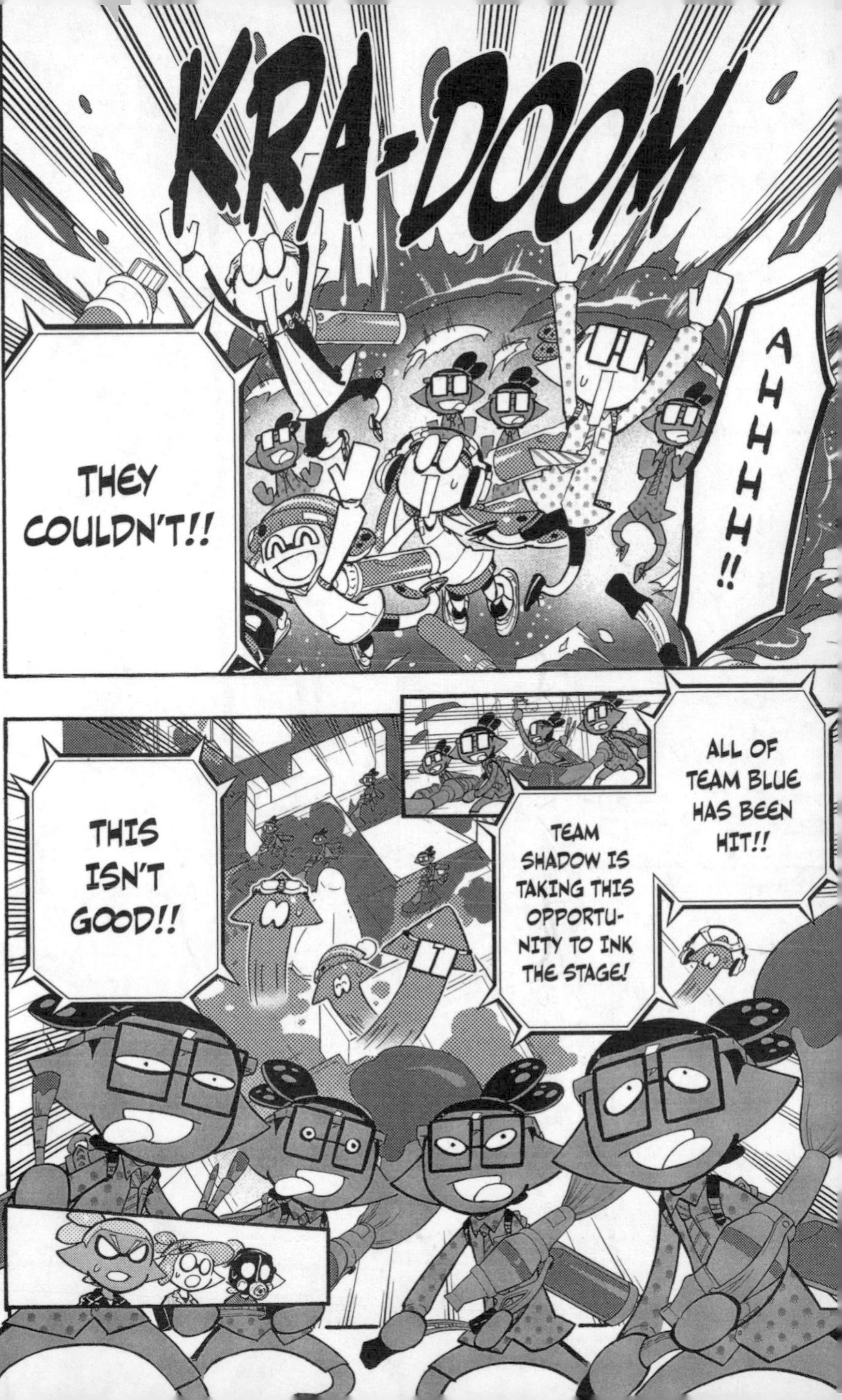
KRA-DOOM
AHHHHH!!
THEY COULDN'T!!
ALL OF TEAM BLUE HAS BEEN HIT!!
TEAM SHADOW IS TAKING THIS OPPORTU-NITY TO INK THE STAGE!
THIS ISN'T GOOD!!

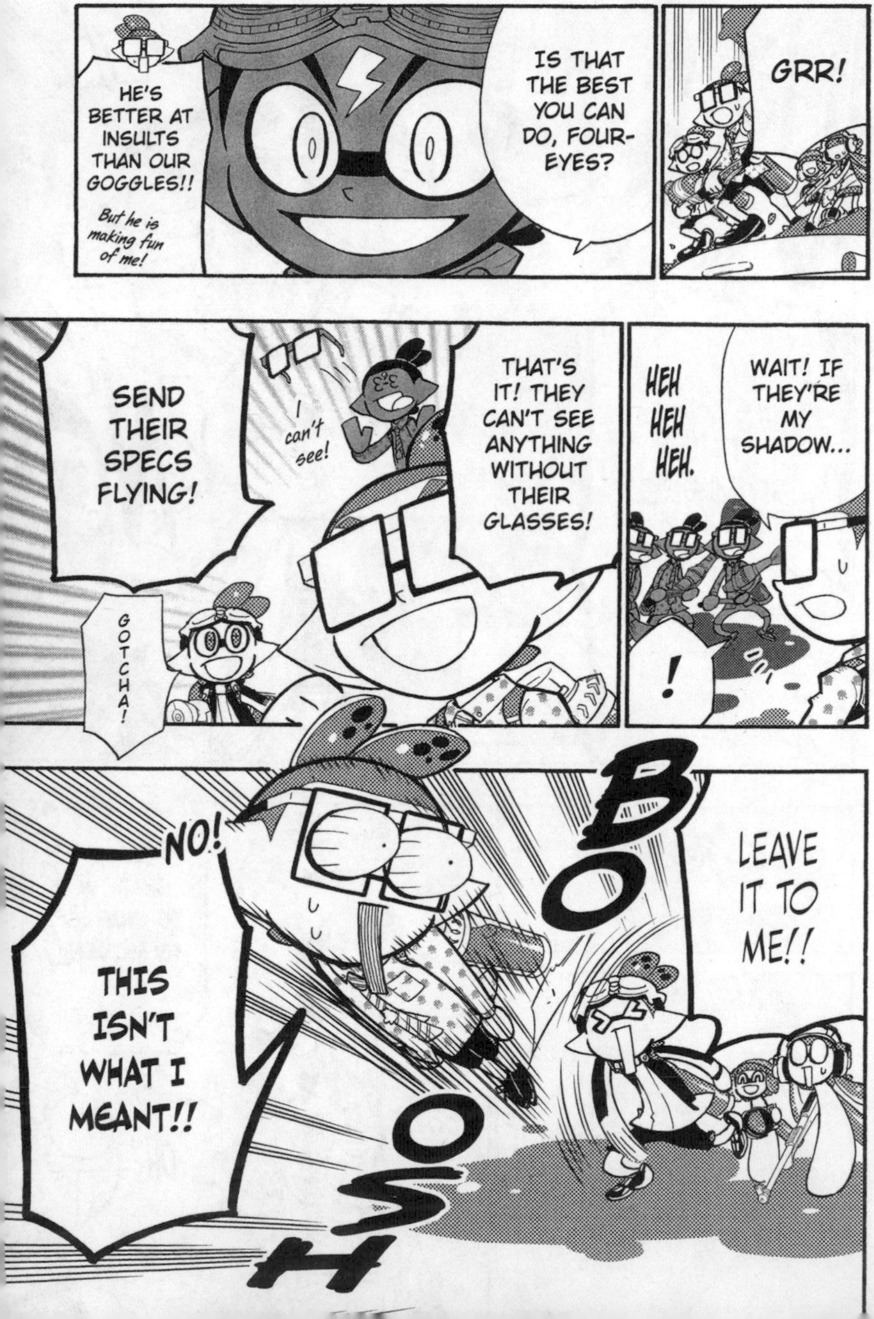
GRR!
IS THAT THE BEST YOU CAN DO, FOUR-EYES?
HE'S BETTER AT INSULTS THAN OUR GOGGLES!!
But he is making fun of me!
WAIT! IF THEY'RE MY SHADOW...
HEH HEH HEH.
!
THAT'S IT! THEY CAN'T SEE ANYTHING WITHOUT THEIR GLASSES!
I can't see!
SEND THEIR SPECS FLYING!
GOTCHA!
LEAVE IT TO ME!!
BOOSH
NO!
THIS ISN'T WHAT I MEANT!!

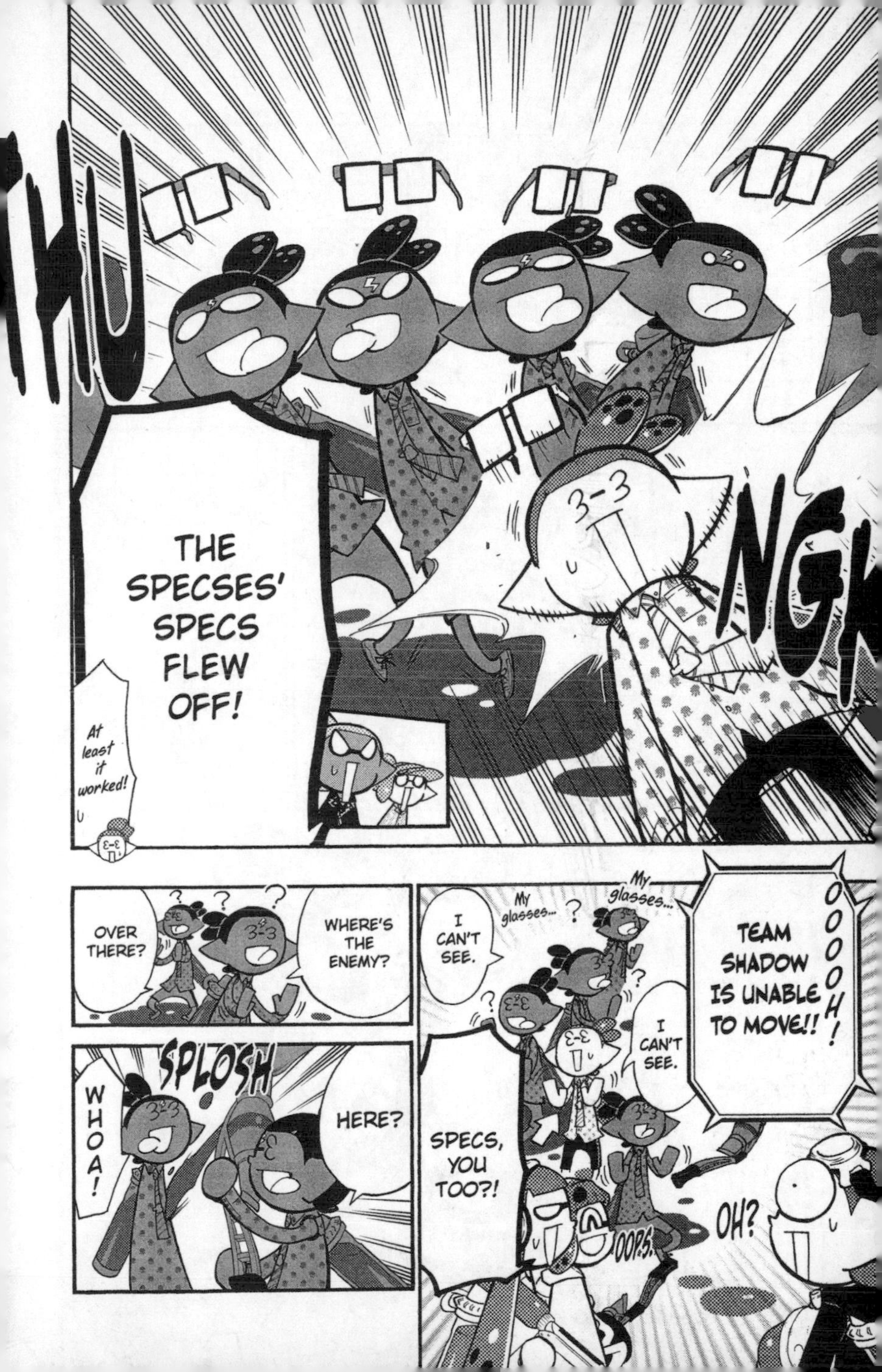
THU
NGK
THE SPECSES' SPECS FLEW OFF!
At least it worked!
OOOOOH!
TEAM SHADOW IS UNABLE TO MOVE!!
My glasses...
My glasses...
I CAN'T SEE.
I CAN'T SEE.
SPECS, YOU TOO?!
OH?
OOPS.
WHERE'S THE ENEMY?
OVER THERE?
HERE?
SPLOSH
WHOA!

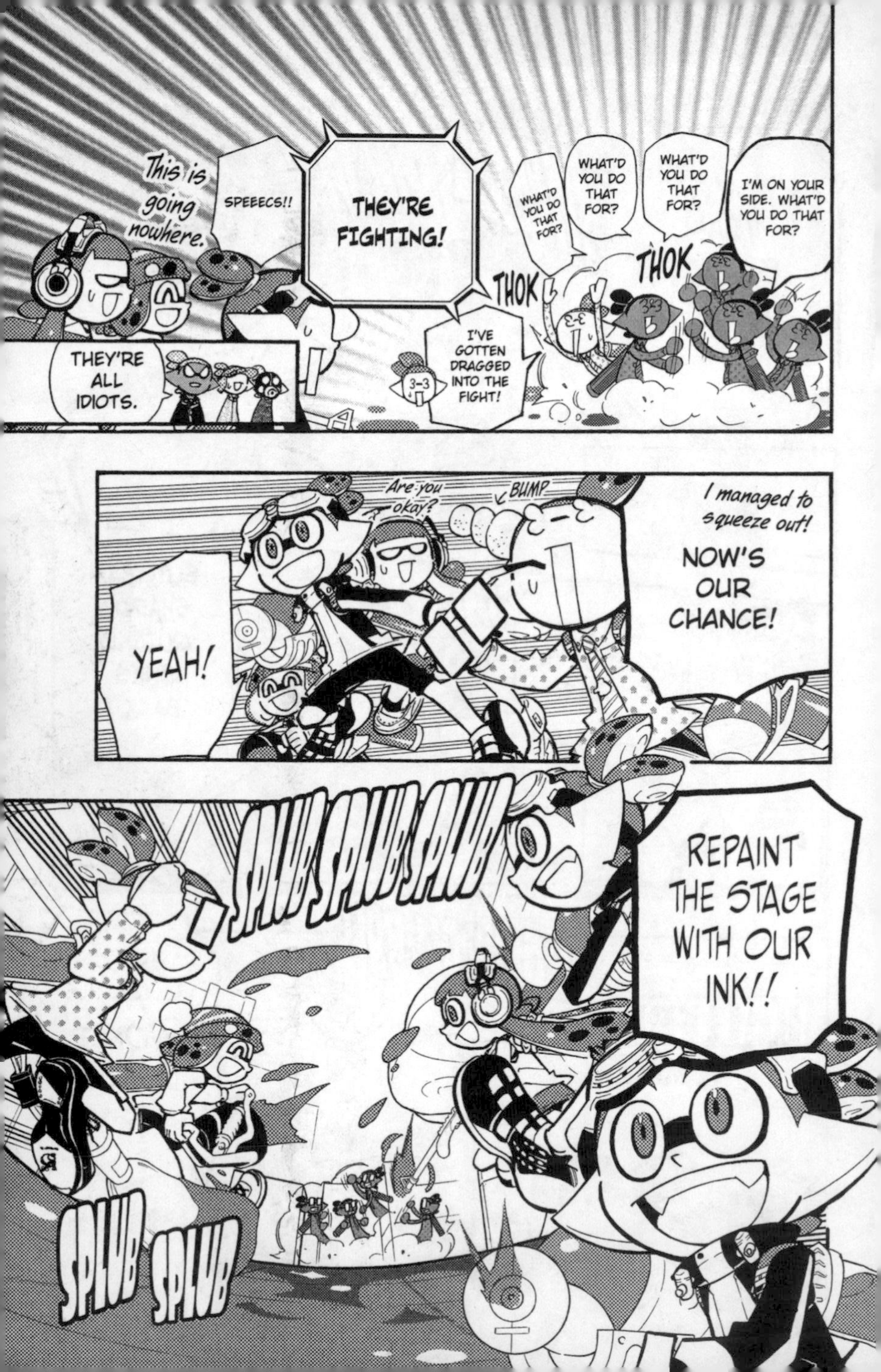
I'M ON YOUR SIDE. WHAT'D YOU DO THAT FOR?
WHAT'D YOU DO THAT FOR?
WHAT'D YOU DO THAT FOR?
WHAT'D YOU DO THAT FOR?
THOK
THOK
I'VE GOTTEN DRAGGED INTO THE FIGHT!
THEY'RE FIGHTING!
SPEEECS!!
This is going nowhere.
THEY'RE ALL IDIOTS.
I managed to squeeze out!
NOW'S OUR CHANCE!
BUMP
Are you okay?
YEAH!
REPAINT THE STAGE WITH OUR INK!!
SPLUB SPLUB SPLUB
SPLUB
SPLUB

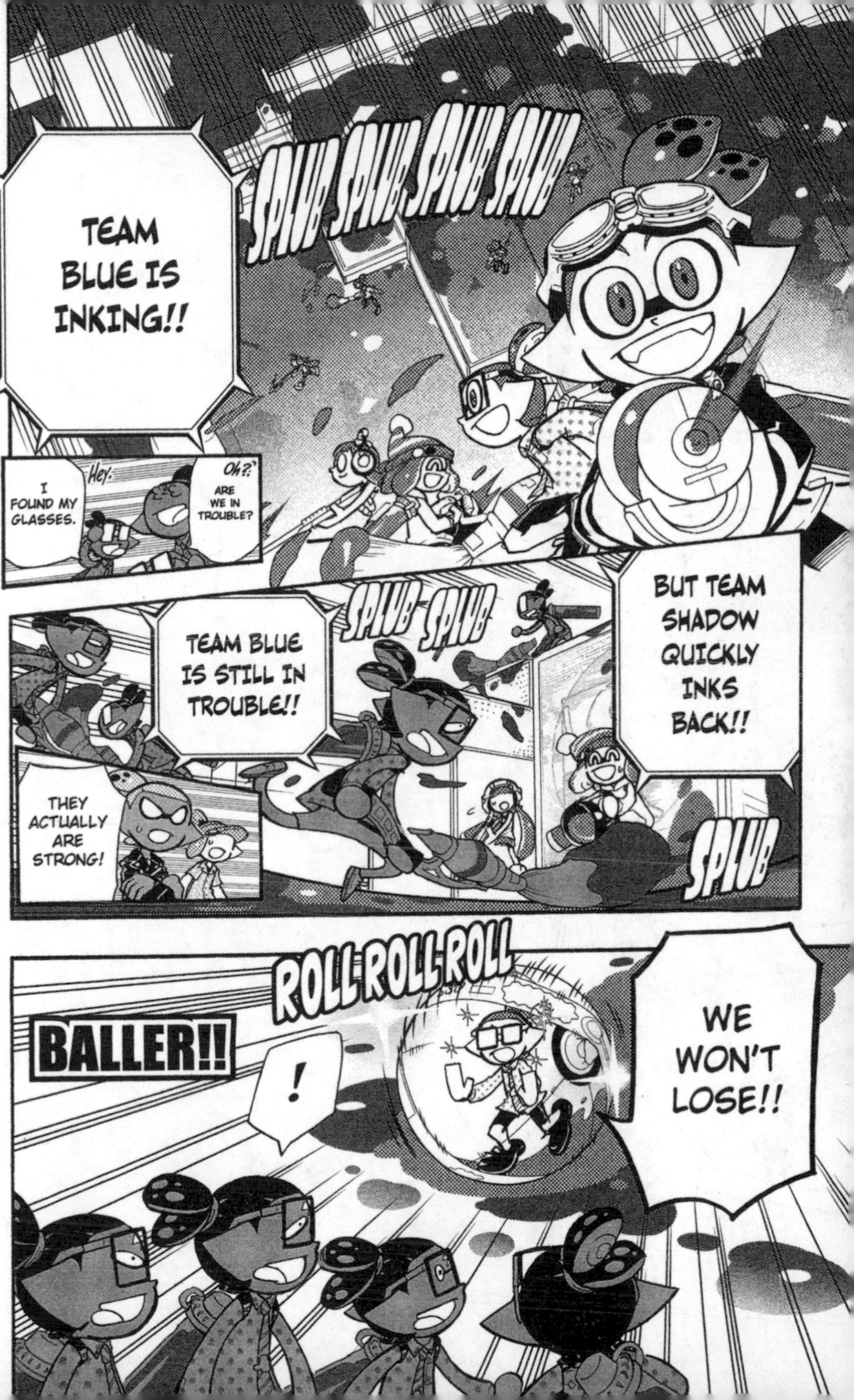
SPLUB SPLUB SPLUB SPLUB
TEAM BLUE IS INKING!!
Oh?!
ARE WE IN TROUBLE?
Hey.
I FOUND MY GLASSES.
BUT TEAM SHADOW QUICKLY INKS BACK!!
SPLUB SPLUB
TEAM BLUE IS STILL IN TROUBLE!!
SPLUB
THEY ACTUALLY ARE STRONG!
WE WON'T LOSE!!
ROLL ROLL ROLL
!
BALLER!!

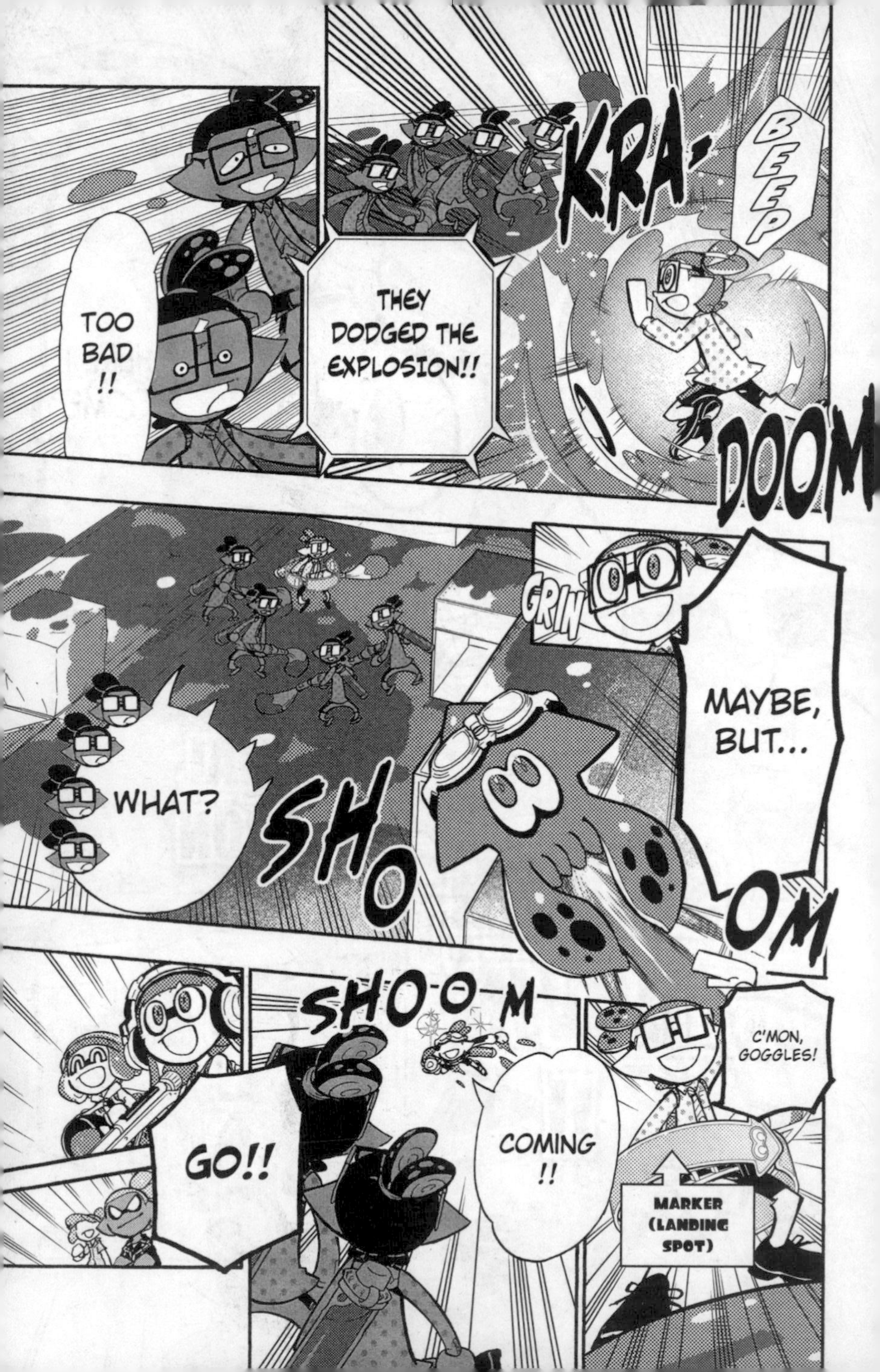
KRA-BEEP
THEY DODGED THE EXPLOSION!!
DOOM
TOO BAD!!
GRIN
MAYBE, BUT...
SHOOM
WHAT?
C'MON, GOGGLES!
MARKER (LANDING SPOT)
SHO-O-OM
COMING!!
GO!!

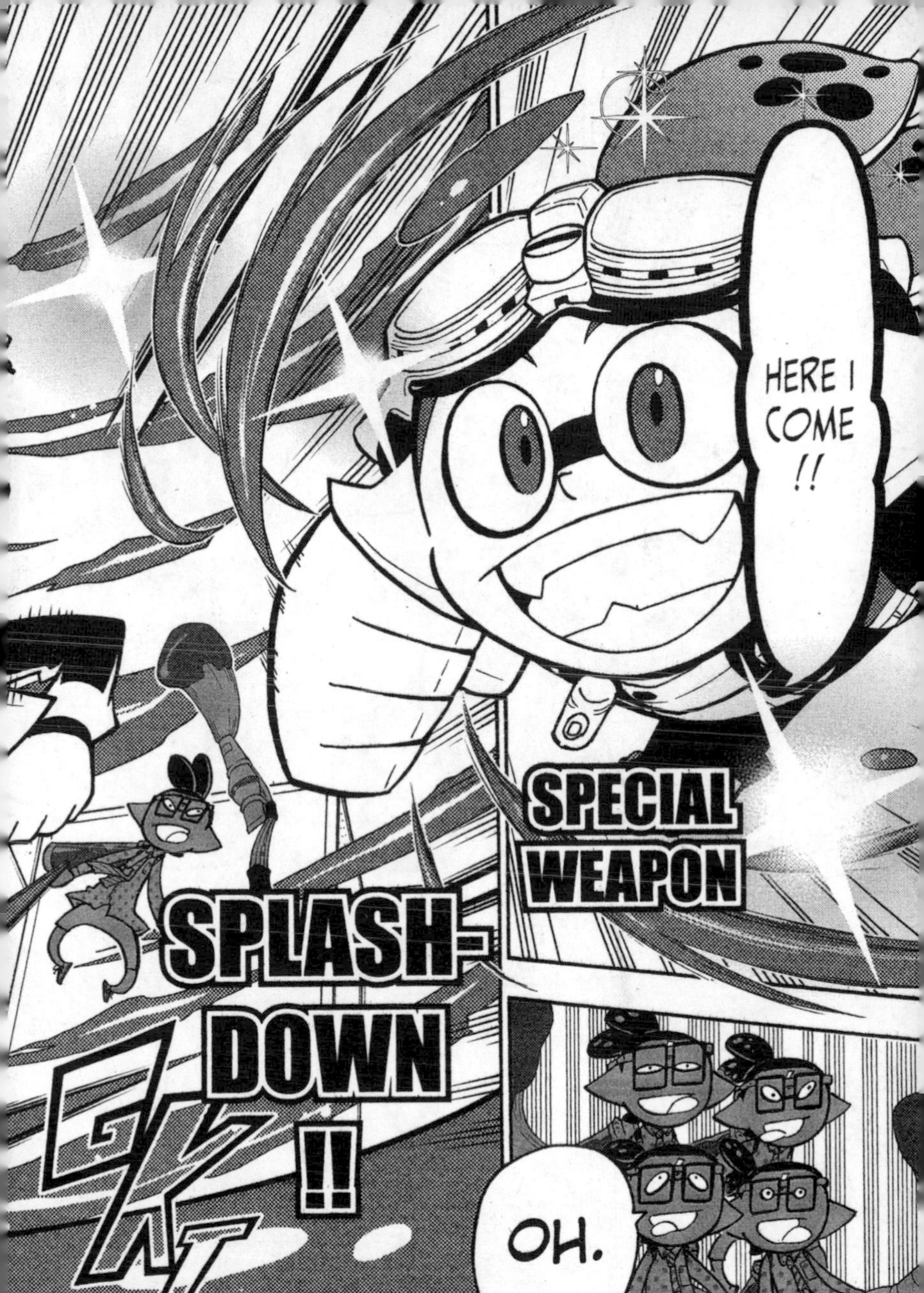
HERE I COME !!
SPECIAL WEAPON
SPLASH-DOWN !!
OH.

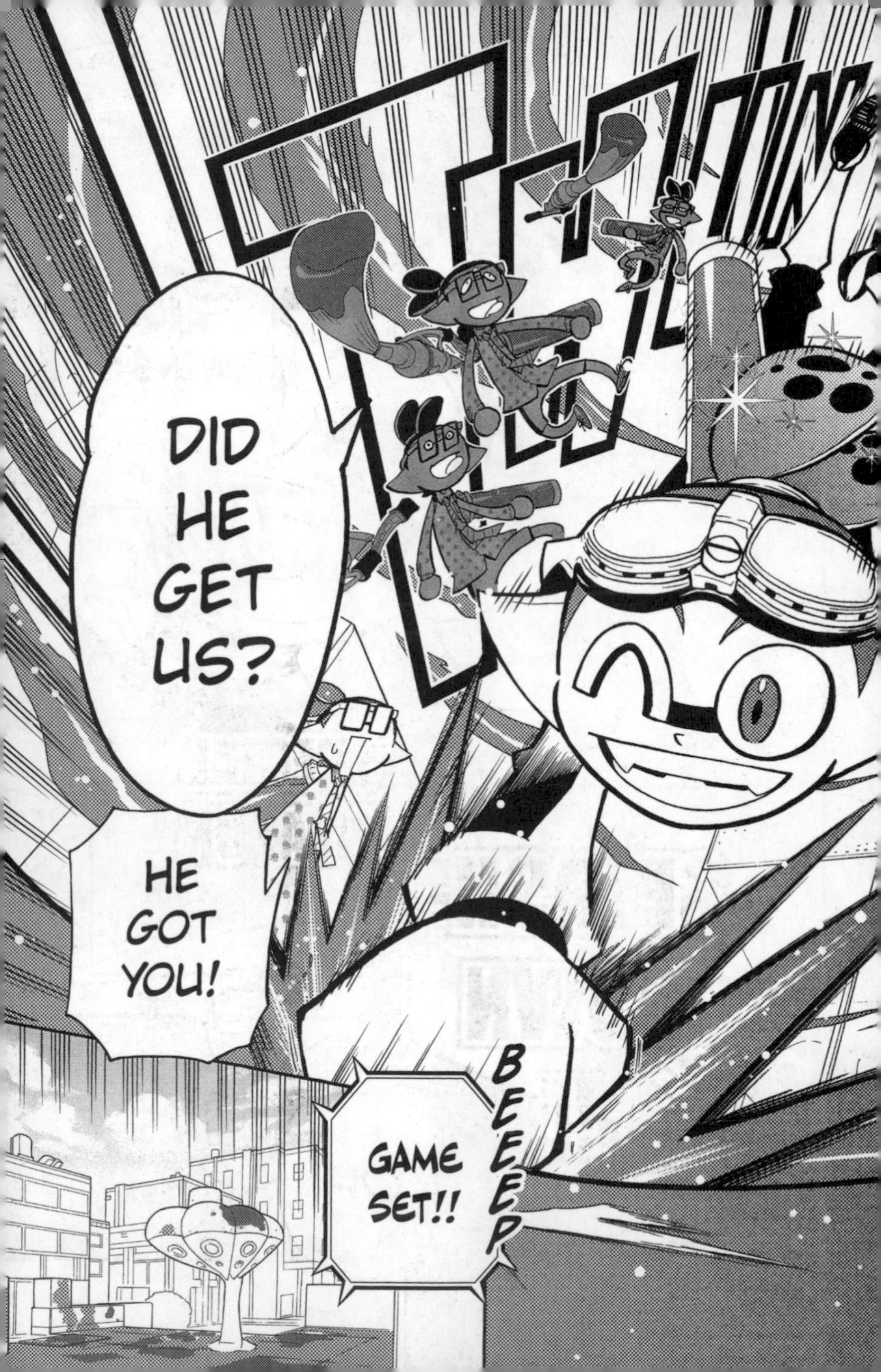
DID HE GET US?
HE GOT YOU!
BEEEEEP
GAME SET!!

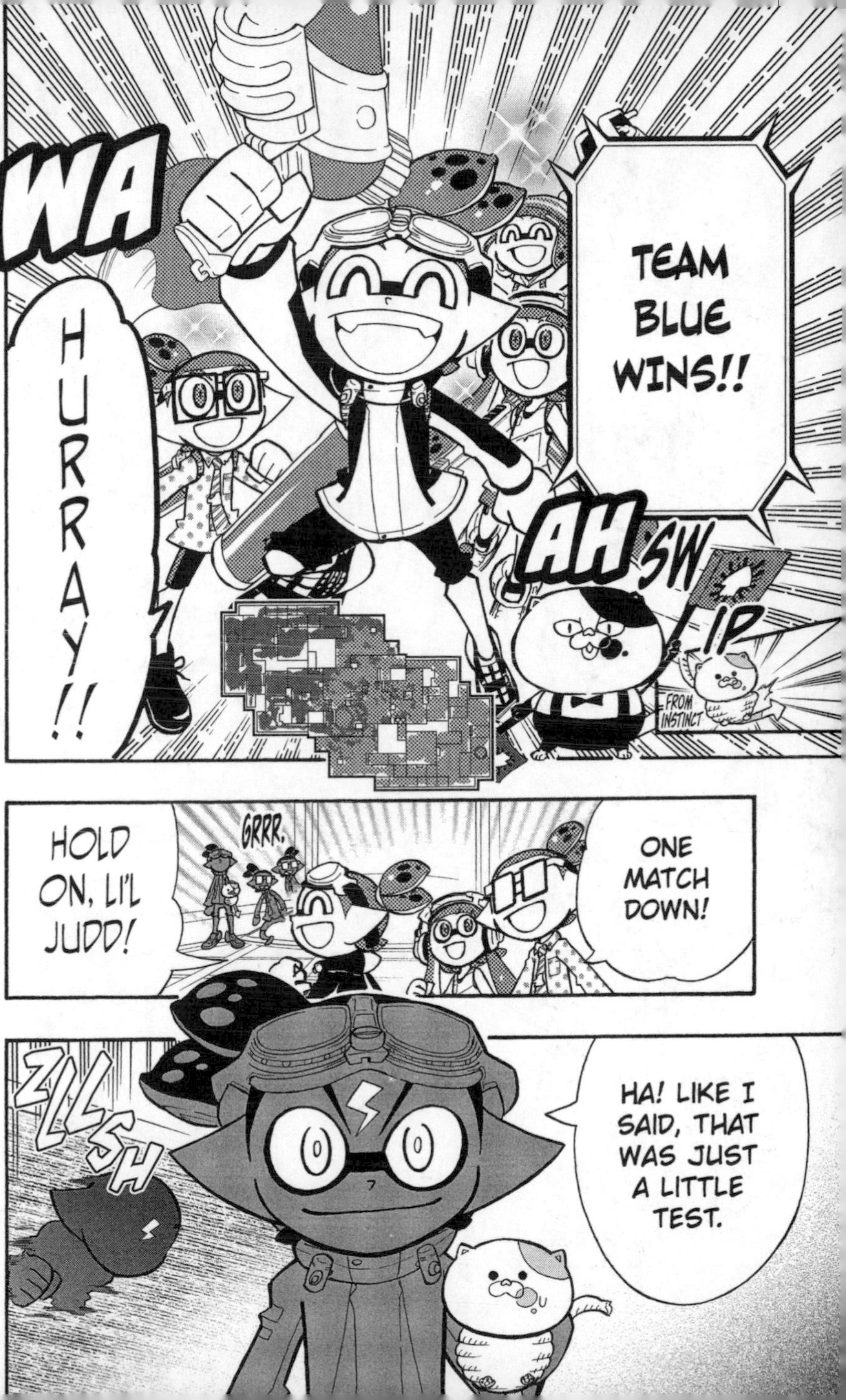
TEAM BLUE WINS!!
AH
SW
IP
FROM INSTINCT
WA
HURRAY!!
ONE MATCH DOWN!
GRRR.
HOLD ON, LI'L JUDD!
HA! LIKE I SAID, THAT WAS JUST A LITTLE TEST.
ZZZSH

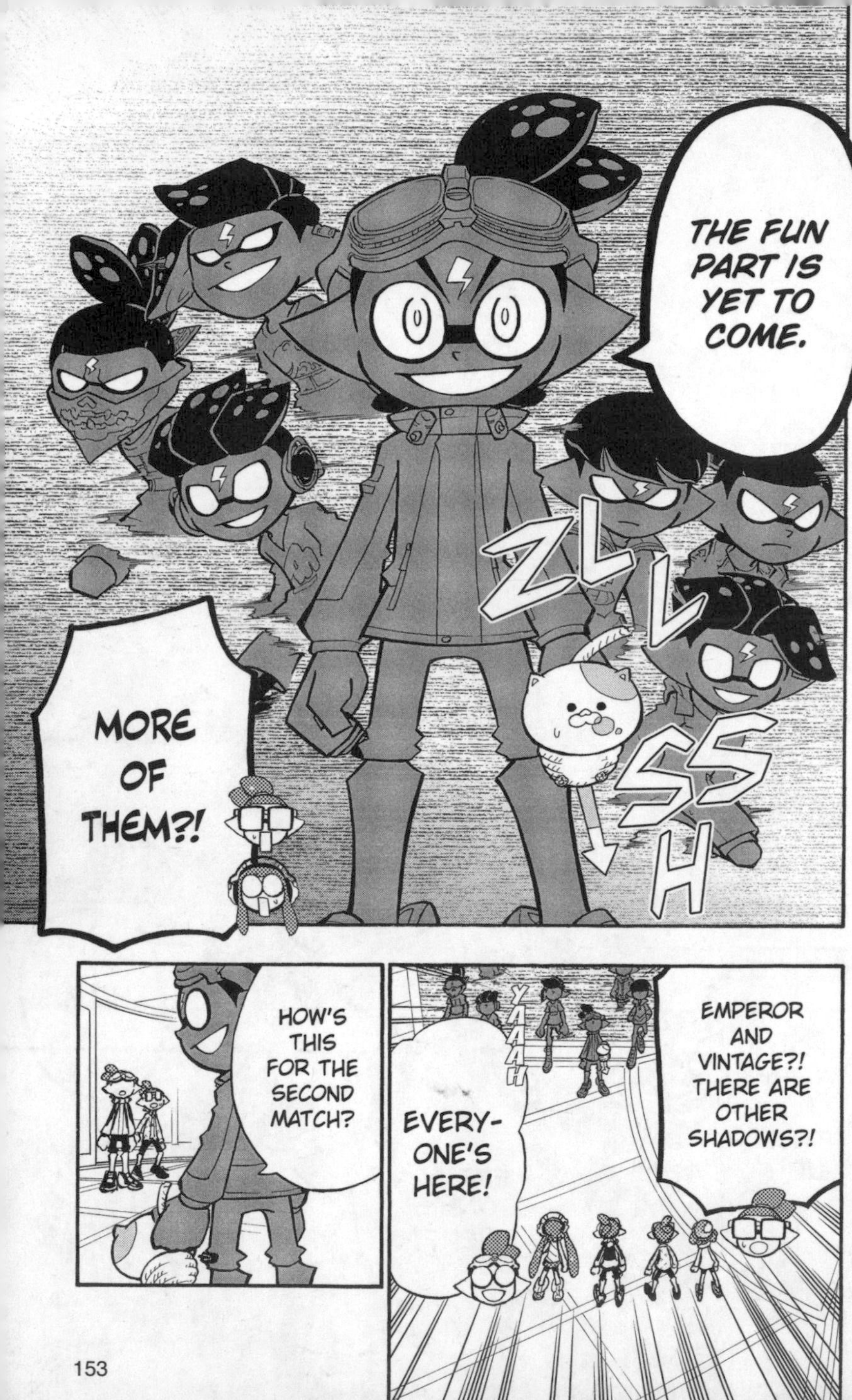
THE FUN PART IS YET TO COME.
ZLLSSH
MORE OF THEM?!
EMPEROR AND VINTAGE?! THERE ARE OTHER SHADOWS?!
YAAAH
EVERY-ONE'S HERE!
HOW'S THIS FOR THE SECOND MATCH?

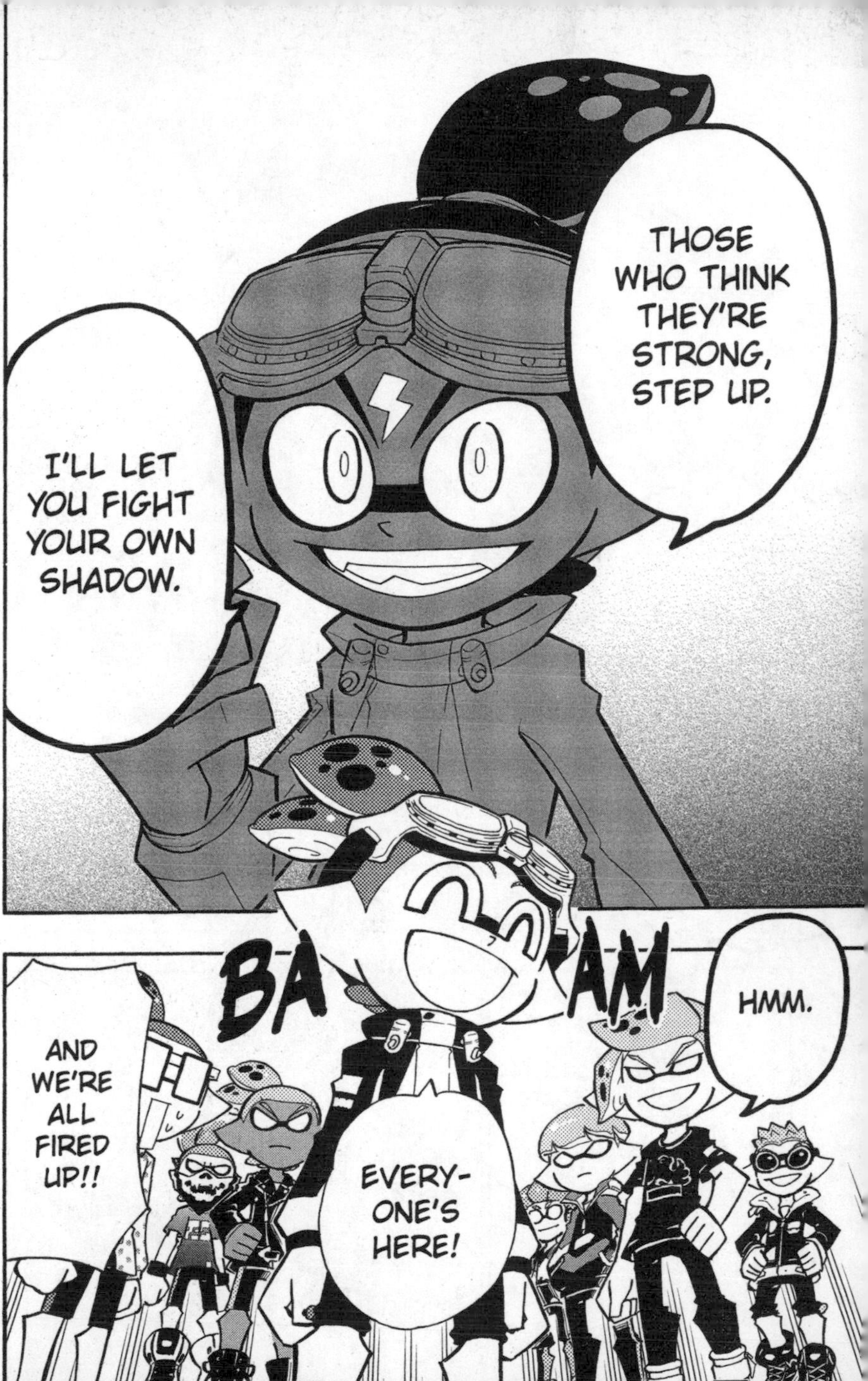
THOSE WHO THINK THEY'RE STRONG, STEP UP.
I'LL LET YOU FIGHT YOUR OWN SHADOW.
HMM.
BA AM
EVERY-ONE'S HERE!
AND WE'RE ALL FIRED UP!!

SPLATOON VOLUME 14 END / CONTINUED IN VOLUME 15

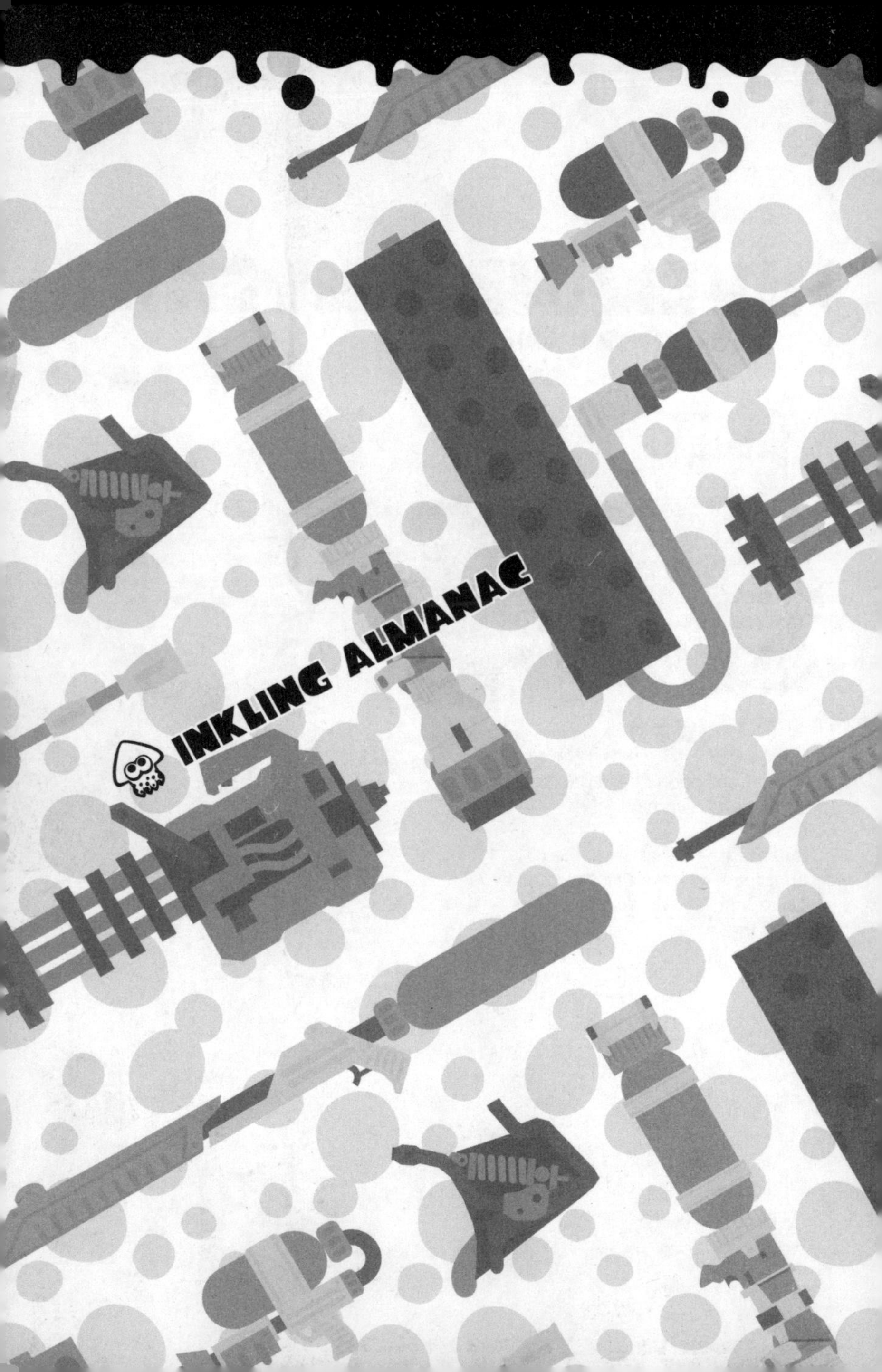
INKLING ALMANAC

HIVEMIND ANTENNA
(INK COLOR: SKY GRAY)

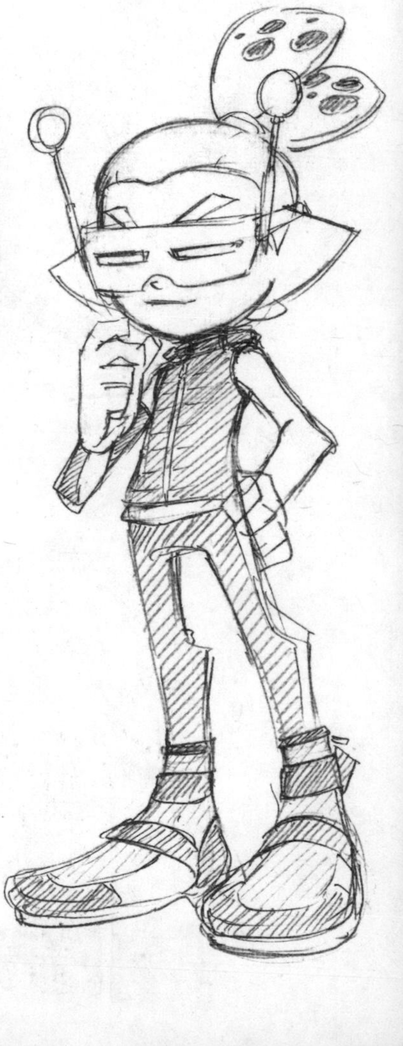

Weapon: Kensa Charger
Headgear: Hivemind Antenna
Clothing: Front Zip Vest
Shoes: Navy Enperrials

INFO

•If your cell phone can't get a signal, stand near Hivemind.

•He has been contacting the other three guardians—Fierce Fishskull, Jetflame Crest, and Eye of Justice—more often these days.

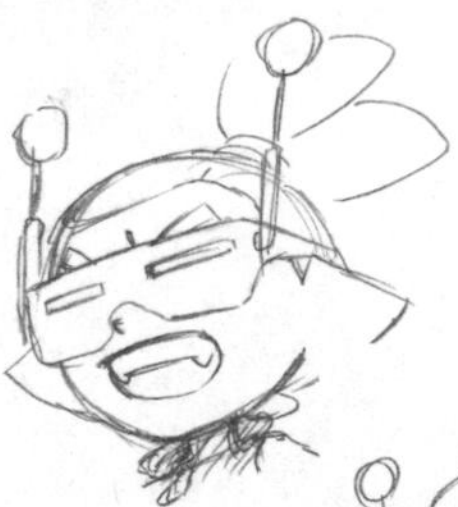

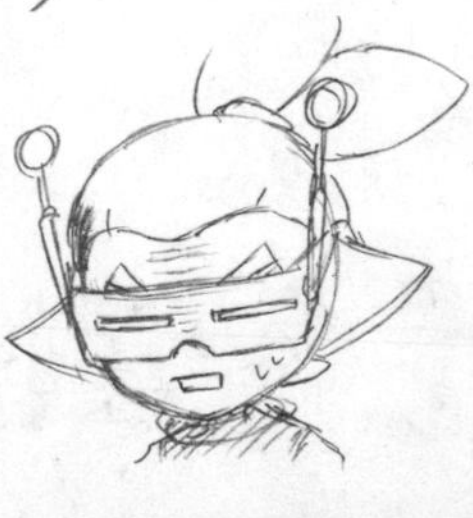

Splatoon 14

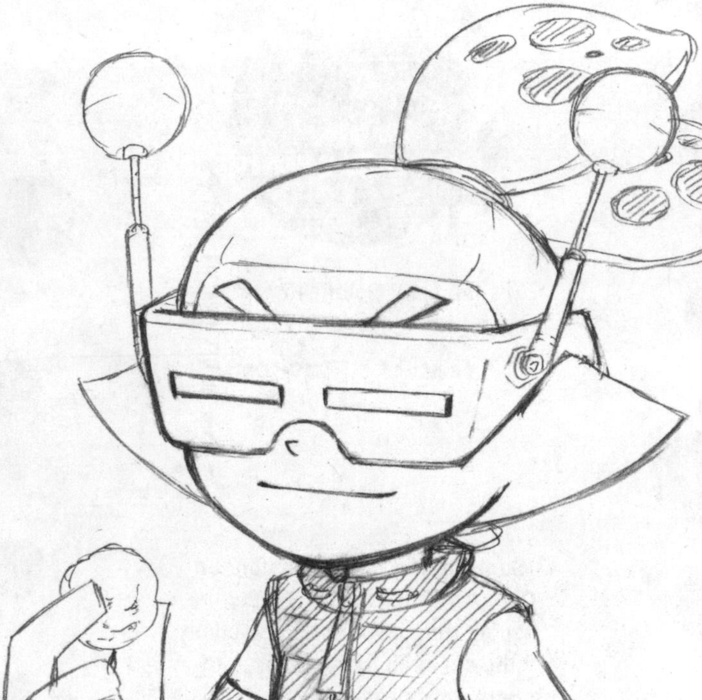

THANK YOU!

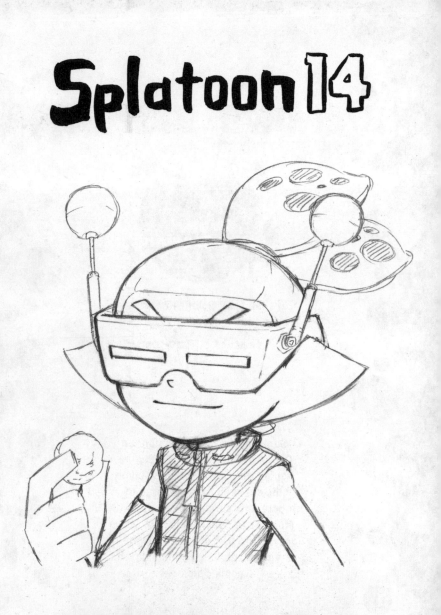

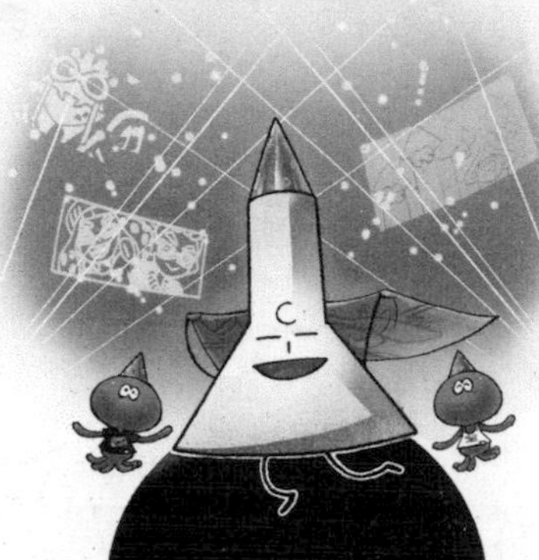

Story Introduction

It's the Final Splatfest! I want to have fun at Inkopolis Square too!

Sankichi Hinodeya

Sankichi Hinodeya was born on October 29 in Nagano Prefecture, Japan. Hinodeya first emerged on the scene in an extra issue of Square Enix's *Gangan Powered* with *Maho Bozu Sankyu* (*Magical Monk Sankyu*). In 2015, Hinodeya began the manga adaptation of Nintendo's hit game *Splatoon*.